AF541316

Tactical Nuclear Weapons
Deterrence Stability between India and Pakistan

Tactical Nuclear Weapons-Deterrence Stability Between India and Pakistan

V. Sahay, Comdt. (Retd.)

Gaurav Book Centre Pvt. Ltd.
NEW DELHI-110002

Publisher
GAURAV BOOK CENTRE PVT LTD
4832/24, Prahlad Lane,S-207 Ansari
Road, Daryaganj, Delhi-110002
Ph.: 43570976, 23278261
Email: gauravbookcentre@gmail.com

Edition: 2024

ISBN: 978-93-83316-34-2

Laser Typesetting
JEE-VEE Graphics, Delhi

Price: 1295/-

Printed
Neeta Press, Delhi

Contents

Preface

Indian and Pakistani diplomacy has reflected the desire within their military-civil establishments to ward off criticism, particularly that which followed periods of high tension. It has been particularly important to project the image of a state that is fully aware and in control of itself.

India has criticized Pakistan's stance on battlefield nukes. Rakesh Sood, former Indian special envoy for disarmament and nonproliferation, said it was "extremely destabilizing for any country to develop tactical nuclear weapons" and that India had no plans to do so. He also argued that Pakistan's nuclear doctrine is "cloaked in ambiguity," undermining confidence between the two countries.

The contrast between India and Pakistan on "no first use" could not be greater. Unlike India, which is both stronger than Pakistan and no pushover where China is concerned, Pakistan is a weak state that is unfortunately growing even weaker as a result of its awful strategic choices. Pakistan's security competition with India, which dates back to the creation of the two countries as independent states, is multi-dimensional in nature and involves territorial, religious, and power-political dimensions. These grievances have combined in unhelpful ways to make Pakistan the anti-status quo power in the Indian subcontinent. Having fought four unsuccessful wars with India in an effort to secure its strategic aims, Pakistan switched to a dangerous and provocative strategy in the last decades of the 20th century—a strategy of supporting terrorist groups aimed at enervating India through "a thousand cuts," even as Pakistan began to feverishly expand its nuclear arsenal in an effort to prevent New Delhi from retaliating with conventional forces.

It is further hoped that the book will prove to be of immense value to teachers, students and researchers.

—*Editor*

1

Introduction

PAKISTAN'S NUCLEAR DIPLOMACY

Although it is a client state of the US and dependent upon it in many critical ways, Pakistan has resolutely rejected US efforts to move it away from nuclear weapons. It is currently under criticism for having blocked talks between 64 countries to limit fissile materials under the Conference on Disarmament (CD) in Geneva. The current posture reflects Pakistani anger at the US-India nuclear deal and the subsequent enhancement in India's capacity to generate fissile materials. It also assumes – perhaps correctly – that the Afghanistan situation makes Pakistan too essential to the US for it to take a hard stance.

Indian and Pakistani diplomacy has reflected the desire within their military-civil establishments to ward off criticism, particularly that which followed periods of high tension. It has been particularly important to project the image of a state that is fully aware and in control of itself.

In fact, nuclear respectability is implicitly and jointly sought by Indian and Pakistan elites, both military and civilian. Their goal is to show that their nukes are in responsible hands, that they can handle nuclear weapons just as well as anyone else, are sternly opposed to proliferation, and they are victims rather than supporters of terrorism. Officials and experts from both countries meet at arms control workshops and seminars, behave civilly (if not cordially) towards each other, and appear to be rational actors. CBMs, nuclear risk reduction measures, etc. have become their standard vocabulary items. The underlying mistrust and hostility is thereby effectively concealed.

Indian establishment intellectuals had grasped the value of creating the responsible actors image much before their Pakistani counterparts. The clinching of the US-India nuclear deal in 2007 owes much to this. Indeed, the Indian strategic analyst C. Raja Mohan had observed years earlier that,

"New Delhi and Islamabad should know that the willingness of the rest of the world to accept them as part of the official nuclear club depends on the ability of India and Pakistan to responsibly manage their own nuclear relationship.....If India and Pakistan want to be taken seriously, they must show results from their nuclear talks."

Musharaf's predecessor as chief of army staff, General Jehangir Karamat, while he was ambassador of Pakistan to the United States, was also keen to show that Pakistan and India are not trigger-happy,

"For those who observe South Asia from the outside it is considered a most dangerous place and a region in which a nuclear exchange could be a reality. It is thought that the India-Pakistan confrontations in 1987, 1990 and 2002, as well as the Kargil conflict in 1999, all had a nuclear dimension of some sort. This is not what most South Asians think".

Nevertheless, Gen. Karamat did admit that during the Kargil crisis, as well as in the crisis that followed the attack by Islamic militants upon the Indian Parliament in December 2001, that statements and signaling through missile tests could have had unintended consequences. As argued in the earlier part of this essay, the velvet gloves are rapidly discarded once the going gets rough. The politeness of diplomats, while welcome, merely hides the visceral feelings beneath.

The success of diplomacy speaks for itself. Giving primacy to its geo-political interests, the US fundamentally changed its posture on India: sanctions imposed in 1998 were gradually withdrawn, criticism became inaudible, a grudging acceptance of nuclear status followed, and then – in a dramatic blow to the Nuclear Non-proliferation Treaty – the US ended up making a special deal that now makes it a supplier of nuclear equipment and materials to India.

Pakistan, while faring not quite so well and not being privileged by a similar deal, was de-facto accepted as a nuclear power with the safety and security of its nuclear arsenal reduced to the level of a nagging, low-level worry.

SAFETY AND SECURITY PAKISTAN'S NUCLEAR ARSENAL

Determined to retain and expand its nuclear capabilities but shaken by the reaction to A.Q. Khan's global nuclear entrepreneurship, in 2004 Musharraf's government had sharply reversed its earlier policy of keeping all nuclear matters under the wrap. It hoped thereby to assure the world that Pakistan's nuclear weapons were in safe hands. A stream of highly placed official visitors made a beeline for Washington's think-tanks and military colleges across the United States. A few years earlier this would have been unthinkable. Visits from top officials of the Strategic Plans Division (SPD), which is charged with the possession, maintenance, and safety of Pakistan's nuclear weapons became routine, and still continue.

It is especially significant that the director general of the SPD, Lt. Gen. Khalid Kidwai, is a visitor to the US. He was, for example, invited to a special guest lecture to the faculty, students, and guests of the Naval Postgraduate School in Monterey where he sought to debunk the notion that Pakistani weapons could fall into the hands of religious extremists, were on hair-trigger alert, or be used irresponsibly. Other Pakistani military officers associated with the nation's nuclear program are paid by US funding sources for writing reports and papers for US think-tanks and research institutes. Still others are in the process of writing books that will reveal the true history of the Pakistani nuclear program xlviii.

To safeguard Pakistan's crown jewels is a relatively recent preoccupation that dates to the September 11, 2001 attack. Although Pakistan's military government insisted that there was no danger of any of its nuclear weapons being taking for a ride, it did not take chances. Several weapons were reportedly airlifted to various safer, isolated, locations within the country. This nervousness was not unjustified – two strongly Islamist generals of the Pakistan

Army (the head of Pakistan's ISI intelligence agency, Lt. General Mehmood Ahmed, and Deputy Chief of Army Staff, General Muzaffar Hussain Usmani), close associates of General Musharraf, had just been removed. The seriousness of betraying the progeny of Pakistan's intelligence services was something that Musharraf feared – and for good reason.

Internationally, there are widespread fears that instability in Pakistan could make its nuclear weapons and stocks of nuclear explosive material dangerously vulnerable to theft. As could be expected, Pakistan's position has been one of emphatic denial: the Foreign Ministry claims that our [nuclear] assets are 100 percent secure, under multiple custody. Soothing words, however, have not taken away a general sense of worry. Pakistan is now in the grip of a full-fledged insurgency by Islamic groups. Some of these view Pakistan's nuclear weapons as belonging to the *Ummah*, rather than Pakistan alonel. This has enhanced the feeling internationally that Pakistan's nuclear weapons, fissile materials, and other nuclear components are unsafe.

The dangers to Pakistan's nuclear weapons are potentially four-fold:

- From India and the US, separately or together. Israel is a distant possibility but not to be ruled out.
- From outside: Islamic militants attacking a nuclear storage site or facility with the purpose of capturing a nuclear weapon.
- From inside: Islamic elements in the army who have responsibility for protecting and operating nuclear sites or facilities.
- From a collaboration between insiders and outsiders.

There is concern in Pakistan of the growing Israeli-Indian strategic alliance, underscored by the supply of four Phalcon AWAC-type systems. These have the capability of tracking Pakistani aircraft over the entire geographical area. India has already acquired two Israeli Green Pine radars, capable of tracking missiles at a distance of 400 km. These are normally used in conjunction with the Arrow II anti-missile system. These early-warning systems could be effectively used by Israel to launch a pre-emptive strike at Pakistan's nuclear facilities with India's direct assistance or by using India as a base. Only an extreme crisis would result in India or the US, whether acting together or separately, to attack a nuclear armed state with all the obvious dangers this contains. Even a massive use of force is unlikely to net all of well-hidden and well-protected Pakistani nuclear weapons. Moreover, the job would be incomplete unless the major nuclear weapon facilities, reactors, and uranium enrichment plants were also destroyed completely. This would involve nothing short of total war.

On the other hand, Islamic extremists may seek a weapon for ultimate use against a US or European city. But, because it would be much easier to arrange, they may seek the destruction of an Indian or Pakistani city, with the hope of provoking total war between Pakistan and India. This would be consistent with the suicide bombing strategy followed by Al-Qaida elsewhere. In the extremist mindset, it is best if infidels are killed. But if Sunni Muslims are killed, they will simply make it to heaven a bit earlier.

Defending against other nations as well as internal enemies poses a difficult security dilemma: Pakistan would like to keep the location and details of its nuclear weapons secret in order to increase their chances of a strike by India, the US, or Israel. On the other hand army insiders are already, by definition, in the know. Perhaps in collusion with an external Islamic group they could be plotting a move unknown to the Nuclear Command Authority (NCA), the SPD, or the Chief of Army Staff. How could such an attempt be foiled? Only partial safety is possible no matter what the technical fix. One obvious mechanism is to reduce the readiness level. Pakistan is widely believed to store the fissile core and bomb mechanisms separately in safely guarded vaults. As early as December 1999, it had requested senior US officials visiting Islamabad for Permissive Action Links (PALs) that are directly integrated into the firing mechanism and electronics of a nuclear weapon, as well as Environment Sensitive Devices (ESDs), in order to enhance protection against unauthorized use or accidental nuclear detonations.

At that time, the US had declined for obvious reasons: these devices make it possible for the weapons to be maintained at a higher state of alert for the same level of safety, thereby increasing the threat perceived by India. But subsequent to a reversal of Pakistan's relationship with the US after 911, it is possible that the US may have acceded to Pakistan's request without demanding that Pakistan reveal the location or details of its nuclear weapons. According to an ISIS report, US Secretary of State Colin Powell had offered nuclear protection assistance to Pakistan after 911li.

Pakistan found the offered technology to be quite rudimentary but nevertheless accepted it under the condition that the end point usage would remain opaque. Other aspects of the assistance included training courses for Pakistani nuclear weapons personnel in US labs where they were instructed on nuclear safety and security issues.

David Albright, a US nuclear security analyst, prescribed the following forms of additional assistance to Pakistan in the aftermath of 911:

"Generic physical protection and material accounting practices; theoretical exercises; unclassified military handbooks on nuclear weapons safety and security; more sophisticated vaults and access doors; portal control equipment; better surveillance equipment; advanced equipment for materials accounting; personnel reliability programs; and programs to reduce the likelihood of leaking sensitive information. In addition, aid could focus on methods that improve the security of nuclear weapons against unauthorized use through devices not intrinsic to the design of the nuclear weapon or through special operational or administrative restrictions. Excluded assistance would include nuclear weapons design information aimed at making more secure, reliable or safer nuclear weapons or devices, PALs, coded launch control devices, and environmental sensing devices."

While technical measures to reduce the chances of nuclear sabotage and accident must undoubtedly be implemented, there is a fundamental tension that cannot be avoided – a perfectly safe nuclear weapon is also one that cannot be used. Hence, by definition, it is useless. In times of crisis and war, when casualties and passions run high, there will be a strong urge to weaken the safety mechanisms in place.

PAKISTANI NUCLEAR STRIKES ON TACTICAL TARGETS

However, there is an undeniably close link between nuclear weapons and a nation's conventional military capabilities. If a nation's conventional capability is relatively low vis a vis a nuclear armed adversary, that nation is likely to adopt a 'first use' strategy to thwart a conventional military offensive that may threaten to undermine its territorial integrity and lead to its break up. This is the situation that Pakistan finds itself in at present. In such a case, the nuclear weapons to be used or threatened to be used would be 'tactical' nuclear weapons against India's mechanised forces inside Pakistani territory. While India may have no intentions of launching a major conventional offensive into Pakistan, given India's conventional superiority (no matter how slender the edge may be), Pakistan has based its national security strategy on the first use of nuclear weapons to prevent its comprehensive military defeat like in 1971 and, consequently, its disintegration as a nation. It is for this reason that Pakistan finds it difficult to accept India's offer of a bilateral no-first-use treaty as a confidence building measure.

In the Indo-Pak context, Indian advocates of tactical nuclear weapons pre-suppose that when pushed to the wall, Pakistan would not hesitate to use nuclear weapons against India's mechanised forces inside Pakistani territory as the 'opprobrium quotient', as General Sundarji called it, would be low since the use of nuclear weapons could be justified as a defensive measure of the last resort. They aver that in response India too should employ only tactical nuclear weapons on Pakistani forces, rather than raise the nuclear ante to full-scale retaliation. Though there is considerable merit in it, in India's overall strategic equation with Pakistan it is a dangerous argument and would completely degrade the potential not only of India's nuclear deterrence but also of India's conventional superiority.

According to the army doctrine published recently by the Army Training Command (ARTRAC), "the Indian Army believes in fighting the war in enemy territory. If forced into a war, the aim of our offensive(s) would be to apply a sledgehammer blow to the enemy. The Indian Army's concept of waging war is to ensure a decisive victory and to ensure that conflict termination places us at an advantageous position." In a future Indo-Pak war in the plains, should India pursue a pro-active strategy and launch an offensive with one or more Strike Corps across the international boundary, supported massively by the IAF, India's mechanised spearheads are likely to achieve major operational level gains in three to five days and strategic gains soon thereafter. Pakistan may then be forced to commit its strategic reserves, that is, either or both the Army Reserves North (ARN) and South (ARS) and risk their destruction in detail or exercise its nuclear option.

Indian analysts are inclined to believe that Pakistan is likely to resort to the early use of nuclear weapons, especially when it can justify their use as a defensive measure of the last resort on its own soil against Indian mechanised forces. If this logic is accepted, India's conventional superiority against Pakistan will stand negated and the Indian military leadership will either have to run the risk of accepting the consequences of a nuclear strike from Pakistan or plan to launch only tactical level limited offensives with shallow objectives so as to avoid crossing Pakistan's perceived nuclear threshold.

Such a course of action would naturally play straight into Pakistan's hands and give that country the freedom to continue to interfere in India's internal affairs through its 'proxy war' in J&K, including the launching of Kargil-type misadventures, without the fear of massive Indian retaliation with conventional forces. Pakistan may even resort to launching trans-international boundary operations in areas such as the Rann of Kutch on one pretext or the other, as it did in the summer months of 1965. The safety provided by India's doctrine of 'no-first-use' of nuclear weapons would further embolden Pakistan to seek tactical advantage.

The Indian army would be left with the option to plan to seize a long though narrow strip of Pakistani territory virtually all along the front without ringing Pakistan's nuclear alarm bells by launching a number of limited, shallow objective offensives. However, this capability is unlikely to dissuade Pakistan from practicing its peculiar brand of jihad through a cocktail of terrorism and aggressive actions across the LoC a la Kargil. The only sensible option may perhaps be to call Pakistan's nuclear bluff and plan to launch Strike Corps operations to achieve strategic gains in as early a time frame as is militarily possible. This approach will need to be combined with a declaratory policy that a nuclear strike against Indian soldiers, even if they are deep inside Pakistani territory, will constitute the use of nuclear weapons against India and will invite massive counter value and counter force punitive retaliation against Pakistan. General Sundarji wrote in 1992 that, "If the damage suffered by Indian forces (due to a Pakistani nuclear strike) is substantial, national and troop morale would demand at least a quid pro quo response. There might even be a demand in some quarters for a quid pro quo plus response."17 However, after over a decade of Pakistan's proxy war and particularly after that country's perfidious intrusions into the Kargil district of J&K in the summer months of 1999, the national mood is much different. Indian public opinion will accept nothing short of the final dismemberment of Pakistan in case that country chooses to cross the nuclear Rubicon and launches a nuclear strike, even if it is on Indian forces.

INDIA'S NUCLEAR AMBITION

The Government of India intends to draw twenty-five per cent of its energy from nuclear power by 2050. This plan includes 20,000 MW of installed capacity from nuclear energy by 2020, and 63,000 MW by 2032. There are currently twenty one operational nuclear power reactors in India, across six states. They contribute less than three per cent of the country's total energy generation, yet radioactively pollute at every stage of the nuclear fuel cycle: from mining and milling to reprocessing or disposal. There is no long-term radioactive waste disposal policy in India.

The inherent risks of nuclear power are made greater in India by the structure of the country's nuclear establishment. he organisation in charge of safety in all nuclear facilities, the Atomic Energy Regulatory Board, shares staff and is provided funds with the organisations it is supposed to be regulating. This compromises its ability to act independently and enforce vigorous safety regulations. In addition, there is little distinction between military and civilian nuclear affairs, and all matters of atomic energy come directly under the Prime Minister, not parliament. This means the nuclear establishment is under no obligation to disclose information on the nuclear power sector to citizens. There's no excuse for this opacity in a country with an ambition to use nuclear energy for electricity.

Regardless of these flaws, India is one of the few countries in the world that is expanding its nuclear power sector at an enormous rate. Seven more nuclear reactors are under construction, of 4800 MW installed capacity. At least thirty-six new nuclear reactors are planned or proposed.

FOREIGN INVESTMENT IN INDIA'S NUCLEAR SECTOR

India's civilian nuclear programme was largely indigenous for many years, but the government is now beckoning foreign investment. It intends to set up 'nuclear parks' supplied by foreign companies and operated-for now-by the Nuclear Power Corporation of India Limited (NPCIL), a government-owned company. These 'parks' are planned to have installed generated capacity of 8,000-10,000 MW at a single site. As the greatest installed capacity at one site is currently only 1,400 MW (Tarapur Atomic Power Station in Maharashtra, with four reactors), this is a huge increase. Russian company Atomstroyexport, a government subsidiary, has reached a deal to build sixteen nuclear reactors in India. From the two of these units, of 1000 MW each, one is operational and the other is currently under construction in Kundankulam, Tamil Nadu.

French company AREVA NP (a joint venture between AREVA and Seimens) have agreed to construct six 1650 MW reactors in Jaitapur, Maharastra. The European pressurised reactors, an untested type of reactor, will have a collective capacity of 9900 MW, making the Jaitapur nuclear power plant the largest in the world. Private US companies GE-Hitachi Nuclear Energy and Westinghouse Electric have been given sites at Kovada in Andhra Pradesh and Mithivirdi in Gujarat, respectively. It should be noted that, while the US seems happy to export nuclear reactors, not a single nuclear plant has been commissioned in the US since the 1979 Three Mile Island accident.

Clean Energy and Climate Change

Nuclear energy is often painted as a 'clean' energy option, and therefore a solution to climate change. Splitting the atom doesn't produce greenhouse gases, but the nuclear fuel cycle is far from clean: it produces radioactive waste that pollutes the environment for generations. Radioactive material has also leaked into the environment in the many accidents at Indian nuclear power plants, suggesting the sector is anything but clean.

As for a contribution to climate change, the expert committee on an integrated energy policy set up by the planning commission takes a dim view of nuclear power prospects: 'Even if a 20-fold increase takes place in India's nuclear capacity by 2031-32, the contribution of nuclear to the energy mix is at best expected to be 5-6 per cent,' they write. In contrast, renewable energy does not pollute the environment, nor produce greenhouse gases. It is the true solution to climate change.

Civil Liability for Nuclear Damage Act, 2010

Greenpeace India's campaign on nuclear energy began with the Civil Liability for Nuclear Damage Bill in 2010. The bill was the last hurdle for the government in opening up India's nuclear power industry to private investors in the USA, and proposed that financial liability for foreign suppliers – in the event of an accident – be capped at Rs. 500 crore. This amount was far lower than demanded by other countries, and even lower than levels of damages sometimes claimed in weather storms. Much of the liability was also transferred to the operator – in this case the Indian government – meaning that compensation would be covered by the taxpayer. It indicated the government's disregard for the safety and well being of Indian citizens in preference of foreign investment.

Through the involvement of Greenpeace and other groups, the terms of the Bill were changed to include supplier liability in addition to the operator liability. India's liability regime is currently unique in that it also holds suppliers accountable.

PAKISTAN AND INDIA: RACE TO THE END

One of the more tenacious conspiracy theories that have taken root in the hothouse of Pakistan's capital is that Osama bin Laden was not killed in the May 2, 2011, Navy SEAL raid on his compound in Abbottabad — that, in fact, he had already been dead for years, killed in the caves of Tora Bora.

According to this theory, the CIA had been keeping bin Laden's corpse on ice, literally, ready to be resurrected at a moment when his "death" could better serve U.S. interests. That moment came when the SEALs decided to conduct a dry run of their long-planned operation to snatch Pakistan's nuclear weapons. Bin Laden's thawing corpse was brought along as cover in case the exercise blew up — and as a devious bit of political theater to besmirch Pakistan's reputation if all went well.

What keep conspiracy theories like this alive are bits and pieces of half-baked evidence that could be construed to support a deeply held belief. In this case, it is the belief — accepted across the board in Pakistan, from the top brass of its military down to the dusty gaggle of taxi drivers who awaited me each morning outside my Islamabad hotel — that the United States has a not-so-secret plan to snatch Pakistan's nuclear arsenal.

The United States, which is duly concerned that Pakistan's nukes could fall into the wrong hands, almost certainly does have a plan to neutralize those weapons in the event of a coup or total state collapse. When the question was put to Condoleezza Rice during her 2005 confirmation hearings to become secretary of state, she replied, "We have noted this problem, and we are prepared to try to deal with it."

"Try" is the key word. Military experts — American, Pakistani, and Indian — agree that grabbing or disarming all of Pakistan's nukes at this stage would be something close to mission impossible. As one senior Pakistani general told me, "We look at the stories in the U.S. media about taking away our nuclear weapons and this definitely concerns us, so countermeasures have been developed accordingly." Such steps have included building more warheads and spreading them out over a larger number of heavily guarded locations. This, of course, also makes the logistics of securing them against theft by homegrown terrorists that much more complicated.

Fears of that terrifying possibility were heightened in August, when a group of militants assaulted a Pakistani base that some believe houses nuclear weapons components. Nine militants and one soldier were killed in a two-hour firefight at the Kamra air force base. The local media immediately floated the theory that this, too, was part of the American plot to steal Pakistan's nukes. But more disturbing than any conspiracy theory is the reality that this was the fourth attack in five years on the Kamra base, just 20 miles from the capital. At least five other sensitive military installations have also come under attack by militants since 2007.

Yet, though the danger of a loose Pakistani nuke certainly deserves scrupulous attention, it may not be the severest nuclear threat emanating from South Asia, as I came to realize after interviewing more than a dozen experts in Pakistan, India, and the United States this summer. Since the 9/11 attacks, preventing the world's most dangerous weapons from falling into the hands of the world's most dangerous actors — whether al Qaeda terrorists or Iranian mullahs — has understandably been America's stated priority. Yet the gravest danger — not only for the region, but for the United States itself — may be the South Asian incarnation of a Cold War phenomenon: a nuclear arms race.

Pakistan, with an estimated 90 to 120 warheads, is now believed to be churning out more plutonium than any other country on the planet — thanks to two Chinese-built reactors that are now online, a third that is undergoing trials, and a fourth that is scheduled to become operational by 2016. It has already passed India in total number of warheads and is on course to overtake Britain as the world's No. 5 nuclear power. Pakistan could end up in third place, behind Russia and the United States, within a decade.

This April, Pakistan tested a short-range ballistic missile, the Hatf IX, a so-called "shoot and scoot" battlefield nuclear weapon aimed at deterring an invasion by India's conventional forces. This development carries two disturbing implications. First, Pakistan now has the know-how to build nuclear warheads compact enough to fit on the tip of a small missile or inside a suitcase (handy for terrorists). Second, Pakistan has adopted a war-fighting doctrine that does not preclude nuking its own territory in the event of an Indian incursion — a dubious first in the annals of deterrence theory.

India, meanwhile, has just tested its first long-range ballistic missile, the Agni-V, with a range of 3,100 miles. In April, the Indian Navy added a new Russian-made nuclear-powered submarine to its fleet and is now building its own nuclear subs. One has already been launched and will enter service next year, and India is determined to add submarine-launched ballistic missiles to its arsenal. This puts India on the verge of joining the elite nuclear "triad" club — states with the ability to survive a first strike by an adversary and deliver a retaliatory strike by land, sea, or air.

India has also said that it has successfully tested an anti-ballistic missile shield that could be deployed "in a short time" to protect New Delhi and Mumbai. The downside of this defensive measure — putting aside the question of effectiveness — is that it invites an adversary to build many more warheads in the hope that a few will be able to slip through the shield.

India claims that it is not really engaged in an arms race — or that, if it is, its opponent is not Pakistan, but China, a nuclear-armed superpower and economic rival with which it shares a disputed border.

The Agni-V was dubbed the "China-killer" in some overheated Indian headlines. China's nuclear ambitions are geared toward deterring the United States and Russia, but it obligingly stirs the pot in South Asia by providing Pakistan with plutonium reactors — in flagrant violation of its obligations as a member of the Nuclear Suppliers Group.

Meanwhile, through a 2008 deal negotiated by George W. Bush's administration, the United States has given India access to nuclear fuel on the international market. In the past, India had been barred from such trade because the Nuclear Non-Proliferation Treaty does not consider its nuclear weapons program legitimate, and its limited supplies of domestic uranium forced it to choose between powering its reactors and building more nuclear weapons. "Power production was the priority; now they can have both," explained Toby Dalton, deputy director of the Nuclear Policy Program at the Carnegie Endowment for International Peace.

With both sides armed to the teeth, it is easy to exaggerate the fears and much harder to pinpoint where the real dangers lie. For the United States, the nightmare scenario is that some of Pakistan's warheads or its fissile material falls into the hands of the Taliban or al Qaeda — or, worse, that the whole country falls into the hands of the Taliban. For example, Rolf Mowatt-Larssen, a former CIA officer now at Harvard University's Belfer Center for Science and International Affairs, has warned of the "lethal proximity between terrorists, extremists, and nuclear weapons insiders" in Pakistan. This is a reality, but on the whole, Pakistan's nuclear arsenal appears to be reasonably secure against internal threats, according to those who know the country best.

To outsiders, Pakistan appears to be permanently teetering on the brink of collapse. The fact that large swaths of the country are literally beyond the control of the central government is not reassuring. But a weak state does not mean a weak society, and powerful internal dynamics based largely on kinship and tribe make it highly unlikely that Pakistan would ever fall under the control of an outfit like the Taliban. During the country's intermittent bouts of democracy, its civilian leaders have been consistently incompetent and corrupt, but even in the worst of times, the military has maintained a high standard of professionalism. And there is nothing that matters more to the Pakistani military than keeping the nuclear arsenal — its crown jewels — out of the hands of India, the United States, and homegrown extremists.

"Pakistan struggled to acquire these weapons against the wishes of the world. Our nuclear capability comes as a result of great sacrifice. It is our most precious and powerful weapon — for our defense, our security, and our political prestige," Talat Masood, a retired Pakistani lieutenant general, told me. "We keep them safe."

Pakistan's nuclear security is in the responsibility of the Strategic Plans Division, which appears to function pretty much as a separate branch of the military. It has its own training facility and an elaborate set of controls and screening procedures to keep track of all warheads and fissile material and to monitor any blips in the behaviour patterns of its personnel. The 15 or so sites where weapons are stored are the mostly heavily guarded in the country. Even if some group managed to steal or commandeer a weapon, it is highly unlikely the group would be able to use it. The greater danger is the theft of fissile material, which could be used to make a crude bomb. "With 70 to 80 kilos of highly enriched uranium, it would be fairly easy to make one in the basement of a building in the city of your choice," said Pervez Hoodbhoy, a distinguished nuclear physicist at Islamabad's Quaid-i-Azam University. At the moment, Pakistan has a stockpile of about 2.75 tons — or some 30 bombs' worth — of highly enriched uranium. It does not tell Americans where it is stored.

"All nuclear countries are conscious of the risks, nuclear weapons states especially so," said Gen. Ehsan ul-Haq, who speaks with the been-there-done-that authority of a man who has served as both chairman of Pakistan's Joint Chiefs of Staff Committee and head of the ISI, its controversial spy agency. "Of course there are concerns. Some are genuine, but much of what you read in the U.S. media is irrational and reflective of paranoia. Rising radicalism in Pakistan? Yes, this is true, and the military is very conscious of this."

Perhaps the most credible endorsement of Pakistan's nuclear security regime comes from its most steadfast enemy. The consensus among India's top generals and defense experts is that Pakistan's nukes are pretty secure. "No one can be 100 percent secure, but I think they are more than 99 percent secure," said Shashindra Tyagi, a former chief of staff of the Indian Air Force. "They keep a very close watch on personnel. All of the steps that could be taken have been taken. This business of the Taliban taking over — it can't be ruled out, but I think it's unlikely. The Pakistani military understands the threats they face better than anyone, and they are smart enough to take care it."

Yogesh Joshi, an analyst at the Institute for Defense Studies and Analyses in New Delhi, agrees: "Different states have different perceptions of risk. The U.S. has contingency plans [to secure Pakistan's nukes] because its nightmare scenario is that Pakistan's weapons fall into terrorist hands. The view from India over the years is that Pakistan, probably more than any other nuclear weapons state, has taken measures to secure its weapons. At the political level here, there's a lot of confidence that Pakistan's nuclear weapons are secure."

The greater concern — not only for India and Pakistan, but for the United States and everyone else — may be the direct competition between the two South Asian states. True, in terms of numbers and destructive capacity, the arms buildup in South Asia does not come close to what was going on during the Cold War, when the United States and the Soviet Union built enough bombs to destroy the planet many times over. India and Pakistan have enough to destroy it only once, perhaps twice.

But in many ways, the arms race in South Asia is more dangerous. The United States and the Soviet Union were rival superpowers jockeying for influence and advantage on the global stage, but these were also two countries that had never gone to war with each other, that had a vast physical and psychological separation between them, that generally steered clear of direct provocations, and that eventually had mechanisms in place (like the famous hotline between Moscow and Washington) to make sure little misunderstandings didn't grow into monstrous miscalculations.

By contrast, the India-Pakistan rivalry comes with all the venom and vindictiveness of a messy divorce, which, of course, it is. The two countries have officially fought three wars against each other since their breakup in 1947 and have had numerous skirmishes and close calls since then. They have a festering territorial dispute in Kashmir. The 1999 Kargil conflict, waged a year after both countries went overtly nuclear, may have come closer to the nuclear brink than even the 1962 Cuban missile crisis. At the height of the showdown, there was credible intelligence that both sides were readying their nuclear arsenals for deployment. Pakistan lost all three of these wars. Its very large army is still only half the size of India's, whose military budget is more than seven times larger than Pakistan's. Pakistan's generals are well aware that in any all-out conventional confrontation with India, they're toast. The guiding ideology of Pakistan's Army — from the generals on down to their drivers — is that India represents a permanent existential threat. This is why Pakistan clings to its nukes and attempts to maintain at least the illusion of what its generals call "bilateral balance."

This conventional asymmetry increases the danger of the nuclear arms race — it feeds India's hubris and Pakistan's sense of failure. Here are two countries headed in opposite directions. India's $1.7 trillion economy is eight times the size of Pakistan's and has grown at an enviable 8.2 percent annually over the last three years, compared to just 3.3 percent for Pakistan.

India is in the forefront of the digital revolution, and while the country's leaders were embarrassed by this summer's massive two-day blackout, Pakistan's broken-down infrastructure struggles to provide citizens with more than a few hours of electricity each day. India, the world's largest democracy, is on the cusp of becoming a global power; Pakistan, with its on-and-off military dictatorships (off at the moment), ranks 13th on Foreign Policy's most recent Failed States Index.

More significant than these statistics is the mindset behind them. India is brimming with confidence. Pakistan is hobbled by fear, paranoia, and a deep sense of inferiority. India's major cities, New Delhi and Mumbai, are modernizing global metropolises. Checking into the Marriott in Pakistan's capital is like checking into a maximum-security prison — high walls topped with razor wire, armed guards in watchtowers. Islamabad today looks and feels like a city under siege where there could be a coup at any moment. This economic and cultural lopsidedness is strikingly reflected in the countries' nuclear competition.

In perhaps no other major power is the military quite so submissive to civilian authority as it is in India. "The civilian side lords it over the military in a manner that often borders on humiliation — and there is no pushback from the military," said

Ashley Tellis, an India expert with the Carnegie Endowment. The reasons for this are rooted in India's long struggle for independence against a colonial master that filled the ranks of its police and army with natives. "The military was seen as a force that served a colonial occupier," said Tellis. With the Indian officer corps' fondness for whiskey, mustaches, and other Briticisms, "the nationalist leadership looked at them as aliens" and took extreme measures to make sure there would be no coups.

From a nuclear standpoint, the result of this dynamic is a command-and-control system that is firmly in the hands of the civilian political leadership, a clearly stated "no first use" policy, and a view that nukes are political weapons — a way to project global power and prestige — not viable war-fighting tools.

In theory, Pakistan's nuclear trigger is also in civilian hands. A body called the National Command Authority, headed by the prime minister, is supposed to be the ultimate decider of whether to initiate a nuclear attack. In reality, however, it is the military that controls the process from top to bottom. Pakistan has never formally stated its nuclear doctrine, preferring to keep the Indians guessing as to when and where it might use nukes. But now it appears to be contemplating the idea of actually using tactical nuclear weapons in a confrontation with India.

The problem with this delicate state of affairs is not simply the two countries' history of war, but Pakistan's tactic of hiding behind its nuclear shield while allowing terrorist groups to launch proxy attacks against India. The 2001 attack on India's Parliament building and the 2008 Mumbai attack are the most egregious examples. Both were carried out by Lashkar-e-Taiba militants based in Pakistan with well-established links to the ISI and were far more provocative than anything the Americans or Russians dished out to each other during the four decades of the Cold War. (More than 160 people were killed in the attack that held India's largest city hostage for 60 hours.) Terrorism is the classic underdog tactic, but Pakistan is certainly the world's first nuclear-armed underdog to successfully apply the tactic against a nuclear rival.

India has been struggling to respond. "For 15 years this country is bleeding from attack after attack, and there is nothing we can do," said Raja Mohan of the Observer Research Foundation, a New Delhi think tank. "The attacks correlate directly to Pakistan's acquisition of nuclear weapons. From the moment they got nukes, they saw it as an opportunity they could exploit. And India has no instruments to punish Pakistan or change its behaviour."

There are encouraging signs that Pakistan may be rethinking this tactic, realizing that over the long run the Taliban and others of its ilk pose a far greater danger to Pakistan than to India. The relentless succession of suicide bombings and attacks on police and military bases and a costly war to wrest control of the Swat Valley from the Taliban seem to have finally convinced Pakistan's military that, in the words of one general, "the threat today is internal, and if it is not pushed back and neutralized, it will continue to expand its influence and we will have an Afghanistan situation inside our own country." But even if the ISI is sincere about ending its relationship with jihadi proxies, India's military planners are still searching for an appropriate weapon with which to punish Pakistan in the event of "another Mumbai."

The problem for India is that even though it holds a huge advantage in conventional forces, its mobilization process is ponderously slow. This shortcoming was humiliatingly exposed after the 2001 attack on the Parliament building, when it took the Indian Army about three weeks to deploy for a retaliatory strike — enough time for the United States to step in and cool tempers on both sides. A potential nuclear crisis had been averted, but in 2004, India, still smarting from its inability to retaliate, announced a new war-fighting doctrine dubbed "Cold Start," which called for the capability to conduct a series of cross-border lightning strikes within 72 hours. The idea was not to hold territory or threaten the existence of the Pakistani state, but to use overwhelming firepower to deliver a punishing blow that would fall short of provoking a nuclear response.

Pakistan's reaction — or overreaction — was to double down on developing its short-range battlefield nuclear weapon, the Hatf IX. Any incursion from India would be met with a nuclear response even if it meant Pakistan had to nuke its own territory. "What one fears is that with the testing of these short-range nuclear missiles—

five in the last couple of months — this seems to indicate a seriousness about using theater nuclear weapons," said Hoodbhoy, the physicist.

While strategists on both sides debate whether the Hatf IX, with a range of 60 kilometers and a mobile multibarrel launch system, would be enough to stop an advancing column of Indian tanks — Hoodbhoy argues that "smaller, sub-kiloton-size weapons are not really effective militarily" — they do agree that it would take more than one missile to do the job, instantly escalating the crisis beyond anyone's control.

The last nuclear weapon state to seriously consider the use of battlefield nuclear weapons was the United States during the first decades of the Cold War, when NATO was faced with the overwhelming superiority of Soviet conventional forces. But by the early 1970s, U.S. strategists no longer believed these weapons had any military utility, and by 1991 most had been withdrawn from European territory.

Pakistan, however, seems to have embraced this discarded strategy and is now, in effect, challenging India to a game of nuclear chicken — which seems to have made India tread carefully. Tellingly, in 2008, when Lashkar terrorists attacked Mumbai, Cold Start was not implemented. These days, Indian officials seem to be backing away from the idea. "There is no Cold Start doctrine. No such thing. It was an off-the-cuff remark from a former chief of staff. I have been defense minister of the country. I should know," veteran Indian politician Jaswant Singh assured me. In a WikiLeaked classified document dated Feb. 16, 2010, Tim Roemer, then U.S. ambassador to India, described Cold Start as "a mixture of myth and reality" that, if implemented, "would likely encounter very mixed results."

Pakistani military planners, however, continue to be obsessed with the idea of Cold Start. It comes up in every conversation about security, and it is the driving force behind the country's program to develop tactical battlefield nukes. For now, the focus is on missile delivery systems, but according to Maria Sultan, director of the South Asian Strategic Stability Institute, an Islamabad think tank, there is growing interest in using nukes in other ways

— such as to create an electromagnetic pulse that would fry the enemy's electronics. "In short, we will look for full-spectrum response options," she said.

The arms race could make a loose nuke more likely. After all, Pakistan's assurances that its nuclear arsenal is safe and secure rest heavily on the argument that its warheads and their delivery systems have been uncoupled and stored separately in heavily guarded facilities. It would be very difficult for a group of mutinous officers to assemble the necessary protocols for a launch and well nigh impossible for a band of terrorists to do so. But that calculus changes with the deployment of mobile battlefield weapons. The weapons themselves, no longer stored in heavily guarded bunkers, would be far more exposed.

Nevertheless, military analysts from both countries still say that a nuclear exchange triggered by miscalculation, miscommunication, or panic is far more likely than terrorists stealing a weapon — and, significantly, that the odds of such an exchange increase with the deployment of battlefield nukes. As these ready-to-use weapons are maneuvered closer to enemy lines, the chain of command and control would be stretched and more authority necessarily delegated to field officers. And, if they have weapons designed to repel a conventional attack, there is obviously a reasonable chance they will use them for that purpose. "It lowers the threshold," said Hoodbhoy. "The idea that tactical nukes could be used against Indian tanks on Pakistan's territory creates the kind of atmosphere that greatly shortens the distance to apocalypse."

Both sides speak of the possibility of a limited nuclear war. But even those who speak in these terms seem to understand that this is fantasy — that once started, a nuclear exchange would be almost impossible to limit or contain. "The only move that you have control over is your first move; you have no control over the nth move in a nuclear exchange," said Carnegie's Tellis. The first launch would create hysteria; communication lines would break down, and events would rapidly cascade out of control. Some of the world's most densely populated cities could find themselves under nuclear attack, and an estimated 20 million people could die almost immediately. What's more, the resulting firestorms would put 5 million to 7 million metric tons of smoke into the upper atmosphere, according to a new model developed by climate scientists at Rutgers University and the University of Colorado.

Within weeks, skies around the world would be permanently overcast, and the condition vividly described by Carl Sagan as "nuclear winter" would be upon us. The darkness would likely last about a decade. The Earth's temperature would drop, agriculture around the globe would collapse, and a billion or more humans who already live on the margins of subsistence could starve.

This is the real nuclear threat that is festering in South Asia. It is a threat to all countries, including the United States, not just India and Pakistan. Both sides acknowledge it, but neither seems able to slow their dangerous race to annihilation.

2

Pakistan's Tactical Nuclear Weapons: The Inevitability of Instability

Hatf IX (Nasr) is a Pakistani ballistic missile which can deliver a sub-kiloton nuclear warhead over a range of 60 km, or 37.3 miles. It is supposed to have entered service in 2013 and is believed to be fully integrated into Pakistan's C3I (command, control, communications and intelligence). Its purported role is as a low-yield battlefield deterrent against mechanised columns. Should India – and the world – take Nasr seriously? The development and deployment of Nasr by Pakistan was inevitable and the impact of this tactical nuclear weapon (tac nuke) on the emerging India-Pakistan deterrence relationship is inherently destabilising.

DEFINING TACTICAL NUCLEAR WEAPONS: THE PAKISTANI CONTEXT

There are four different yardsticks by which tac nukes could be defined and classified. The first is the range of the missile: it must be short range, that is less than 80-100 km. The second is yield of warhead, conventionally benchmarked at less than 5 kilotons (kT) with reference to a 1994 US Congressional definition prohibiting R&D in US nuclear weapons laboratories below this yield. The third is function – Pakistan would use its tactical nuclear weapons in an anti-armour role; bunker busting is the primary role envisaged by US proponents of research into low yield nuclear weapons. The fourth yardstick is impact, which in the case of tac nukes is limited to the immediate battlefield, or in other words, the sub-theatre.

Tactical Nuclear Weapons: Problem than a Solution?

Why are tac nukes usually seen as a problem rather than as a solution? In the first place, they lower the nuclear threshold by blurring the distinction between conventional and nuclear war. Secondly, tac nukes accentuate the 'always-never dilemma' inherent in all nuclear weapons: they must always work when you want them to, yet never be used when you do not want them to be used. The possibility of unauthorised or accidental use increases significantly with tac nukes: unlike ballistic missile submarines (SSBNs), whose commanders have delegative control, in the case of tac nukes delegative control may go down to subaltern/NCO levels under battlefield conditions. Thirdly, battlefield deployment of tac nukes, especially in situations of rapid armour movement, creates an enormous pressure to 'use them or lose them'. Finally, there is a much greater possibility for tac nukes to fall into 'wrong hands' due to theft, pilferage or sabotage.

Given these problems, all of them well known for decades, why has Pakistan gone down the tac nuke route? In order to understand why, it is important to underline that Pakistan has, from even before South Asia's overt nuclearisation, signalled a nuclear doctrine of not only first use but also early use. This doctrine has created problems for Pakistan, whose nuclear planners have had to grapple with the issue of nuclear thresholds, that is the point beyond which Pakistan would have no option but to use its nuclear weapons. As far back as 2002, the Landau Network–Centro Volta team (Cotta-Ramusino and Martellini) had identified four Pakistani thresholds: geographic (space threshold), military, political (domestic destabilisation) and even economic. Tac nukes are Pakistan's solution to the military threshold.

PAKISTAN'S TACTICAL NUCLEAR WEAPONS: HERE TO STAY

There are three essential features of Pakistan that suggest that its tac nukes are here to stay. Firstly, as the weaker power in the India-Pakistan dyad, Pakistan faces significant conventional asymmetries. Only nuclear weapons provide Pakistan with a sense of strategic parity with India. Faced with the possibility of an Indian armoured thrust in the plains or desert sectors, Pakistan is signalling that it will use its tactical nuclear weapons despite their escalatory potential.

Secondly, Pakistan is a quintessential 'homeland state' with deep existential anxieties. Its entire national identity has been constructed as a homeland for an endangered people facing a historically implacable foe. No matter how many internal security challenges it faces, Pakistan will not drop its guard vis-à-vis India and will always give the external threat primacy. In such an identity construction, nuclear weapons give Pakistan and its people the assurance of national survival and civilizational certitude that they are second to none. Furthermore, they encapsulate the sense of 'we will all go together when we go' – akin to the Samson Option of that other nuclearised homeland state, Israel.

Finally, Pakistan is a revisionist power that has systematically pursued asymmetric strategies to overturn the territorial status quo. In this context, the nature of the 'Kashmir issue' comes into sharp focus. As a wise person once said of the Kashmir issue, 'Kashmir is with India, the issue is with Pakistan.' While admittedly a neat play on words, this observation identifies two core elements in the 'shadow of the future': (1) The Kashmir issue will be resolved only when Pakistan considers it resolved; (2) any change in the territorial status quo would be inimical to India. Pakistan's dilemma is the nuclear weapons give it strategic parity but also buttress the territorial status quo. This explains why Pakistan has no compunction in deliberately shortening its nuclear fuse vis-à-vis India by deploying tac nukes.

PAKISTAN BUILDING 'BATTLEFIELD NUKES' TO DETER INDIA

As the world remains focused on preventing a nuclear arms race in the Middle East, South Asia's dangerous nuclear rivalry—between India and Pakistan—grows ever more deadly. General Khalid Kidwai, a top advisor to the Pakistani government, said this week that Pakistan needed short-range tactical nuclear weapons, also known as "battlefield nukes" to deter nuclear archrival India.

Kidwai said that "having tactical weapons would make war less likely," at aconference on nuclear security organized by the Carnegie Endowment for International Peace in Washington. Kidwai administered Pakistan's nuclear and missile weapons program for fifteen years.

Pakistan's tactical weapon developmentincludes the Nasr Missile, which has a range of around 37 miles (60 kilometers) and reflects concerns in Pakistan that "India's larger military could still wage a conventional war against the country, thinking Pakistan would not risk retaliation with a bigger nuclear weapon."

Pakistan especially fears and aims to neutralize India's "Cold Start" doctrine, a type of blitzkrieg that aims to advance fast enough into Pakistan to seize key installations before a retaliatory nuclear strike.

Unlike India, which has a no first use nuclear doctrine, Pakistan has repeatedlysaid that it would retaliate against India with nuclear weapons if enough of its territory were lost. Tactical nuclear weapons would also neutralize Indian forces on the battlefield, even in Pakistan itself, and would seriously disrupt India's tactical maneuverability.

Trending Offers and Articles

India has criticized Pakistan's stance on battlefield nukes. Rakesh Sood, former Indian special envoy for disarmament and nonproliferation, said it was "extremely destabilizing for any country to develop tactical nuclear weapons" and that India had no plans to do so. He also argued that Pakistan's nuclear doctrine is "cloaked in ambiguity," undermining confidence between the two countries.

Despite Kidwai's assertion that such weapons would make war unlikely, Peter Lavoy, a former U.S. defense official questioned if "whether such intermingling of conventional forces and nuclear weapons in a battlefield could increase the risk of nuclear war."

Kidwai's statement is in line with Pakistan's recent aggressive expansion of its nuclear and ballistic missile programs. Pakistan's nuclear weapons program is a major cause for concern for the rest of the world, amid fears that its weapons can fall into the wrong hands. Kidwai, however, rejected this and insisted that adequate safeguards were in place. However, Pakistan's aggressive expansion of its nuclear capacity could continue to make South Asia a much more dangerous place, escalating tensions with India. Earlier in March, Pakistan tested a Shaheen-III missile, which has a range of about 1,700 miles. This would enable Pakistan to hit any part of India with a nuclear warhead, while also placing Israel within range.

Shahid Latif, a retired commander in the Pakistani Air Force, said that "now, India doesn't have its safe havens anymore." According to the *Bulletin of Atomic Scientists*, Pakistan actually has more nuclear weapons—120—than India (110). This is despite its more meager resource and economic base, and in line with thefamous statement made by former Pakistani Prime Minister Zulfikar Ali Bhutto in 1972, that "even if we have to eat grass, we will make nuclear bombs."

GROWING NUCLEAR CAPABILITIES WITH NO END IN SIGHT

In contrast to the United States and the former Soviet Union, China historically maintained a small nuclear force consisting primarily of land-based missiles whose warheads were stored separately, with the delivery vehicles maintained routinely in un-alerted status in silos or caves. This relatively relaxed posture was viewed as sufficient to protect Chinese security during the Cold War because Beijing believed that the positive externalities of mutual U.S.-Soviet nuclear deterrence bestowed on China sufficient protection. Because even a small number of survivable nuclear weapons capable of reaching an adversary's homeland could wreak unacceptable damage, Chinese leaders sought to maintain relatively modest forces that through a combination of opacity, sheltering, and sometimes limited mobility, could survive the remote contingencies of direct nuclear attack at a time when these dangers were limited principally by the political constraints of strong bipolar competition.

With the ending of the Cold War and with the progressive rise of Chinese power, Beijing—whether it publicly admits it or not—

has come to view the United States as its principal strategic competitor. Given China's recognition of the sophistication of U.S. nuclear and conventional forces in the face of Beijing's desire to reclaim the strategic primacy it once enjoyed in Asia, Chinese nuclear modernization became inevitable. This modernization, which consists principally of efforts to increase the survivability of its nuclear deterrent in the face of what it perceives to be a formidable U.S. nuclear threat supplemented by other major regional dangers from Russia, India, and other prospective nuclear powers, has taken the following form: the deployment of new land-based solid-fueled ballistic missiles of varying ranges (to include intercontinental-range ballistic missiles); ballistic missile submarines with weapons capable of reaching the continental United States; new highly survivable nuclear weapon storage sites; and a robust national command and control system that incorporates a resilient, dedicated nuclear command and control segment.

The number of nuclear warheads in the Chinese arsenal has also progressively increased as the nuclear delivery systems have been augmented, but there still significant uncertainties about the existence and the number of nuclear gravity bombs and tactical nuclear weapons in the Chinese arsenal. The total size of the Chinese nuclear weapons inventory today is widely believed to consist of some 250 nuclear warheads, but the accuracy of these or any other numbers is debatable. China has a substantial fissile material stockpile consisting of some 16 metric tons of highly enriched uranium and some 1.8 metric tons of weapon-grade plutonium, so there are no practical constraints on its ability to produce an arsenal of any size it chooses. Given the choices China makes in regard to delivery systems, it could deploy anywhere up to an additional 150 warheads over the next ten years.

At arsenal levels of such size, the Chinese nuclear force will be oriented fundamentally towards deterring nuclear use (or the threat of use) against China by maintaining a survivable retaliatory capacity during conflicts with any nuclear-armed state and by maintaining the capacity for escalation dominance vis-à-vis weaker nuclear adversaries. Toward these ends, China will continue to reiterate its "no first use" nuclear policy, though what that doctrine means precisely is unclear.

China today views the United States as its principal active nuclear and conventional threat, followed by India in the nuclear realm. Russia remains a latent nuclear threat and although it was historically an important driver of Chinese nuclear planning, Russia has receded considerably in Chinese calculations today. North Korea, Taiwan, and Japan remain longer-term sources of strategic uncertainty for Beijing, with nuclear threats remaining a current or prospective challenge in all three cases. The most pressing practical contingencies involving Chinese nuclear use in the prospective future, however, involve employment against U.S. forces to forestall defeat or signal a willingness to risk further escalation in the context of a successful U.S. intervention in a Taiwan crisis or in another crisis of similar magnitude in East Asia (for example, on behalf of Japan), and the use of tactical (or other) nuclear weapons in a conflict with India.

INDIA

The rivalry between China and India since their birth as modern states after the Second World War created the preconditions for a nuclear rivalry between them—a competition that was inflamed when China first tested nuclear weapons in 1964 driven by its antagonism to the United States and its emerging split with the Soviet Union. The first Chinese nuclear test, coming two years after India's defeat in the 1962 Sino-Indian conflict, precipitated the Indian nuclear weapons program, which in turn first demonstrated its capacity in 1974. Despite the supposed Chinese disdain of India, Beijing began to systematically target India with nuclear weapons after the latter's first nuclear test, and sometime in the late-1980s transferred a nuclear weapon design and fissile material to Pakistan, at least in part as a strategy of containing India. New Delhi responded to the Chinese challenge with additional nuclear tests in 1998, declared itself to be a nuclear weapon state, and began to overtly develop its nuclear deterrent since—aimed at both China and Pakistan.

India today is believed to possess an arsenal of some 100 nuclear weapons, though this figure is highly uncertain. The country is thought to have produced close to 600 kilograms of weapons-grade plutonium, though it is unclear whether all this material has been machined into warheads. India can produce extremely large quantities of weapons-grade plutonium, should it chose to use its power reactors currently outside of safeguards for this purpose. To date, however, there is no evidence that India has embarked on any crash program to enlarge its nuclear arsenal, despite its having the technical capacity to do so. If India persists in producing about 5-6 nuclear weapons annually (as it is believed to have done since 1998), the India nuclear deterrent would consist of some less than 200 nuclear weapons by 2025—assuming the public assessments of its current inventory are correct. These weapons will be deployed aboard primarily mobile, solid-fueled, ballistic missiles of up to intermediate range, though these will be supplemented by a limited number of legacy gravity weapons and a small but growing number of sea-launched ballistic missiles. All Indian nuclear weapons currently are maintained routinely in de-mated condition, though whether this posture will persist after the four ballistic missile submarines are eventually inducted into its arsenal is unclear.

The heart of India's current nuclear modernization program, which is centered on developing and inducting mobile, sold-fueled intermediate-range ballistic missiles, deploying ballistic missile submarines, developing a ballistic missile defense system, building weapon storage and integration sites, and completing its command and control network, is aimed principally at refurbishing its deterrence capability vis-à-vis China. The threats emerging from Pakistan are significant, but Indian policy makers judge that their current deterrent against Islamabad as generally adequate. The deterrence gap versus China, however, is considerable and it will not be bridged until India acquires the capacity to range the Chinese heartland with missiles of adequate reach.

Even when the effort to reach this goal is completed—an endeavor that will continue well beyond 2025—it is likely that New Delhi will persist with its currently relaxed nuclear posture so long as current trends in Sino-Indian and Indo-Pakistani relations persist. This posture is predicated on the requirement of a "minimum" deterrent (whose numerical size is not publicly known) and a strict "no first use" policy (which is likely to subsist durably because of India's general conventional military superiority over Pakistan and its still substantial, though decaying, operational military superiority over China along their disputed border). As long as these conditions obtain, there is little incentive for India to violate its "no first use" policy, which is oriented fundamentally towards deterring nuclear attack (or threats of attack) emerging from Pakistan and China.

PAKISTAN

The contrast between India and Pakistan on "no first use" could not be greater. Unlike India, which is both stronger than Pakistan and no pushover where China is concerned, Pakistan is a weak state that is unfortunately growing even weaker as a result of its awful strategic choices. Pakistan's security competition with India, which dates back to the creation of the two countries as independent states, is multi-dimensional in nature and involves territorial, religious, and power-political dimensions. These grievances have combined in unhelpful ways to make Pakistan the anti-status quo power in the Indian subcontinent. Having fought four unsuccessful wars with India in an effort to secure its strategic aims, Pakistan switched to a dangerous and provocative strategy in the last decades of the 20th century—a strategy of supporting terrorist groups aimed at enervating India through "a thousand cuts," even as Pakistan began to feverishly expand its nuclear arsenal in an effort to prevent New Delhi from retaliating with conventional forces.

The post-2001-02 shift in Indian policy, which holds out the threat of conventional retaliation to Pakistani-supported terrorist attacks (despite the overarching presence of nuclear weapons in the subcontinent), has only deepened Pakistan's dependence on nuclear weapons further, resulting in an acceleration of its weapons program. Today, the Pakistan arsenal includes both gravity weapons and ballistic missiles of up to medium range as well as cruise missiles, glide bombs, and a plethora of new and diverse tactical nuclear weapons. The Pakistani nuclear arsenal is judged by many reputable scholars to consist of some 90-110 weapons, though at the current pace of growth the force could easily expand to over three times that number within a decade.

Pakistan's strategic weaponry is believed to be deployed in de-mated condition routinely in peacetime. Whether that posture will apply to the newer tactical systems is unclear. Pakistan's nuclear doctrine, unlike India or China's, is centered fundamentally on first use, and it is oriented primarily towards defeating India's conventional superiority in the event of conflict. Although Pakistan's nuclear forces are intended, strictly speaking, for deterrence and not war fighting, Islamabad's emerging tactical capabilities could inadvertently push Pakistan towards the latter.

The external dangers of deterrence breakdown, which could precipitate the catastrophe of Pakistani nuclear use against India, are complemented by internal dangers as well. Pakistan's internal fissures, it is often feared, could bleed into its armed forces, resulting in risks to the security of its nuclear weaponry. Although the Pakistani military has made enormous investments in enhancing nuclear security (aided by the United States) in recent years, fears about the loss or compromise of its nuclear weaponry because of domestic dangers still persist—and not unreasonably so.

TAKING STOCK

When all three states are synoptically considered, therefore, the following contingencies remain the most pressing from the viewpoint of U.S. strategic interests for the reasons adduced below:

1) Chinese use or threats of use of nuclear weaponry to deter U.S. military intervention on behalf or Taiwan or other American allies in Asia. Of the three nuclear weapons states that are the subject of this testimony, only China conceives of its nuclear arsenal as having direct utility for deterring U.S. military operations directed against its interests at various locations along the Asian rimland. Any contingency that brings U.S. forces in confrontation with China would represent a dangerous predicament and would require both local conventional and overall nuclear superiority for political and military success. Any failure on this score could not only precipitate immediate

operational reverses that would frustrate the realization of U.S. political aims, but it could lead over time to the erosion of the U.S. alliance system in East Asia, the future acquisition of nuclear weapons by current American allies, and the eventual loss of American primacy in the Indo-Pacific. For all these reasons, preparing seriously to ensure success in this contingency should remain at the top of American strategic priorities. The recent innovations centered on the "AirSea Battle" concept indicate that the Pentagon has taken the emerging Chinese threats to the U.S. ability to aid its East Asian allies seriously, though it is unclear whether force planning for nuclear escalation vis-à-vis China has been adequately integrated into the current war plans. If this lacuna is real, it could prove costly in the context of a conflict—and could undermine the confidence of the allies in the viability of the U.S. nuclear umbrella.

2) Pakistani "use" of nuclear weapons as cover to support continued terrorist attacks against India. Although this contingency derives from Pakistan's ability to exploit the deterrence capability inherent in its nuclear reserves for revisionist ends—and represents the dominant threat levied by the Pakistani military against India now for some three decades—it embodies the most likely route to nuclear deterrence breakdown in South Asia. Neither Indian nor U.S. nuclear capabilities are directly useful in defeating this threat, but U.S. and international political pressure on Pakistan, which has been employed episodically, might offer a means of mitigating its worst dangers. The most likely antidote that could alter such Pakistani behavior, however, would be the rising costs of terrorist blowback within Pakistan—which is, unfortunately, an expensive way of getting Pakistan to change course.

3) Pakistani nuclear use against India or against Indian military forces in the context of Indian retaliation against Pakistani-supported terrorist attacks against India. This contingency arises if India decides to retaliate against Pakistan through the large scale use of military force for

punitive purposes. Any significant employment of Indian military force obviously carries the risk of a Pakistani nuclear response, which is why Indian leaders have shied away from exercising major conventional war options that require especially the large scale use of land forces. Should India contemplate major military operations, however, it is likely that the United States would intervene, but mainly through energetic diplomacy as it did in 2001-02 and again in 2008. It is unlikely that the United States would choose to intervene militarily to prevent either conflict escalation or nuclear weapons employment for a host of operational reasons, though some kinds of trans-or post-conflict assistance might be feasible: in such circumstances, the most important U.S. capabilities that would be relevant would be intelligence, surveillance and reconnaissance (ISR) assets, capabilities required for noncombatant evacuation operations, and Nuclear Emergency and Support Teams (NEST) and other assets essential for post-detonation assistance and recovery (if nuclear use has occurred). Because of the large numbers of U.S. citizens normally resident or traveling in India, and the complexity of evacuation operations in a nuclear environment, this scenario can be more stressing than is commonly realized. The most useful U.S. contribution towards preventing a Pakistani use of nuclear weapons in such a scenario—and the Indian nuclear retribution that would result thereafter—would be to press Pakistan to exit the terrorism business or risk being left alone (or, even worse, the object of international sanction) if a major Indian military response ensues in the aftermath of any pernicious terrorist attack. Other than this, there is little that the United States can do to preserve deterrence stability between two asymmetrically-sized states where the gap in power promises to become even wider tomorrow than it is today.

4) Pakistani loss of control over nuclear assets in the context of conventional military operations against India OR a compromise of nuclear security in peacetime in Pakistan. This scenario, which has been discussed considerably in

recent years both in India and in the United States, would also be highly complex in the demands it places on the U.S. military, depending on the details of the contingency. U.S. ISR elements, special operations forces, and other quick reaction capabilities would be highly relevant in such a contingency—as would close coordination with the government of Pakistan and its armed forces. The United States has already aided Pakistan significantly in regards to nuclear weapons protection, but there are obvious limits to further assistance beyond a point, not least because of the deep-rooted Pakistani fears about the United States seeking access and information about the location of Pakistan's nuclear weaponry.

5) Chinese or Indian nuclear coercion against the other in the context of a border crisis OR in the limiting case, the actual use of nuclear weapons to stave off battlefield defeat. This last contingency, admittedly remote today, would put a high premium on U.S. ISR assets as well as, obviously, active U.S. diplomacy. At the present, it is unlikely that the United States would find itself involved in such a conflict except as a concerned bystander, but if this situation were to change as U.S.-Indian ties grow deeper over time, U.S. conventional and nuclear forces might acquire new roles for extended deterrence and reassurance with respect to India. Until then, however, U.S. ISR capabilities and diplomacy would represent the instruments most relevant to coping with such a scenario.

IMPLICATIONS FOR THE UNITED STATES

The broad range of nuclear challenges arising from a consideration of the problems involving China, India and Pakistan suggest several important conclusions as far as U.S. strategic forces are concerned.

First, U.S. nuclear forces will continue to remain the ultimate backstop where American national security is concerned. The notion that these forces will become irrelevant any time soon, or that their abolition can be contemplated, is a dangerous fantasy. Eliminating nuclear weapons globally must instead take a backseat to protecting U.S. nuclear dominance and maintaining the effectiveness of the U.S. nuclear deterrent over the long term.

Second, the progressive growth of Chinese, Indian, and Pakistani nuclear forces over the next ten years—and the likelihood of further proliferation elsewhere in years to come—implies that any further reduction of U.S. nuclear forces beyond the New Start treaty ought to be eschewed. Given the complexity of the emerging nuclear environment—a world that is best described as asymmetric nuclear multipolarity—the United States must seek to maintain the requisite superiority of the total force that permits it to achieve conventional success in regional contingencies while preserving the advantages currently enjoyed by U.S. nuclear forces. Given the onerous U.S. extended deterrence commitments in Europe and Asia, American nuclear parity with Russia must not diminish to a point where parity with China slinks into reach.

Third, the United States must think seriously about the threat of nuclear deterrence breakdown in Asia as a time when the continent will host many nuclear powers whose arsenals vary in capacity, architecture and doctrine. The desire to reduce the salience of nuclear weaponry in global politics is estimable. That means that U.S. nuclear weapons ought not to be brandished unnecessarily. However, it does not imply forgetting that U.S. nuclear weapons are still essential for deterring not only nuclear attacks (or the threats thereof) on the United States and its allies but also major conventional attacks as well, while still remaining useful as tactical warfighting instruments in certain specific, admittedly limited, contingencies where conventional weapons currently remain ineffective. As a general rule, therefore, the desire to reduce the salience of nuclear weapons in world politics should not extend to devaluing the utility of nuclear weapons for deterrence because these instruments will continue to remain the ultima ratio in an environment that only promises more, not less, proliferation.

'PAKISTAN COULD HAVE 200 NUCLEAR WEAPONS BY 2020'

While many states are downsizing their nuclear stockpiles, Asia is witnessing a buildup. Pakistan, located in a region "most at risk of a breakdown," has the fastest-growing nuclear program, as Gregory Koblentz tells DW. The US-based Council on Foreign Relations titled *Strategic Stability in the Second Nuclear Age,* author Gregory D. Koblentz, an expert on arms control and non-proliferation, identifies South Asia as the region "most at risk of a breakdown in strategic stability due to an explosive mixture of unresolved territorial disputes, cross-border terrorism, and growing nuclear arsenals."

In this context, Pakistan has the fastest-growing nuclear program in the world. And as Koblentz says in a DW interview, by 2020, the Islamic Republic could have a stockpile of fissile material that, if weaponized, could produce as many as two hundred nuclear devices, roughly equivalent to the size of the United Kingdom's nuclear arsenal.

ASIA AS A WHOLE IS WITNESSING A NUCLEAR WEAPONS BUILD-UP

The only four countries currently expanding their nuclear arsenals are China, India, Pakistan and North Korea. Although each nation's buildup is motivated by different reasons, the combination makes Asia the center of a new nuclear arms race.

China has been increasing and diversifying its nuclear arsenal since the end of the Cold War. This buildup is part of a broader effort to modernize the Chinese military and is also motivated by advances in the US' military capabilities such as long-range precision strike systems and missile defenses.

Major developments include the introduction of road-mobile intercontinental ballistic missiles and a new generation of nuclear submarines armed with ballistic missiles. These new forces should significantly improve the survivability of China's strategic nuclear forces.

India and Pakistan's slow-motion arms race picked up speed in 1998 when both countries conducted multiple nuclear tests. The ensuing nuclear and missile buildup by both countries shows no signs of abating. Last month, Pakistan tested two missiles capable of carrying nuclear warheads: the 900-kilometer range Shaheen-1A (Hatf-IV) and the 1,500-kilometer range Shaheen 2 (Hatf-VI).

Altogether, Pakistan has deployed or is developing eleven different nuclear delivery systems including ballistic missiles, cruise missiles, and aircraft. India is also fielding an increasingly capable array of ballistic and cruise missiles to complement its nuclear-capable aircraft. Both states are also expanding their capacity for producing highly enriched uranium and plutonium, the two key materials needed to produce nuclear weapons.

North Korea is the newest member to the nuclear club. Although North Korea started with a much smaller base of nuclear and missile technology than China, India or Pakistan, it has exerted enormous effort to develop a nuclear warhead small enough to be delivered to the continental United States by a ballistic missile.

In your report you identify South Asia as the region "most at risk of a breakdown in strategic stability." Why is this the case? South Asia is the region most at risk of a breakdown in strategic stability due to an explosive mixture of unresolved territorial disputes, cross-border terrorism, and growing nuclear arsenals. While the United States and Soviet Union were engaged in a fierce competition during the Cold War, India and Pakistan face more severe security challenges than those of the other nuclear weapon states. The status of the Muslim-majority province of Jammu and Kashmir in India remains a source of dispute between the two states. India and Pakistan have already fought three conventional wars since they gained independence in 1947, including two over Kashmir.

Since their nuclear tests in 1998, India and Pakistan have fought one low-intensity war (the 1999 Kargil War) and experienced two serious crises spurred by terrorist attacks launched from Pakistan (the 2001 attack on the Indian Parliament and the 2008 Mumbai attack). The geographic proximity of the two countries complicates crisis management since the flight times of ballistic missiles is measured in minutes. Finally, while both states claim to seek only a credible minimum nuclear deterrent, regional dynamics have driven them to pursue an array of nuclear and missile capabilities.

Rivalry between India and Pakistan

One of the most dangerous aspects of Indo-Pakistani rivalry

is the introduction of tactical nuclear weapons in South Asia. During the next Indo-Pakistani conflict, the "fog of war" could take the shape of a mushroom cloud. After the 1999 Kargil War, India developed a new doctrine of rapid, limited conventional military operations designed to punish Pakistan but remain below Pakistan's presumed nuclear threshold.

In response, Pakistan has begun deploying tactical nuclear weapons, such as the Nasr (Hatf IX) short-range ballistic missile, to deter even limited Indian military intervention. Since the conventional military imbalance between India and Pakistan is expected to grow thanks to India's larger economy and higher gross domestic product (GDP) growth rate, Pakistan's reliance on nuclear weapons to compensate for its conventional inferiority will likely be an enduring feature of the nuclear balance in South Asia.

One of the most worrisome risks introduced by Pakistan's deployment of tactical nuclear weapons, especially acute during a crisis, is what Scott Sagan calls the "vulnerability/invulnerability paradox."

Pakistani nuclear doctrine calls for the deployment of road-mobile missiles during a crisis to protect them from an Indian first strike. But these weapons will become more vulnerable to theft or terrorist takeover once they leave the security of a military garrison.

The risk that terrorists could breach Pakistan's nuclear security is magnified by the strong presence of domestic extremists and foreign jihadist groups in Pakistan, their demonstrated ability to penetrate the security of military facilities, and evidence that these groups have infiltrated the Pakistani security services.

Another worrisome development is that the Pakistani practice of storing its nuclear warheads separately from launchers, which has provided a strong barrier to nuclear escalation in the past, may be eroding. The introduction of tactical nuclear weapons may lead Pakistan to loosen its highly centralized command and control practices. Due to their short-ranges (the Nasr/Hatf-IX has a range of about 60 kilometers), these types of weapons need to be deployed close to the front-lines and ready for use at short-notice.

Granting lower-ranking officers greater authority and capability to arm and launch nuclear weapons raises the risk of unauthorized actions during a crisis. Another risk is inadvertent escalation. There is the potential for a conventional conflict to escalate to the nuclear level if the commander of a forward-deployed, nuclear-armed unit finds himself in a "use it or lose it" situation and launches the nuclear weapons under his control before his unit is overrun.

How fast is Pakistan's nuclear weapons' stockpile growing? While there are significant uncertainties about the scope and sophistication of Pakistan's nuclear weapon program, the country appears to have the most aggressive program in the world for producing nuclear material for military purposes. According to the Stockholm International Peace Research Institute, Pakistan currently has enough fissile material, in the form of highly enriched uranium and plutonium, for about 100-120 nuclear weapons.

However, Pakistan is expanding its capability to produce even more weapons-grade material. By 2020, it could have sufficient weapons-grade uranium and plutonium to manufacture more than 200 nuclear weapons, roughly equivalent to the size of the United Kingdom's nuclear arsenal.

Although Pakistan initially focused on the uranium route to nuclear weapons, in recent years it has focused more on the plutonium pathway. Pakistan currently has three reactors at the Khusab nuclear site, 200 kilometers south of Islamabad, capable of producing enough plutonium for six to seven nuclear weapons a year.

In addition, Pakistan is constructing a fourth reactor at this site and expanding its ability to reprocess the spent fuel from these reactors to obtain additional plutonium. Once all four reactors and associated reprocessing facilities are complete, Pakistan will be able to produce an estimated 10-12 bombs-worth of plutonium a year.

Where is Pakistan getting the material it needs to develop these weapons? Pakistan has a well-developed covert procurement network to obtain the materials it needs to fuel its nuclear and missile programs. During the 1970s, the Pakistani metallurgist

Abdul Qadeer Khan obtained critical information about centrifuges being developed by the Anglo-Dutch-German consortium URENCO. Khan used his personal contacts and a list of URENCO's European suppliers to obtain vital material for the uranium enrichment program for several decades.

China also provided important assistance in the early 1980s in the form of highly enriched uranium and the design for an early-generation nuclear weapon. China has also been the source of key technologies (such as ring magnets) for the centrifuge program and for the construction of the Khusab plutonium production reactors. The Institute for Science and International Security has also documented a number of recent cases of American, Pakistani, Chinese, and Israeli citizens violating US export control laws by attempting to ship dual-use materials to Pakistan.

Are there any international attempts or strategies to halt the nuclear arms build-up in the region? The nuclear and missile arms race in South Asia has not received the same level of international concern as developments in Iran or North Korea. The US tried to prevent arms racing between India and Pakistan after their 1998 nuclear tests but that effort fell to the wayside as other issues gained higher priority.

The terrorist attacks on September 11 and the US invasion of Afghanistan pushed nuclear issues low down on the list of important issues in US-Pakistani relations. Similarly, the rise of China and the potential for greater economic relations eclipsed nuclear weapon issues in US relations with India.

THE DEVELOPMENT OF NUCLEAR WEAPONS

Unfortunately, I think that South Asia will remain at high risk for a nuclear crisis of some sort for the next five to ten years. Kashmir will continue to be a source of conflict between India and Pakistan. That territory has existential implications for both countries and will not be resolved in the foreseeable future.

Although Pakistan experienced its first democratic change of government in 2013, the country's history of military coups will limit the ability of Prime Minister Nawaz Sharif and his successors to challenge the authority of the military establishment on defense and foreign policy issues. In addition, elements of the Pakistani government, such as the Inter-Service Intelligence agency, actively resist efforts at rapprochement with India. At the same time, India has not gone out of its way to assuage Pakistan's sense of vulnerability to its much larger and richer neighbor or pursue confidence-building measures that could reduce nuclear risks on the subcontinent.

The next crisis between India and Pakistan could be sparked by a cross-border military incursion, a mass-casualty terrorist attack, or a high-profile assassination. The growth of nuclear and missile capabilities on the subcontinent since 1998 has increased the risk that such a crisis could escalate in unforeseen and dangerous ways.

As India and Pakistan deploy new nuclear forces, such as cruise missiles, tactical nuclear weapons, and sea-based nuclear missiles, new challenges to crisis stability, deterrence, and command and control will arise. If India and Pakistan don't change their current trajectory, a nuclear crisis, or even worse, is likely to occur.

OVERCOMING PAKISTAN'S NUCLEAR DANGERS

Since the earliest days following the nuclear tests by India and Pakistan in 1998, policymakers in the United States and Europe have struggled to envision a realistic path by which Pakistan might achieve some measure of nuclear normalization. Perhaps unexpectedly, the turbulent U.S.-Pakistani relationship of the last several years and Pakistan's rapidly growing nuclear arsenal have revived rather than dampened interest in a normalization deal. The logic of such a deal hinges on the argument that bringing Pakistan into line with global nonproliferation norms could be a valuable inducement to shaping its behavior in the region.

Mark Fitzpatrick's Overcoming Pakistan's Nuclear Dangers is the latest serious attempt to grapple with the question of how the international community might deal with one of the most problematic nuclear-armed states. The majority of the book is dedicated to a carefully drawn analysis of the various risks of Pakistan's nuclear enterprise. Only in the last dozen pages does Fitzpatrick connect these risks—in particular, the growing arsenals in India and Pakistan and the potential for an arms race on the subcontinent—to the larger argument that, despite the evident challenges, Pakistan should be offered a path to nuclear normalization. Ten years after Abdul Qadeer Khan's proliferation network was shut down, he writes, "it is fair to ask how long Pakistan must pay the price for that failure." This conclusion, which Fitzpatrick admits represents a revision of his own views on the subject, has drawn the most critical attention.

In making his argument, Fitzpatrick, a former acting U.S. deputy assistant secretary of state for nonproliferation who now is with the International Institute for Strategic Studies, sensibly begins with a well-prioritized assessment of the actual risks of Pakistan's nuclear program. He concludes that media assessments probably have overblown the likelihood of nuclear terrorism and that advances in Pakistan's nuclear security and safety infrastructures have received far too little attention. Appropriately, he worries more about the developing arms race on the subcontinent, evidenced by Pakistan's rapidly growing stockpiles of fissile material and India's "inherent advantage" in facilities for uranium enrichment and spent fuel reprocessing, which can be used in civilian or military nuclear programs; by India's robust ballistic and cruise missile programs; by Pakistan's introduction of tactical nuclear weapons; and by the development of sea-based nuclear deterrents.

Fitzpatrick's chapter on Indian-Pakistani nuclear competition highlights the growing risks of misperception and command-and-control failures in an environment with new delivery mechanisms and intentionally ambiguous nuclear doctrines. His analysis suggests at a minimum that the next crisis on the subcontinent may escalate more quickly and unpredictably than those of the past.

Fitzpatrick concludes that, in order to deal with these growing dangers, Pakistan and the international community should "make mutually reinforcing adjustments" by which Islamabad adopts global nuclear norms in exchange for recognition as a "normal nuclear country." Entirely apart from the details of terms and implementation, there is considerable value to rekindling debate about such a deal. Pakistanis in government, academia, and think tanks spend an enormous amount of time calculating the conditions under which their country might gain global legitimacy as a responsible nuclear state. A generation of nuclear strategists is coming of age in Pakistan convinced that the United States is committed to maintaining a discriminatory regime or, worse, rolling back Pakistan's nuclear capability altogether.

That alone is reason enough for credible voices in the United States and Europe to signal that the international community seeks a path for bringing Pakistan in from the cold. At the very least, talking about normalization reinforces to Pakistan the major benchmarks that any deal would likely require in order to win international approval, namely, binding limitations on fissile material production and nuclear testing.

Further, holding out the future prospect of full normalization provides incentives for Pakistan's continued responsible participation in other areas of the global nuclear order, such as its acceptance of International Atomic Energy Agency safeguards on its civilian nuclear facilities and its contributions to the nuclear security summits.

Scholars who have previously considered the contours of a possible deal for Pakistan have shared two basic and mutually reinforcing assumptions. First, Pakistan's proliferation record and history of using proxies against Afghanistan and India necessitate that any agreement include conditions more robust than the ones contained in the 2005 U.S.-Indian nuclear deal. Second, any deal would face daunting if not insurmountable challenges on account of the deep mistrust between Islamabad and Western capitals and the still-evolving strategic competition between Pakistan and India.

On the first point, Fitzpatrick does not stray far from conventional wisdom. He sets a high bar for a nuclear normalization deal, requiring Pakistan to agree to end fissile material production, drop its veto over initiating fissile material cutoff treaty (FMCT) negotiations in Geneva, sign the Comprehensive Test Ban Treaty (CTBT), and cease its support for groups that conduct terrorism. Tellingly, he does not discuss how this latter condition would be evaluated or verified.

On the second point—the political and strategic challenges of a deal—Fitzpatrick is frustratingly vague. Fundamental questions about the incentives for Pakistan and the United States and other nuclear-armed states are addressed casually or not at all. Ultimately, this reflects the book's signature weakness: it fails to seriously acknowledge or address the reality that the incentives for Pakistan and the international community to pursue a nuclear normalization agreement are exceptionally weak.

With regard to Pakistan, there is no question that its political and military elites seek international recognition as stewards of a responsible nuclear state. It is less clear that those elites believe that the path to such recognition must involve effective restrictions on the size of Pakistan's arsenal. India, operating under very different geopolitical conditions, negotiated an exceptionally favorable deal with the United States and members of the Nuclear Suppliers Group (NSG) that neither restricted its fissile material production nor bound it by treaty to a cessation of nuclear testing. Pakistan may well wager that it can hold out for a more lenient deal, even if that takes 10 years or more.

Indeed, there is virtually no evidence to suggest that Pakistan is ready to foreclose fissile material production in the short term, even if it withdraws its objection to the start of FMCT negotiations. Fitzpatrick suggests that Pakistan may expect that it can attain fissile material sufficiency by 2020—that is, stockpile enough material to generate a "minimum, credible deterrent" in perpetuity. Members of the Pakistani nuclear establishment, however, have been exceptionally careful not to signal a sufficiency threshold, and the competition that the book describes is unpredictable enough to make Pakistani planners nervous about making that assessment prematurely.

Pakistan may not yet have determined how many low-yield, plutonium-based tactical nuclear weapons it needs to assure its desired deterrence effects against Indian conventional force incursions or if those numbers may need to increase in the future. Alternately, if India moves forward aggressively in developing ballistic missile defense technologies, Pakistan may wish to build up an arsenal of low-yield nuclear cruise missiles and would want to have on hand the requisite plutonium stocks to do so. Fitzpatrick argues that agreeing to an FMCT might appeal to Pakistan if the treaty locks in a level of relative parity between it and India in the size of their fissile material stockpiles. This seems unlikely. Particularly after the U.S.-Indian nuclear deal, Pakistan has articulated its concern that even under FMCT strictures, India would be able to utilize unsafeguarded power-reactor plutonium for military purposes. It has also insisted repeatedly in talks in the Conference on Disarmament that an FMCT must address existing stockpiles, not simply future production. Although many outside observers believe that Pakistan already has exceeded the capabilities necessary to establish a credible deterrent against India, officials within the Pakistani nuclear establishment see few incentives to agree to a fissile material cutoff at this time and may believe that even stockpile parity with India would leave Pakistan at a disadvantage.

The second key reason that Pakistan faces weak incentives for a nuclear normalization deal with the international community is that, while remaining outside the bounds of the nuclear Nonproliferation Treaty (NPT), Islamabad already has gained the benefits of civilian nuclear cooperation through deals with China. Notably, China, with which Pakistan also has long-standing economic and military ties, has pledged to construct two large nuclear power plants in Karachi, and deals for additional plants may well follow. China joined the NSG in 2004 and has justified its provision of nuclear equipment to Pakistan by claiming that it was "grandfathered" by earlier Chinese-Pakistani agreements. This is a tendentious reading of NSG guidelines, but neither China nor Pakistan has faced significant diplomatic or economic consequences for the growing civilian energy partnership. Pakistan quite rightly assumes that, as a practical matter, it does not need an NSG exception to realize the fruits of civilian nuclear cooperation and is unlikely to give up much to the United States to attain what it has already secured from China.

As for the United States, there are a number of reasons to believe that the moment is not right for nuclear normalization with Pakistan. Over the last decade, two developments have colored the politics of such a decision. First, there is not a clear consensus about the value of the U.S.-Indian nuclear deal. Nonproliferation advocates continue to worry that the deal diluted the global nuclear order and the utility of the NPT. For their part, some advocates of the U.S.-Indian bilateral relationship are disappointed that the deal did not do more to bolster trade or widen security cooperation. In truth, it may be too soon to assess the long-term impact of the agreement. Nevertheless, the short-term political impact seems obvious: there is little appetite to expend the political capital necessary for another deal with a non-NPT state anytime soon.

Second, the years since 2005 have been tumultuous for the U.S.-Pakistani relationship. As a result, the prevailing mood in the U.S. policy community is that inducements offered to Pakistan are fundamentally ineffective in shaping Pakistan's behavior except in highly specific circumstances. The kinds of conditions that the U.S. Congress would likely want to see as part of a nuclear normalization deal—for example, long-overdue and targeted actions against extremist groups operating inside and outside of Pakistan—have proven over the last decade to be politically toxic to the bilateral relationship, difficult to verify, and easily evaded. Most U.S. policymakers have come to believe that if Pakistan wants to be recognized as a "normal" country, it must ultimately deal with its internal threats under its own initiative and in response to its own incentives, not under inducements tied to nuclear cooperation or conditional financial assistance.

Where does all of this leave the prospects for a normalization deal? If Fitzpatrick is right and the greatest risks of Pakistan's nuclear program are related to its growing arsenal and its arms race with India, then an agreement on a fissile material cutoff should be the minimum baseline condition required by the international community. At least in the near term, Pakistan is unlikely to agree even to this minimal condition, as evidenced by the hardening of its stance on FMCT negotiations. A deal might be viable if the United States had something compelling to offer, but it does not. China is already providing nuclear cooperation outside the scope of the NPT, and the nonmaterial benefits of international recognition of Pakistan's nuclear status are too vague and fleeting to affect its strategic calculations at this time.

Add India's incentives to the mix, and the prospects for a deal of the kind Fitzpatrick proposes wane even further. Pakistan has made it clear that it will not agree to a fissile material cutoff or sign the CTBT without agreement by India to do the same. New Delhi has shown little enthusiasm for furthering Pakistan's quest for nuclear legitimacy and must consider its strategic competition with China in any decision to permanently halt fissile material production or testing. Having already received an NSG exception, India is not inclined to support any carve-outs for Pakistan in the international nuclear regime.

In short, Fitzpatrick's proposal of a nuclear normalization deal for Pakistan is disappointingly unrealistic. Although his analysis is provocative, a more rigorous examination of the policy incentives—and the politics—would have pointed to the conclusion that a deal that could provide tangible benefits to Pakistan and the West almost certainly is unworkable, at least for now. Where Fitzpatrick gets it right is in highlighting the risks that continue to accrue from the strategic competition on the subcontinent.

His book stands as a careful corrective to those who have focused on nuclear terrorism in Pakistan while downplaying the troubling implications of an accelerating arms race in South Asia. Until Pakistan is satisfied with the credibility of its deterrent against India—something that will happen only when it begins to re-evaluate its assumptions about internal and external threats—deals that offer little more than a generalized promise of nuclear recognition will continue to fall short.

3

Tactical Nuclear Weapons: Lessons for India & Pakistan

Even though 50,000 to 60,000 nuclear warheads were produced since the arguably senseless bombing of Hiroshima and Nagasaki in 1945, some basic human survival instinct "repeatedly stayed the finger that might have pushed the button." The world's abhorrence for nuclear weapons is now so widespread and deep-rooted that even if battlefield or tactical nuclear weapons (TNWs) were to be used against a purely military target in a conflict in future, the effect would be strategic. In fact, the impact would be geo-strategic as the explosion of even a single nuclear weapon anywhere on earth would be one too many and would not be acceptable to the international community. The employment of nuclear weapons as useful weapons of war was always doubtful; it is even more questionable today. Given the widespread abhorrence for nuclear weapons, the Nuclear Rubicon cannot be lightly crossed now and whichever nation decides to cross it will have to bear the consequences.

According to authors William R. Van Cleave and S. T. Cohen, "... the term tactical nuclear weapons in the closest approximation refers to battlefield nuclear weapons, for battlefield use, and with deployment ranges and yields consistent with such use and confined essentially in each respect to the area of localised military operations." Some air-dropped nuclear glide bombs, carried by fighter-bombers, have been known to have yields of over one megaton. Parts of NATO's erstwhile TNW forces, including

Pershing missiles, were on constant readiness alert as part of the Quick Reaction Alert force. The line dividing tactical (including theatre) and strategic nuclear weapons is rather blurred. While a strategic strike can be conducted with weapons of low yield, a tactical strike can be effected with virtually any class of nuclear weapons – though the results achieved may not be commensurate with the effort put in. For example, hitting a forward military airfield with an Inter Continental Ballistic Missile (ICBM) would be a gross overkill and would result in extremely high collateral damage. In fact, the phrase 'tactical use of nuclear weapons' would convey a more accurate sense of the intended use rather than 'use of tactical nuclear weapons'.

In the public perception, the most popular TNWs have been the 8 inch (203 mm) M-110 and the 155 mm M-109 atomic artillery weapons, and the Lance and Honest John Short Range Ballistic Missiles (SRBMs). At the upper end of the range scale were the Pershing missiles with a range of 160 to 835 km. These were intermediate range theatre SRBMs. The erstwhile Soviet and Warsaw Pact forces had their own corresponding TNWs. Among the better known ones were the FROG and Scud series of rockets and missiles. In addition, there was a category of weapons known as 'mini-nukes'. These had yields from 0.05 to 0.5 kilotons. TNWs, particularly those of the US and its NATO allies, were nuclear warfighting weapons and formed an important part of NATO's strategy of flexible response or 'first use' policy. These weapons were among the first that would have been used in the early stages of a NATO-Warsaw Pact war.

Reasons Advocated for Use

During the Cold War, the proponents of TNWs justified their requirement on these grounds: they deter the use of TNWs by the enemy; they provide flexible response over the whole range of possible military threats; they offer nuclear military options below the strategic level; they help to defeat large-scale conventional attacks; and, they serve the political purpose of demonstrating commitment to the allies. The opponents of TNWs asserted that these 'more usable' weapons would lower the nuclear threshold and make nuclear use more likely. Fears of collateral damage in the extensively populated and developed NATO heartland spurred European opposition to TNWs. Many European political and military leaders convincingly argued that NATO would be better off without TNWs. Alain Enthoven, economist and former US Assistant Secretary of Defense for Systems Analysis, wrote: "Tactical nuclear weapons cannot defend Western Europe; they can only destroy it… there is no such thing as tactical nuclear war in the sense of sustained, purposive military operations…"

There are other compelling reasons too for leaving TNWs out of the nuclear arsenal.

Firstly, these are extremely complex weapons (particularly sub-kiloton mini-nukes, because of the precision required in engineering) and are difficult and expensive to manufacture and support technically. Inducting them into service even in small numbers would considerably raise the budget of the strategic forces.

Secondly, the command and control of TNWs needs to be decentralised at some point during war to enable their timely employment. Extremely tight control would make their possession redundant and degrade their deterrence value. Decentralised control would run the risk of their premature and even unauthorised use – Kissinger's 'mad major syndrome'.

Thirdly, since the launchers must move frequently to avoid being targeted, dispersed storage and frequent transportation of TNWs under field conditions, increases the risk of accidents. Lastly, the employment of conventional artillery and air-to-ground precision weapons by the enemy may damage or destroy stored nuclear warheads.

Reasons for Discarding TNWs

It was for many good reasons that the US and its NATO allies and the Soviet Union and Warsaw Pact forces developed, produced, stockpiled in large numbers and planned to use tactical nuclear weapons as weapons of war. It was also for many good reasons that the weapons were never put to use. (TNWs exist in arsenals of both nations still and the Russians have refused to negotiate any arms control US makes concessions on Ballistic Missile Defence

(BMD). Even the mini-nukes and the so-called 'clean' enhanced radiation neutron bombs would have, if used in substantial numbers in a European war, afflicted a few hundred million civilians, including future generations, with long-term radiation sickness of incalculable magnitudes. Even the professed military utility of blunting a major armoured offensive is debatable as the attacker would ensure that he does not present a concentrated target before the bulk of tactical nuclear weapons, or at least their delivery systems, have been destroyed in an initial phase that itself would turn out to be apocalyptic. Even then, the attacker would concentrate rapidly for short durations only at the point of decision and then disperse quickly. For instance, in the well-developed, semi-urban terrain of Punjab on both the sides of the Indo-Pak boundary, collateral damage would be unavoidable. Hundreds of thousands of civilian casualties would be unmanageable for an army fighting a war.

Political and diplomatic reasons also militate against the use of tactical nuclear weapons. A nuclear posture with a first use option – NATO's in Europe (it still is first use as per the latest Deterrence and Defence Posture Review (DDPR) and Pakistan's current nuclear policy – is both repugnant and dangerous. It is also inherently destabilising and naturally escalatory. With the megamedia revolution public opinion is bound to undermine the credibility of the use of tactical nuclear weapons and, as deterrence is more than anything else a mind game, the lack of credibility does nothing for enhancing deterrence. Rather it creates new dangers.

The command and control of tactical nuclear weapons has naturally to be decentralised during war to enable their timely employment. Extremely tight control would make their possession redundant and degrade their deterrence value by several orders of magnitude. Decentralised control would run the risk of their premature and even unauthorised use based on the discretion of field commanders, however discerning and conscientious they may be.

Dispersed storage and frequent transportation under field conditions, since the launchers must move from hide to hide to avoid being easily targeted by the enemy, increases the risk of accidents as well as complicate nuclear security. The employment of conventional artillery and air-to-ground precision weapons by the enemy may damage or destroy forward stored nuclear warheads and, though the probability is low, may even set off a nuclear explosion.

INDIA AND PAKISTAN: CONTRASTING APPROACHES

India has wisely opted not to go down the TNW route, but Pakistan has chosen to acquire these dangerous weapons. The Pakistan army's continuing efforts to arm the 60-km Hatf-9 (Nasr) SRBM with nuclear warheads will adversely impact deterrence stability on the Indian subcontinent as tactical nuclear weapons are inherently destabilising and invariably escalatory. The Nasr missile was first tested in April 2011 and then a few times since then and is reported to be a replica of the Chinese M-20. According to Pakistani analysts, the Hatf-9 (Nasr) missile is their answer to India's Cold Start doctrine as the use of TNWs will stop India's armoured spearheads advancing into Pakistan in their tracks. They miss the centrality of India's no first use doctrine completely: even one nuclear strike – whether in India or against Indian forces – will invite 'massive retaliation', which Pakistan can ill afford.

Because of their inherent destructiveness, their indiscriminate nature and their gruesome genetic effects extending to future generations, nuclear weapons must never be used again. Hence, those who attempt to make them 'usable' by claiming to limit their effects to soldiers on the battlefield, presumed to be justifiable targets even for otherwise forbidden weapons, are on the wrong path. According to Air Cmde Jasjit Singh, "Any nuclear weapon, of any quality, mode of delivery or yield, used against any type of target, will result in a strategic impact to which the logical response would be the use of nuclear weapons, more often than not, on an overwhelming scale." The tactical nuclear weapons carpet cannot now be rolled back; it must not at least be unrolled any further. India and Pakistan must learn from the mistakes of the West and not take the lead in repeating them without justifiable political and military gains.

THE LOOMING THREAT IN SOUTH ASIA: NUCLEAR POSTURES OF INDIA AND PAKISTAN

When assessing nuclear weapon risks, the international community is currently preoccupied with Iranian development – this week's negotiations in Oman are the latest effort to quell their ambitions – and North Korean provocation. Although Tehran and Pyongyang are indeed a cause for concern, it is the current nuclear postures of Islamabad and New Delhi that should worry us the most. The development of tactical nuclear weapon capability and ambiguous nuclear-use policies on both sides continue to fuel tensions and increase the likelihood of nuclear exchange.

Recent literature suggests Pakistan has increasingly sought and acquired tactical nuclear weapon capabilities. In 2011, Islamabad introduced the "Nasr" missile, a 60 km-range truck-mounted ballistic weapon capable of carrying a sub-kiloton warhead. Pakistan is also currently developing a short-range nuclear-capable sea-based missile system. Islamabad's intensified work on tactical nuclear weapons is meant to deter India's conventional attack and achieve second-strike capability. In response, India also escalated its work on tactical nuclear capabilities, including the 150-km range Prahaar tactical ballistic missiles and the 750-km Shourya hypersonic missiles. Last month, the Defense Research and Development Organization (DRDO) also tested its new nuclear-capable cruise missiles capable of skirting enemy air-defense systems. Some argue that nuclear developments on the Indian side serve the purpose of securing counterforce or escalation dominance over Pakistan. Ultimately, Pakistan and India's advancement of their respective tactical weapon capability is particularly worrisome as it dramatically lowers the threshold for the use of nuclear weapons by making the unthinkable – a nuclear conflict – more acceptable and thus more plausible.

These new nuclear capabilities are especially worrying given the current ambiguity of nuclear postures in India and Pakistan. Pakistan's nuclear posture is primarily designed to counter the Indian threat; it pledges no-first use against non-nuclear weapon states, but does not rule out first-use against nuclear-armed aggressors. Perhaps most worryingly, Pakistan's nuclear posture is based on the conviction that it must remain intentionally vague about its nuclear red lines in order to maintain deterrence against India's conventional superiority. Islamabad outlines four red lines that could potentially drive it to nuclear first use, including a conventional attack by India, destruction of a large part of Pakistan's air or land forces, and economic or political destabilization resulting from Indian interference. By being deliberately unclear about its nuclear red lines, Pakistan reserves significant room for interpretation when it comes to nuclear-use. This posture not only reaffirms India's fears but also further lowers the threshold for nuclear weapons use.

India's nuclear posture is based on a no-first-use policy and a commitment to maintaining only credible minimum deterrent forces – largely viewed as a sign of restraint and stability. However, India's no-first-use policy seems to be nothing more than a political statement. While India's official nuclear doctrine declares that it will refrain from using nuclear weapons first, it officially admits a readiness to utilize them in case of a biological or chemical weapons attack. In addition, the size of India's deterrent nuclear force far exceeds what would be 'minimally' required to counter Pakistan's capabilities. This is because India's nuclear policy is envisaged to counter China's much larger arsenal. This raises questions about New Delhi's claim of possessing nuclear weapons solely for defensive purposes vis-à-vis Pakistan.

In addition to its tactical nuclear arsenal, India has made progress in developing its ballistic missile defense system and the DRDO has admitted it is currently developing Multiple Interdependently Targetable Reentry Vehicles (MIRVs) for some of the Agni strategic ballistic missiles. Ultimately, the development of defensive capabilities along with MIRV-equipped nuclear missiles looks like ambition to achieve a disarming first strike capability – a blatant negation of New Delhi's official posture.As Vipin Narang argues, coupling MIRVs and ballistic missile defense (BMD) could enable a state to consider first-strike strategies that use multiple warheads to target an adversary's nuclear arsenal and then rely on BMD to intercept any missiles that survived the disarming strike.Although there is no confirmation that this is India's thinking, these planned capabilities fuel Islamabad's concerns over the survivability of its nuclear forces.

The nuclear postures of India and Pakistan facilitate an atmosphere of mistrust and uncertainty which, when coupled with the introduction of tactical nuclear weapons and the lack of mutual understanding of red lines, increases the likelihood of a nuclear conflict sparked by miscalculations and misperceptions of intentions. Bearing in mind that both sides have little regular communication on nuclear issues, hostile and ambiguous signaling is a major factor contributing to the risk of nuclear war. As reciprocal indications of mistrust escalate tensions, a seemingly minor border skirmish might spiral into nuclear exchange. Ultimately, without a clear formulation of nuclear postures and thus without mutual understanding of the other's intentions, the risk of nuclear conflict between India and Pakistan will continue to increase.

15-YEARS AFTER POKHRAN II: DETERRENCE CHURNING CONTINUES

For over two decades, a dominant section of western analysts harped on the volatilities of the India and Pakistan nuclear dyad, often overselling the 'South Asia as a nuclear flashpoint' axiom, and portending a potential nuclear flare-up in every major stand-off between the two countries. The turbulence in the sub-continent propelled such presages, with one crisis after another billowing towards serious confrontations, but eventually easing out on all occasions. While the optimists described this as evidence of nuclear deterrence gradually consolidating in this dyad, the pessimists saw in it the ingredients of instability that could lead to a nuclear conflict. Though there is no denial of the fact that the three major crises since the 1998 nuclear tests – Kargil (1999), the Parliament attack and Operation Parakram (2001-2002) and the Mumbai terror strike (2008) – brought the two rivals precariously close to nuclear showdowns, not once had their leaderships lost complete faith in the efficacy of mutual deterrence. Fifteen years after the nuclear tests, it is relevant to examine if deterrence remains weak in this dyad or has consolidated towards greater stability.

A complex deterrence matrix

With its history of deep-rooted hostility, the South Asian binary went through a tumultuous evolution of deterrence structures and postures. The early years were marked by limited war and terror strikes literally validating the western notion of an unstable region. India's perceptibly transparent no-first-use (NFU) doctrine was met with a policy of strategic ambiguity from Pakistan, which preferred to keep its nuclear first-use option open and at the same time refusing to declare its threshold(s). The proclaimed aim was to deter India at all levels of military action – sub-conventional, conventional or nuclear. India's military might was cited as justification for such postural asymmetry. The unprofessed objective though was to carve out a space to sustain the low-intensity conflict (Kashmir insurgency and terror strikes in Indian heartland) while mitigating any Indian retaliation. With its nuclear brinkmanship behaviour fuelling global paranoia, the early years of nuclearisation and its primal instability was proving to benefit Pakistan with no decisive Indian challenge to its sub-conventional influx.

Many Indian analysts highlighted this as evidence of the doctrinal imbalance, with some questioning the efficacy of nuclear deterrence against Pakistan and a few others even demanding a review of India's NFU posture. Though the Indian leadership upheld the NFU as sacrosanct, the need to challenge the *status quo* began to be felt after the 2001-2002 crises. Largely attributed to the 'lessons' of Operation Parakram (which proved to be a costly mobilisation effort with scope for rapid escalation), the Indian Army initiated a major doctrinal shift at the conventional level through what is termed as the 'Cold Start' strategy. With its plan for rapid battle-group thrusts into Pakistani territory without hitting its perceived nuclear tripwires, the military leadership conceived the possibility of calling Pakistan's 'nuclear bluff' by taking its response to Pakistani soil. Though backed by an incipient belief that the space for a limited conventional war exists, Cold Start embodied India's resolve to alter the deterrence landscape without disturbing the nuclear doctrinal framework.

Albeit the feasibility of this strategy was consistently doubted, its signalling spin-off was immense as Pakistan began to doubt the credibility of its brinkmanship behaviour and ability to sustain the LIC without inviting India's retaliation. Through an assortment of political campaigns (by hyping the Cold Start as escalatory) and technological responses (Nasr tactical nuclear missile, Babar and Ra'ad cruise missiles), Pakistan struggled to project confidence in its deterrent. The lack of a unitary effort from the security establishment to promote the Cold Start and the Indian Army eventually having to disown it (by renaming as proactive strategy) largely denoted the efficacy of Pakistan's campaign, aided in some measure by the western alarmists.

Yet, its introduction marked a complex game of deterrence: while one actor propagated a proactive nuclear posture to feed its sub-conventional plan, the other responded with a proactive conventional posture for a range of non-nuclear responses. The official silence on Cold Start matched by Pakistan's refusal to brand the Nasr as a tactical nuclear response only added to this complexity, until the recent articulation by the Chairman of India's National Security Advisory Board (NSAB).1 By clarifying that India will not differentiate between tactical and strategic nuclear weapons and will consider any such use against its forces or territory as a first-strike (implicitly inviting nuclear retaliation), the security establishment has belatedly implied the existence of its proactive strategy. The next stage in this deterrence churning could come in the form of Pakistan's response to the latest Indian posturing, even as western observers anticipate India's proactive military plan to see action after the next major terror strike.

While its tryst with doctrinal realignments continues, India initiated a decisive new level of posturing, with greater implications for the deterrence calculus, by introducing ballistic missile defence (BMD) into the scene. Although India's BMD programme originated out of concerns on Pakistan's missile prowess and the China-Pakistan proliferation nexus, the rapid advances on India's BMD platforms has emerged as a potent challenge to Pakistan's deterrent. Despite the fact that interception technologies are still evolving and are yet to guarantee leak-proof protection, the Indian programme is geared towards developing an extended area defence capability, and possibly a nationwide shield, that could limit the damage from Pakistani (and Chinese) missiles, if not absolute destruction. With no technological counter of its own, but for the nascent cruise missile inventory (with limited engagement scope against BMD systems), Pakistan realises that India's pursuit of a multi-tier interception network will negate its first-strike advantage, and could provide India with greater defensive depth, which it argues, could encourage India towards pre-emption. Besides the fact that even a failed first-use might invite Indian retaliation, the shift in the deterrence calculus is such that even a marginally-effective Indian BMD could diminish the combative edge of Pakistan's strategic forces.

Similar to its response to the Cold Start, Pakistan is now projecting missile defence as causal for instability and had reportedly argued against its deployment at the recent talks on nuclear Confidence Building Measures (CBMs). Consequently, Pakistan attempted a weakly-devised signalling effort in May 2012 by declaring a survivable second-strike capability on its naval platforms.2 While the strategic component of its naval platforms remains unclear, the fact that Pakistan declared a second-strike alternative (after years of reliance on its first-strike posture) is intrinsically a reflection of its desperation on the Indian BMD. However, with no takers for this signalling effort,3 Pakistan may now be left with fewer options, including: (a) developing its own BMD capability, which could be too costly for its sinking economy,4 and (b) seek technological assistance from China or acquisition of its air and missile defence systems.

What's in store?

Fifteen years of nuclear South Asia was all about a paradoxical deterrence seesaw that was intense, yet not unstable enough to cause its failure. After the gains that Pakistan accrued from the initial asymmetry, the scales are now favouring India with its doctrinal rejuvenation and technological advances. Events like the Indo-US nuclear deal, the Abottabad operation and restoration of democracy in Pakistan have also impacted this turnaround. While Pakistan attempted to match India's nuclear deal advantage by feverishly augmenting its fissile stocks, the Abottabad operation eroded the credibility of its Army and diminished its leverage in the India-Pakistan reconciliation process. With its leading political parties now favouring improved relations with India, there is scope for a postural balancing that could contribute to greater stability between the two nuclear neighbours. President Zardari's suggestion for Pakistan's adoption of a NFU posture is one such step that the new civilian government could consider in this direction.

However, as is a well known fact, it will be the Pakistani army which will have the final say on nuclear policy issues. Besides resisting any such proposal to alter its nuclear policy, the army will have the strongest urge to counter India's recent gains by triggering newer crises. But with conditions no longer favouring any strategy of brinkmanship, the onus may now shift on to the civilian government to devise a postural transformation that could project Pakistan as a more responsible and rational nuclear power. This is an imperative forced upon Pakistan not just by the current strategic environment, but also will be a factor in determining its future status in the normative structures of the non-proliferation regime.

4

India, Pakistan and Tactical Nuclear Weapons: Irrelevance for South Asia

Tactical nuclear weapons (TNW) have little utility in the South Asian context since neither India nor Pakistan's nuclear doctrines are based on those of the Cold War superpowers, the US and the Soviet Union. American nuclear analysts used to sit around and talk about limited nuclear wars where countries fired a few warheads and then sat down to negotiate. In actual fact that is all such discussions ever led to for throughout the Cold War the US relied on Mutual Assured Destruction (MAD) which involved wiping out large amounts of the opponent's industry and population. Despite the increased accuracy of nuclear delivery systems and vastly improved command and control infrastructure, the US never varied from the concept of MAD since it became clear that there was no such a thing as a limited nuclear war.

In the South Asian context, MAD as operationalised by the US and the Soviet Union makes little sense. Nor do TNW, which are the nuclear war fighter's fantasy weapons. Neither India nor Pakistan has accuracy levels that are similar to those of the superpowers and neither country has a comparable command and control system, or adequate protection for its leadership, to engage in a Western style nuclear exchange.

Instead, if Pakistan were to initiate a limited nuclear exchange with a few tactical missiles then India, fearing the worst, would have to hit Pakistan with everything it has and here the nuclear logic of Chairman Mao's China comes into play. Mao's China recognised that Beijing could not get into an expensive nuclear arms race with the West or for that matter the Soviet Union. What the country required was to have the guaranteed capability to take out a few cities in an opponent's territory and this would be enough to deter the other side. Thus a minimum deterrent capability that took out 6-10 cities was seen as ensuring deterrence.

In the South Asian case, the numbers are even smaller. An Indian attack that decimated Lahore, Islàmabad, and Karachi would essentially leave Pakistan with an economy and society that is in the 19th century. A similar Pakistani attack on Mumbai or New Delhi would put back India's developmental efforts by a couple of decades as not only would the nation struggle to recover but foreign investors would flee the country. One may argue, therefore, that nuclear deterrence has been achieved by both sides and neither has to worry about feeling vulnerable in this spectrum of conflict.

So what do TNW give either side? The answer is a higher level of instability and a much lower level of deterrence. For Pakistani TNW to be credible against an Indian attack (the Cold Start scenario), they would have to be armed and ready at the border and have to be handed to fairly low-level military officers who were authorised to use them. This is inherently destabilising since if Pakistani positions were being overrun a major or colonel would be left with the unpleasant choice of either using them and precipitating an all-out nuclear war or surrendering them to the Indian military. Since the latter would be unacceptable to any military command, the former would be the only real option left for these officers. In fact, if faced with a large scale conventional attack one has to expect the Pakistani leadership to fear the worse and launch everything they have rather than let us use a few bombs and face large scale Indian retaliation.

HOW DANGEROUS ARE PAKISTAN'S TACTICAL NUCLEAR WEAPONS?

October of last year marked the fiftieth anniversary of the 1962 Cuban missile crisis. Many Asian policymakers will read the lessons of that harrowing episode with some self-satisfaction. When India and Pakistan conducted their nuclear weapon tests in 1998, foreign analystsrepeatedly told them that, as poor countries with weak institutions, they could not be entrusted with such awesome weaponry. Nascent nuclear powers were simply less reliable stewards than their Cold War counterparts. Over a decade on, and multiple crises later — Kargil in 1999, a military standoff in 2001-2, and the Mumbai attacks of 2008 — India and Pakistan have experienced nothing quite as perilous as the Cuban scare.

U.S. officials claim that Pakistan readied nuclear weapons during the Kargil conflict without the knowledge of then-Prime Minister Nawaz Sharif. But, even at the height of their crises neither India nor Pakistan have attempted, as the U.S. did in 1962, anything quite as foolish as depth-charging nuclear-armed submarines or scrambling aircraft equipped with nuclear air-to-air missiles towards hostile airspace. The dawn of Asia's nuclear age has been calmer than that of Europe, and far calmer than the nuclear alarmists predicted.

But, as Paul Bracken and others have warned, we should not get complacent. When India tested its Agni-V missile in April, I and others raised a number of potential issues: Indian scientists were making cavalier statements of nuclear posture best left to political leaders, and the development of multiple warheads for each missile (known as MIRVs) and missile defense technology could all be destabilizing if not handled extremely carefully. India has legitimate deterrence requirements vis-a-vis China, but it would be counterproductive for this to become an open-ended expansion.

Pakistan's nuclear trajectory is, however, altogether more worrying.

This issue is usually framed in terms of numbers. Pakistan possesses what is thought to be the fastest-growing nuclear arsenal in the world and if present trends continue, could equal or surpass Britain's stockpile within a decade. So far, the Western world has viewed this expansion as a nonproliferation issue, not a security one. But, over the longer-term, that could change. As a recent report from the EU Non-Proliferation Consortium noted, "EU members might have military facilities within reach of Pakistani longer-range missiles ... or temporary bases and personnel" and, "in the case of a deterioration in Pakistan's relations with the West, this could be a subject of concern." Pakistan is free to dismiss European and American anxieties, but this will only reinforce the country's longer-term isolation.

There is also a second, more serious concern. Pakistan is developing a new generation of tactical nuclear weapons (TNWs) that target not Indian cities, but Indian military formations on the battlefield. The purpose of these, as former Pakistani Ambassador to the United States Maleeha Lodhi explained in November, is "to counterbalance India's move to bring conventional military offensives to a tactical level." The idea is that smaller nuclear weapons, used on Pakistani soil, would stop invading Indian forces in their tracks.

The rise of tactical nuclear weapons has been well documented over the past two years. What has received less scrutiny, however, is the doctrine on which this rise has been based. Pakistan's nuclear advocates make the case that their approach is no different than NATO's Cold War nuclear posture towards the Soviet Union, and like NATO is the inevitable result of a conventionally weaker country trying to negate its more powerful adversaries' conventional advantage. But the problem is that this comparison misses some key facts.

First, NATO never intended to physically block a Soviet invasion with tactical nuclear weapons. By the 1960s, it had become clear that NATO would still lose even if it unleashed nukes. This goes for Pakistan too. According to one calculation, it would take up to 436 Pakistani nuclear weapons just to halt a single Indian armored division — a clearly absurd number, that leaps higher still if one assumes lower yield weapons and more dispersed Indian formations. Moreover, as Michael Krepon recently wrote, "Pakistan lacks the real-time surveillance capabilities to destroy [moving] armored columns, except where they are funneling into bridge crossings of water barriers."

Second, NATO came to understand that tactical nuclear use would devastate the countries supposedly being defended. As the saying went, "the shorter the [nuclear] range, the deader the

Germans." Substitute "Punjabis" for "Germans", and you have a clearer idea of the problem. The key insight is that NATO's focus was on using nuclear weapons to send political signals — namely, to signal resolve with actions short of a strategic nuclear exchange — not to win on the battlefield. This distinction tends to be lost in discussions of Pakistan.

Third, tactical nuclear weapons are understood to be especially credible precisely because their forward deployment makes them so vulnerable. NATO, aware of this "use them or lose them" dilemma, pre-delegated launch authority for at least some of its tactical nuclear weapons — specifically, atomic demolition munitions — in Germany in the late 1950s.

There is some evidence that Pakistan has or will soon follow suit. In 2005, for instance, Feroz Hassan Khan, a senior official in Pakistan's Strategic Plans Division (SPD), explained that "partial pre-delegation" of weapons would be an "operational necessity because dispersed nuclear forces as well as central command authority ... are vulnerable." The SPD is widely admired for its professionalism, but pre-delegation inevitably dilutes command and control of nuclear weapons, however competent officials might be.

The differences between NATO in the 1950s and Pakistan in the 2010s should be obvious. Despite Germany's Cold War problems with domestic terrorism, and occasionally questionable base security in NATO countries, it was hardly as if the Rhineland was wracked with jihadists. NATO's military officers were also unquestionably under the command of elected civilian leaders.

Fourth, and finally, NATO's reliance on tactical nuclear weapons was short-lived. After 1979, the Alliance withdrew more and more of these weapons from Europe. In fact, from 1980 to 1990 NATO removed a third of its nuclear weapons from Europe, much of this coming in the early part of the decade when the USSR was unveiling a new offensive military doctrine (ironically, elements of which are echoed in India's Cold Start army doctrine today). But NATO felt able to do this because its conventional military capabilities were improving, thanks to Western technological superiority over the Russians.

Pakistan, by contrast, is conventionally falling behind in terms of military spending and technology. The gap between Indian and Pakistani military spending continues to grow. This suggests that Pakistan will continue to emphasize tactical nuclear weapons, which will entrench the risks laid out here. To be sure, India has also shown an interest in short-range nuclear-capable missiles (for instance, the *Prahaar*), but with nowhere near the same enthusiasm, and in a context in which Indian civilians are wary to entrusting the armed forces with such weapons in an operational context.

The Pakistani military argues that it needs to defend against India's Cold Start. But Cold Start — itself of questionable feasibility — is about shallow incursions, hardly comparable to nation-threatening Soviet thrusts to the Atlantic. As the nuclear historian George Perkovich recently wrote, "the willingness to risk a breakdown in nuclear deterrence would only be rational if the threat that is being countered or deterred is of an existential scale. To risk suicide to redress a threat that is not itself mortal would be irrational." A state cannot just choose to costlessly re-define all lesser threats as mortal ones. Simply reducing the nuclear threshold lower and lower is an unsustainable and unnecessary strategy, and can make it more rather than less likely that deterrence will fail in the event of a crisis.

Pakistan already has sufficient numbers and types of nuclear weapons to ensure its survival, and, like NATO before it, to send political signals through limited nuclear use even if a war does break out. Yet Pakistan's present course, premised on a series of misunderstandings of tactical nuclear weapons, will increase friction with those nations who count themselves allies of Pakistan and generate new risks quite out of proportion to anything the country might gain.

INDIA AND PAKISTAN ARE BUILDING UP THEIR ARSENALS, AND ONE TERROR ATTACK COULD IGNITE AN ALL-OUT WAR

Iranian negotiators met in Vienna with leaders from the United States, Russia, France, China, the U.K. and Germany, and got down to the tricky business of finding a way out of a growing nuclear standoff. It was touted as the most promising opportunity in years to reach a deal that would, once and for all, put the brakes on what many fear are Iran's secret plans to build a nuclear bomb.

That deal, however, never materialized. When the talks ended on Nov. 24, the best U.S. Secretary of State John Kerry could offer was some promising rhetoric: "Today, we are closer to a deal that would make the entire world... safer and more secure," he said.

But while the world's major powers fretted over Iran's "breakout" potential—the time it would take to produce enough fissile material to build one nuclear device—a report by the Council on Foreign Relations, timed to come out during the Vienna talks, warned that other countries have not only broken out, but appear to be running wild. This is the reality of the "second nuclear age," the report stated. Even as the traditional nuclear powers reduce their stockpiles, emergent states in Asia—Pakistan and India, in particular, but also North Korea and China—are becoming increasingly tangled in a new arms race, one that is much more complex and difficult to control than what the world witnessed in the second half of the 20th century.

According to the report, Pakistan currently has the world's fastest-growing nuclear arsenal, with enough ûssile material to build 120 bombs and the potential to build at least 80 more by 2020. India has the ability to build 110 nuclear devices, but is also reported to have ramped up its production capacity.

Iran, according to the report, is only one piece in an increasingly complex nuclear puzzle. There is reason to be concerned about its nuclear program, of course. A brooding Middle Eastern Cold War pitting Shia-led Iran against Sunni Saudi Arabia poses some serious international security threats. If Iran does "break out," the experts say, the Saudis will be sure to follow, igniting another nuclear arms race in what is the most unstable region in the world. (Pakistan's nuclear program, reportedly, owes its success to Saudi funding.)

More worrying for the near term, however, is the existing arms race. While Indian and Pakistani arsenals are paltry compared to the word's nuclear powerhouses (Russia and the United States have thousands of strategic warheads deployed), the threat they pose to global security is more dire, considering the geopolitical challenges of the region. The potential for nuclear conflict between India and Pakistan has hovered over the world since 1998, when Pakistan first entered the nuclear club. The two rivals have fought three conventional wars since 1947 and have come dangerously close to a fourth.

Over the past 15 years, the environment has shifted dramatically. Pakistan's struggle with Islamist extremism and its consequences for India, including a devastating 2008 shooting rampage in Mumbai, are redefining the military landscape. India has moved away from its defensive posture and embraced a more "proactive strategy," says Walter Ladwig, assistant professor in the department of war studies at King's College London. "Their new military doctrine, originally called Cold Start, has been evolving since 2003," he says. "It remains the foundation of India's military procurement, including modernizing its conventional capabilities to allow for a more mobile and offensive response against Pakistan in the event of another attack inside India."

Pakistan, concerned by the fact that it cannot compete in conventional military terms against a much richer India, has responded by developing its nuclear capability to include tactical warheads, giving it the ability to strike back with precision nuclear weapons targeting advancing Indian troops, without resorting to all-out nuclear war. "India's strategy has created a lot of consternation in Pakistan," says Ladwig, who has written extensively on the evolution of India's military. "The U.S. has put pressure on India to back away from the Cold Start strategy."

While Indian authorities have disavowed the Cold Start name, the strategy itself remains intact, Ladwig adds, but will take many years to reach operational levels. The Indian army, he says, is still too outdated to achieve the desired goals of a Cold Start offensive at the moment, but, 10 or 15 years down the road, things could change dramatically.

If that happens, which appears likely, considering India's current rate of weapons procurement, it would push the nuclear Armageddon clock forward significantly, warn experts such as Ladwig and the authors of the Council on Foreign Relations report.

The chain of events that could lead to a nuclear confrontation are relatively straightforward: In the event of a large-scale terrorist attack in India blamed on Pakistan-based militants, Indian authorities would demand action (as they did following the Mumbai attack). Pakistan would almost certainly deny involvement. Under Cold Start, India would (unlike after Mumbai) launch a military strike inside Pakistan. The goal would be to disorient the Pakistanis and, before they could recover, control a buffer zone inside Pakistan 10 to 15 km wide—providing it a strong position for any negotiations.

But, as Ladwig points out, "an operational Cold Start capability could lead Pakistan to lower its nuclear red line, put its nuclear weapons on a higher state of readiness, develop tactical nuclear weapons or undertake some equally destabilizing course of action." For Pakistani generals, Cold Start might not look like a limited operation, but rather a prelude to a wider invasion or a tactic to subjugate Pakistan to India's will. Neither side would want to use its nuclear weapons, but the trigger could be as simple as an overzealous Pakistani artillery commander armed with a tactical nuke, or a miscommunication on the Indian side.

For the time being, the potential for that scenario to play out remains low, says retired colonel Baseer Malik, a military analyst in Islamabad. "India knows it outmatches Pakistan in conventional terms," he says. "But, in terms of nuclear, it is a different story. India would not be so short-sighted as to provoke Pakistan in this way. They know how quickly things could escalate."

The threat of escalation now has as much to do with advances in conventional weapons as it does with nuclear imbalances. "Strategic stability is no longer just a product of the interaction between comparable nuclear forces," the Council on Foreign Relations report says, "but, increasingly, between nuclear forces and non-nuclear technologies, such as missile defences, anti-satellite weapons, conventional precision-strike weapons, and cyberweapons."

Thankfully, the worst-case scenario for India and Pakistan is not likely to play out any time soon. India's modernization of its conventional arsenal is still in its infancy, says Ladwig. But as long as it aggressively pursues advanced weaponry, Pakistan will feel threatened and respond with the expansion of its nuclear option. With no end in sight to the animosity between the two countries, the end result can only be bad.

TACTICAL NUCLEAR WEAPON AND DETERRENCE STABILITY IN SOUTH ASIA

The New Delhi's declassification of Cold Start Doctrine in April 2004, upsurge in anti-missile program, and gigantic investment in the conventional weaponry obliged Islamabad to reciprocate by manufacturing and testing a credible-cum-transparent new weapon-NASR missile on April 19, 2011. The NASR missile test has stimulated a debate about the tactical nuclear weapons role in the deterrence stability between India and Pakistan.

The test of the NASR missile has constructive contribution to consolidating the credibility of Pakistan's nuclear deterrence. The Director General of the Strategic Plans Division (SPD), Lieutenant General (Retired) Khalid Ahmed Kidwai stated that "the test was a very important milestone in consolidating Pakistan's strategic deterrence capability at all levels of the threat spectrum." He added that "in the hierarchy of military operations, the NASR Weapon System now provides Pakistan with short-range missile capability in addition to the already available medium and long range ballistic missiles and cruise missiles in its inventory." The range and nuclear warhead characteristics of the NASR missile indicate that it is a tactical nuclear weapon that could be used in the battlefield.

Hypothetically, the NASR missile would be used to deter or inflict punishment on mechanized forces such as the armored brigades and divisions envisaged in India's Cold Start Doctrine. In addition, this successful test of the missile manifested that Pakistan has succeeded scientifically in miniaturizing its nuclear weapon designs to the extent that these can be launched by tactical and cruise missiles. It seems that there would be shells for artillery guns carrying atomic explosives deployed on India-Pakistan border. More precisely, Pakistani defensive formation would be capable to use nuclear strikes to annihilate adversary's aggressing rapid cavalry/armored thrust in the Southern desert theatre or tacking an advantage of a short distance from border to takeover Lahore.

India's revisionist-grand-strategy and Pakistan's status-quo-oriented tactics at the technical level of grand strategy may be perilous for the current deterrence stability between India and Pakistan. Indeed, the continuing arms race between the strategic peers is not a constructive activity for the prevailing deterrence stability in South Asia. India's obsession with the military buildup, regional hegemony and Great Power status in the global politics desist it to enter into a regional arms control arrangement with Pakistan, which is imperative for deterrence stability between the belligerent neighbors. Conversely, Pakistan's resilience to guard its sovereignty by sustaining the prevalent balance of terror with its eastern neighbor through the development and test of tactical nuclear weapons and maintaining its firm stance on the Fissile Material Cut-off Treaty (FMCT) in the Conference on Disarmament at Geneva frustrate both India and United States.

Washington is very much determined to build India as a counterweight Asian power to balance the rising China in Asia in particular and global politics in general. Though Pakistan has no right to question and change the Americans perceptions about the perceived role of India in the Asian affairs, it can vigilantly solidify its own defensive fence through its indigenous military buildup infrastructure, and, in some cases, by purchasing weapons from the friendly states to prevent the Indian aggression.

The strategic competition between India and Pakistan requires that the latter should maintain a balance of terror with former. It is an open secret that once the balance of power skewed in favor of India, it would launch a hegemonic war against Pakistan. The gradual fattening of the Indian military muscle, therefore, naturally exacerbates the military vulnerability of Pakistan.

The Pakistani defense planners continuously endeavor to preserve the balance of terror to sustain the deterrence stability between the belligerent neighbors in South Asia. That is why, after realizing the intrinsic threat of the Indian Cold Start doctrine, Islamabad revised its nuclear doctrine and introduces a tactical nuclear weapon (NASR) in its nuclear posture. Ironically, the propaganda against Pakistan's tactical nuclear weapons has become a routine feature in the national, regional and global strategic discourse and media. Many analysts have been negatively portraying Pakistan's NASR missile invention. The disturbing issue in this debate is that majority of the contributors lack information, and also failed to grasp the dynamics of strategic environment of India and Pakistan. The strategic pundits intoxicated with the concept of 'minimum nuclear deterrence' confidently plead that India's military buildup would not destabilize Pakistan's defensive fence because of its strategic nuclear arsenal. They tried to establish that Islamabad's anxiety over India's anti-missile program and Cold Start Doctrine has been due to its strategic alarmist miscalculations. In addition, many security observers, without conducting basic research on the weapon system and critically examining the strategic environment of Pakistan, had haughtily concluded that Pakistan's pursuit for a new generation of nuclear weapon i.e. tactical nuclear weapon for its deterrence credibility contains ingredients of instability. These analysts have failed to realize the causes and timing of the NASR missile test. Nevertheless, the biased conclusions based on the ignorant and erroneous premises are perilous for the regional stability.

Indeed, new generation of weapon create power transition and intensify security dilemma between the strategic competitors. Hence, the new generation of weapon taxes the strategic stability and could jeopardize deterrence stability. Conversely, in certain cases, if the new generation of weapon is introduced as a reaction to the strategic revisionist state's military buildup, particularly, designs to defend the balance of power or status of the strategic environment, it bolsters the strategic stability.

To conclude, that the tactical nuclear weapons of Pakistan are deterrence stabilizers in South Asia.

PAKISTAN'S NUCLEAR POSTURE: IMPLICATIONS FOR SOUTH ASIAN STABILITY

Terrorists from Lashkar-e-Taiba—a group historically supported by Pakistan—laid siege to Mumbai in November 2008, crippling the city for three days and taking at least 163 lives. But India's response was restrained; it did not mobilize its military forces to retaliate against either Pakistan or Lashkar camps operating there. A former Indian chief of Army Staff, Gen. Shankar Roychowdhury, bluntly stated that Pakistan's threat of nuclear use deterred India from seriously considering conventional military strikes.

Pakistan's asymmetric escalation nuclear posture aims to credibly threaten the first use of nuclear weapons on Indian ground forces—likely on Pakistani soil—to deter significant Indian conventional action against Pakistan. Even though Pakistan claims to Securitystore its nuclear weapons in demated form, they can be assembled and mated rapidly as a crisis unfolds to credibly threaten early first use. Although both India and Pakistan have been *de facto* nuclear weapons states since the 1980s, it was only Pakistan's operationalization of an aggressive first-use nuclear posture in 1998 that created significant instability at both lower and higher levels of conflict.

To maintain the credibility of this posture, Pakistan devolves nuclear assets to the envisioned end users in the Pakistan military. Although the release of nuclear weapons is nominally subject to the authority of the National Command Authority (NCA), there may be few physical impediments preventing lower-level military commanders from releasing nuclear weapons if they deem it necessary. This arrangement would ensure the usability of Pakistan's nuclear weapons even if the NCA were decapitated or otherwise out of communication. As such, it is unlikely that Pakistan has robust permissive action links (PALs) that require centralized authorization, given that its command-and-control architecture may not be reliable enough to support such negative controls. Instead, if Pakistan employs PALs, they likely would be weak, bypassable locks similar to early-generation U.S. devices that could be circumvented in a crisis or conflict scenario.

Pakistan thus deters Indian conventional action through two complementary mechanisms: (1) the threat of authorized nuclear first use in a conventional conflict at some unspecified, but relatively early, threshold; and (2) the "mad-man" mechanism wherein a lower-level military commander decides to take matters into his own hands and release nuclear weapons at a threshold earlier than the NCA may otherwise enforce.

Since 1998, Pakistan's leadership has believed that this asymmetric escalation nuclear posture prevented India from escalating conflicts or retaliating with significant conventional force, following a series of Pakistani or Pakistani-affiliated provocations. In the 1999 Kargil War, the second phase of the Operation Parakram Crisis in June 2002, and after the 2008 Mumbai attacks, Indian leaders contemplated significant conventional retaliatory strikes against Pakistan but ultimately refrained from military action, partly out of fear of uncontrollable escalation to the nuclear level.

Since Pakistan's adoption of an asymmetric escalation posture, South Asia has barreled toward increasing instability. Elements within Pakistan—whether explicitly or implicitly backed by the state—can now provoke India even in its metropolitan heart with virtual impunity, shielded by Pakistan's nuclear posture. While India's assured retaliation nuclear posture has not deterred these provocations, Pakistan's nuclear posture has neutralized India's conventional options for now; limited retaliation would be militarily futile, and more significant conventional retaliation is simply off the table.

THE CURRENT PRICE OF DETERRENCE

Pakistan's deterrence success comes at a significant price to its security and the region's. To ensure the credibility of the asymmetric escalation nuclear posture, Pakistan faces an unholy deterrence/management trade-off. In particular, the Army is forced to cede both nuclear assets and some degree of authority to lower-level officers to ensure that its nuclear weapons are usable if necessary. Many of the risks to Pakistan's nuclear assets are well known: insider-facilitated theft, risks during transportation, and risks during crises. Especially in a crisis, the emphasis on usability may shift so severely for deterrence purposes that the risk of theft and unauthorized or accidental nuclear use may rise significantly. Perhaps the scariest implication of these arrangements is that extremist elements in Pakistan have a clear incentive to precipitate a crisis between India and Pakistan, so that Pakistan's nuclear assets become more exposed and vulnerable to theft. Terrorist organizations in the region with nuclear ambitions, such as al-Qaida, may find no easier route to obtaining fissile material or a fully functional nuclear weapon than to attack India, thereby triggering a crisis between India and Pakistan and forcing Pakistan to ready and disperse nuclear assets—with few, if any, negative controls—and then attempting to steal the nuclear material when it is being moved or in the field, where it is less secure than in peacetime locations.

THE FUTURE PRICE OF DETERRENCE

India's revisions to its conventional doctrine also pose significant future risks. To redress its perceived inability to retaliate against Pakistan-backed conventional and subconventional attacks, India's military is moving toward its much-vaunted "Cold Start" doctrine, which envisions prepositioning holding and armored units closer to the international border to enable surprise offensives against Pakistan from a "cold start." The aim is to reduce Indian mobilization times to enable the Indian military to rapidly achieve limited objectives below Pakistan's nuclear threshold and before international pressure forces Indian offensives to halt. Although Cold Start is still several years away from being fully in place, there are two worrisome implications of India's move to this revised conventional posture.

First, the pressure and ability for India to act quickly once Cold Start is in place could allow military logic to outpace political deliberation. One of the key features of Indian restraint in Kargil and Operation Parakram, as well as after the Mumbai attacks, was that the political leadership had time to deliberate and, in some cases, override the military. In a Cold Start world, the emphasis on maintaining the element of surprise could result in the Indian military quickly dragging India's political leadership into a conflict, ceding escalation control to the Indian and Pakistani militaries with potentially catastrophic consequences.

Second, India's move toward Cold Start fails to appreciate the dynamic coupling of Pakistan's nuclear posture to India's conventional posture. The Pakistan Army is obviously not sanguine about a conventional posture whose sole aim is to enable surprise offensives against Pakistan. Given Pakistan's fears that any Indian military operations may threaten the existence of the state, there is little distinction between limited and total war. Thus, to deter Indian surprise offensives, Pakistan could be forced to move to a ready nuclear deterrent on near hair-trigger alert. In such a scenario, Pakistan's asymmetric escalation nuclear posture would move to a permanent crisis footing, where the overriding emphasis on rapid usability would result in Pakistan's nuclear weapons being highly exposed and even more vulnerable to theft and unauthorized or accidental use. This could be an intolerable risk for regional and international security.

Unfortunately, there may be limited steps the United States can take to remedy the situation, given Pakistan's fears of U.S. intentions regarding its nuclear weapons. Nevertheless, to the degree possible, the United States and other nuclear powers should take whatever steps possible to improve the safety and security of Pakistan's nuclear posture without sacrificing deterrent power. Second, the international community should lean on India to abandon its Cold Start conventional doctrine. Although Pakistan-backed terrorist attacks against India is unacceptable, India's solution should focus on improving domestic intelligence and law enforcement to prevent such attacks, rather than on developing a conventional posture that enables rapid surprise retaliation and that spawns significant risk of uncontrollable escalation past the nuclear threshold.

5

Indian and Pakistani Nuclear Forces

It is difficult to determine the actual size and composition of India's and Pakistan's nuclear arsenals, but NRDC estimates that both countries have a total of 50 to 75 weapons. Contrary to the conventional wisdom, we believe India has about 30 to 35 nuclear warheads, slightly fewer than Pakistan, which may have as many as 48.

Both countries have fission weapons, similar to the early designs developed by the United States in the late 1940s and early 1950s. NRDC estimates their explosive yields are 5 to 25 kilotons (1 kiloton is equivalent to 1,000 tons of TNT).

By comparison, the yield of the weapon the United States exploded over Hiroshima was 15 kilotons, while the bomb exploded over Nagasaki was 21 kilotons. According to a recent NRDC discussion with a senior Pakistani military official, Pakistan's main nuclear weapons are mounted on missiles. India's nuclear weapons are reportedly gravity bombs deployed on fighter aircraft.

NRDC's Nuclear Program initially developed the software used to calculate the consequences of a South Asian nuclear war to examine and analyze the U.S. nuclear war planning process. We combined Department of Energy and Department of Defense computer codes with meteorological and demographic data to model what would happen in various kinds of attacks using different types of weapons.

10 Bombs on 10 South Asian Cities

For our first scenario we used casualty data from the Hiroshima bomb to estimate what would happen if bombs exploded over 10 large South Asian cities: five in India and five in Pakistan. (The results were published in "The Risks and Consequences of Nuclear War in South Asia," by NRDC physicist Matthew McKinzie and Princeton scientists Zia Mian, A. H. Nayyar and M. V. Ramana, a chapter in Smitu Kothari and Zia Mian (editors), "Out of the Nuclear Shadow" (Dehli: Lokayan and Rainbow Publishers, 2001).)

Estimated nuclear casualties for attacks on 10 large Indian and Pakistani cities

City Name	*Total Population Within 5 Kilometers of Ground Zer Injured*	*Number of Persons* —	*Number of Persons Severely Killed*	*Number of Persons Slightly Injured*
		INDIA		
Bangalore	3,077,937	314,978	175,136	411,336
Bombay	3,143,284	477,713	228,648	476,633
Calcutta	3,520,344	357,202	198,218	466,336
Madras	3,252,628	364,291	196,226	448,948
New Delhi	1,638,744	176,518	94,231	217,853
Total India	14,632,937	1,690,702	892,459	2,021,106
		PAKISTAN		
Faisalabad	2,376,478	336,239	174,351	373,967
Islamabad	798,583	154,067	66,744	129,935
Karachi	1,962,458	239,643	126,810	283,290
Lahore	2,682,092	258,139	149,649	354,095
Rawalpindi	1,589,828	183,791	96,846	220,585
Total Pakistan	9,409,439	1,171,879	614,400	1,361,872
		INDIA AND PAKISTAN		
Total	24,042,376	2,862,581	1,506,859	3,382,978

The 15-kiloton yield of the Hiroshima weapon is approximately the size of the weapons now in the Indian and Pakistani nuclear arsenals. The deaths and severe injuries experienced at Hiroshima were mainly a function of how far people were from ground zero. Other factors included whether people were in buildings or outdoors, the structural characteristics of the buildings themselves, and the age and health of the victims at the time of the attack. The closer to ground zero, the higher fatality rate. Further away there were fewer fatalities and larger numbers of injuries. The first nuclear war scenario by superimposing the Hiroshima data onto five Indian and five Pakistan cities with densely concentrated populations.

As in the case of the bombs dropped on Hiroshima and Nagasaki, in this scenario the 10 bombs over Indian and Pakistani cities would be exploded in the air, which maximized blast damage and fire but creates no fallout. On August 6, 1945, the United States exploded an untested uranium-235 gun-assembly bomb, nicknamed "Little Boy," 1,900 feet above Hiroshima. The city was home to an estimated 350,000 people; about 140,000 died by the end of the year. Three days later, at 11:02 am, the United States exploded a plutonium implosion bomb nicknamed "Fat Man" 1,650 feet above Nagasaki. About 70,000 of the estimated 270,000 residents died by the end of the year.

Ten Hiroshima-size explosions over 10 major cities in India and Pakistan would kill as many as three to four times more people per bomb than in Japan because of the higher urban densities in Indian and Pakistani cities.

24 Ground Bursts

In January, NRDC calculated the consequences of a much more severe nuclear exchange between India and Pakistan. It first appeared as a sidebar in the January 14, 2002, issue of Newsweek ("A Face-Off with Nuclear Stakes"). This scenario calculated the consequences of 24 nuclear explosions detonated on the ground – unlike the Hiroshima airburst – resulting in significant amounts of lethal radioactive fallout.

Exploding a nuclear bomb above the ground does not produce fallout. For example, the United States detonated "Little Boy" weapon above Hiroshima at an altitude of 1,900 feet. At this height, the radioactive particles produced in the explosion were small and light enough to rise into the upper atmosphere, where they were carried by the prevailing winds. Days to weeks later, after the radioactive bomb debris became less "hot," these tiny particles descended to earth as a measurable radioactive residue, but not at levels of contamination that would cause immediate radiation sickness or death.

Unfortunately, it is easier to fuse a nuclear weapon to detonate on impact than it is to detonate it in the air — and that means fallout. If the nuclear explosion takes place at or near the surface of the earth, the nuclear fireball would gouge out material and mix it with the radioactive bomb debris, producing heavier radioactive particles. These heavier particles would begin to drift back to earth within minutes or hours after the explosion, producing potentially lethal levels of nuclear fallout out to tens or hundreds of kilometers from the ground zero. The precise levels depend on the explosive yield of the weapon and the prevailing winds.

For the second scenario, we calculated the fallout patterns and casualties for a hypothetical nuclear exchange between India and Pakistan in which each country targeted major cities. We chose target cities throughout Pakistan and in northwestern India to take into account the limited range of Pakistani missiles or aircraft.

15 Indian and Pakistani cities attacked with 24 nuclear warheads

Country	*City*	*City Population*	*Number of Attacking Bombs*
India	New Dehli (national capital)	250-500 thousand	1
India	Bombay (provincial capital)	> 5 million	3
India	Delhi (provincial capital)	> 5 million	3
India	Jaipur (provincial capital)	1-5 million	2
India	Bhopal (provincial capital)	1-5 million	1
India	Ahmadabad	1-5 million	1
India	Pune	1-5 million	1
Pakistan	Islamabad (national capital)	100-250 thousand	1
Pakistan	Karachi (provincial capital)	> 5 million	3
Pakistan	Lahore (provincial capital)	1-5 million	2
Pakistan	Peshawar (provincial capital)	0.5-1 million	1
Pakistan	Quetta (provincial capital)	250-500 thousand	1
Pakistan	Faisalabad	1-5 million	2
Pakistan	Hyderabad	0.5-1 million	1
Pakistan	Rawalpindi	0.5-1 million	1

The target cities, include the capitals of Islamabad and New Dehli, and large cities, such as Karachi and Bombay. In this scenario, we assumed that a dozen, 25-kiloton warheads would be detonated as ground bursts in Pakistan and another dozen in India, producing substantial fallout.

The devastation that would result from fallout would exceed that of blast and fire. NRDC's second scenario would produce far more horrific results than the first scenario because there would be more weapons, higher yields, and extensive fallout. In some large cities, we assumed more than one bomb would be used.

NRDC calculated that 22.1 million people in India and Pakistan would be exposed to lethal radiation doses of 600 rem or more in the first two days after the attack. Another 8 million people would receive a radiation dose of 100 to 600 rem, causing severe radiation sickness and potentially death, especially for the very young, old or infirm. NRDC calculates that as many as 30 million people would be threatened by the fallout from the attack, roughly divided between the two countries.

Besides fallout, blast and fire would cause substantial destruction within roughly a mile-and-a-half of the bomb craters. NRDC estimates that 8.1 million people live within this radius of destruction. Most Indians (99 percent of the population) and Pakistanis (93 percent of the population) would survive the second scenario. Their respective military forces would be still be intact to continue and even escalate the conflict.

Thinking the Unthinkable

After India and Pakistan held nuclear tests in 1998, experts have debated whether their nuclear weapons contribute to stability in South Asia. Experts who argue that the nuclear standoff promotes stability have pointed to the U.S.-Soviet Union Cold War as an example of how deterrence ensures military restraint.

NRDC disagrees. There are major differences between the Cold War and the current South Asian crisis. Unlike the U.S.-Soviet experience, these two countries have a deep-seated hatred of one another and have fought three wars since both countries became independent. At least part of the current crisis may be seen as Hindu nationalism versus Muslim fundamentalism.

A second difference is India and Pakistan's nuclear arsenals are much smaller than those of the United States and Russia. The

U.S. and Russian arsenals truly represent the capability to destroy each other's society beyond recovery. While the two South Asia scenarios we have described produce unimaginable loss of life and destruction, they do not reach the level of "mutual assured destruction" that stood as the ultimate deterrent during the Cold War.

The two South Asian scenarios assume nuclear attacks against cities. During the early Cold War period this was the deterrent strategy of the United States and the Soviet Union. But as both countries introduced technological improvements into their arsenals, they pursued other strategies, targeting each other's nuclear forces, conventional military forces, industry and leadership. India and Pakistan may include these types of targets in their current military planning. For example, attacking large dams with nuclear weapons could result in massive disruption, economic consequences and casualties. Concentrations of military forces and facilities may provide tempting targets as well.

INDIA'S NUCLEAR DEVELOPMENTS MEAN FOR PAKISTAN

The deployment of nuclear-powered ballistic submarines will enhance India's strategic deterrent capabilities, particularly against Pakistan. According to Shane Mason, this development will inevitably prompt Islamabad to try and tilt the strategic balance in the Indian Ocean region in its own favor.

With the induction of the nuclear-powered ballistic missile submarine (SSBN) INS Arihant scheduled for the first half of 2013, and with plans to add at least three more indigenously-built SSBNs to India's naval forces by 2025, New Delhi is poised to begin a gradual strategic shift toward the Indian Ocean. The formal induction of the Arihant is a powerful first step towards establishing a sea-based nuclear deterrent, whereby the Indian armed forces—currently able to deliver nuclear weapons via fighter aircraft and surface-to-surface missiles—will add the capability of firing submarine-launched ballistic and cruise missiles.

Such an arrangement will go a long way towards reinforcing India's already robust second-strike capability, and places it in a small group of states with maritime nuclear forces. It may take a full decade, and the acquisition of at least three or four more submarines, until India has a true operational maritime nuclear capability, but this is clearly a new strategic direction.

Ultimately, and most importantly for regional stability, the completion of India's maritime deterrent skews the India-Pakistan nuclear competition in favor of India. But how, specifically, will the deployment of Arihant, and India's future fleet of nuclear-capable submarines, impact Pakistan's strategic calculus in both short-and long-term planning?

Consequences for Pakistan

In the immediate future, Pakistan will have to act fast to counter the strategic advantages India will gain with the induction of the Arihant and other SSBNs. Pakistan has been working to integrate the French-built Khalid-class submarines into its strategic forces for several years, but significant hurdles remain. Specifically, missile tubes have to be modified to handle nuclear-capable missiles like the Babur cruise missile, and the navy needs to be integrated into the country's existing nuclear command and control architecture, which is currently dominated by the army.

While India will be able to deploy nuclear-propelled submarines over the next few decades, no credible evidence suggests Pakistan has made plans to do the same. Instead, naval planners have focused on acquiring more sophisticated conventional submarines, like the recently announced purchase of six submarines from China with modern air-induced propulsion systems. Pakistan's focus on conventional submarines underscores the country's financial constraints when it comes to military procurement, especially for the historically overlooked Pakistani Navy.

Once deployed, the Arihant and future Indian SSBNs will increase India's strategic depth—something that Pakistan currently lacks, vis-à-vis its eastern neighbor. Virtually undetectable and able to stay underwater for months at a time, nuclear submarines are nearly invulnerable to even the most modern anti-submarine warfare technology and offer a qualitative advantage to a country's nuclear deterrent. Sea-based delivery platforms reinforce a country's ability to retaliate after absorbing a nuclear first strike, and likely dissuade an adversary from attempting a dangerous preemptive attack against its nuclear assets. Assuming a survivable command, control, and communications network, the future fleet of Indian SSBNs will add depth to the country's nuclear deterrent.

India's nascent nuclear monopoly in the Indian Ocean is likely to force officials in Pakistan's National Command Authority to temper their recently emboldened outlook toward nuclear doctrine and strategy.

Recent missile developments suggest at least some officials in the Strategic Plans Division (SPD) believe its forces can use nuclear weapons without necessarily evoking a nuclear response from Delhi. In particular, Pakistan's recent addition of nuclear-capable, tactical ballistic missiles like the Nasr signal Islamabad's confidence that a counterforce nuclear strike—say, against Indian troops who had crossed the international border as part of India's conventional "Cold Start" doctrine, which envisions limited, punish-and-withdrawal operations against targets inside Pakistan—would not escalate to higher levels of retaliation.

This logic hinges on the assumption that a defensive nuclear attack against foreign troops on its own soil would be protected by international law, thereby profoundly complicating India's decision to respond with a nuclear strike of its own. While such thinking would have been risky before, India's nuclear submarines, equipped with nuclear-capable missiles, render such logic even more dubious.

How Pakistan Can Respond?

In the medium-to long-term, Pakistan will feel forced to counter India's SSBNs in order to reestablish strategic balance in the Indian Ocean. Pakistan can choose to respond to India's sea-based deterrent in a number of possible ways. First, Pakistan can acquire SSBNs from friendly countries, or build them indigenously. China, an historical ally with decades of experience in maritime nuclear technology, would be a likely partner in any Pakistani effort to acquire nuclear submarines. Although such cooperation would be deeply unsettling in New Delhi and Washington, and China's own struggles operationalizing SSBNs represent a significant hurdle, Beijing would welcome the opportunity to reinforce Pakistan's deterrent posture, while also increasing its own strategic presence on India's western flank. Considering the desperate state of the Pakistani economy, however, cost constraints appear to rule out this possibility, and most certainly preclude an indigenous program in the foreseeable future.

The most likely Pakistani response, and the policy option it seems poised to pursue, is to equip newly purchased conventional submarines with nuclear-capable cruise and ballistic missiles. In addition to the aforementioned purchase of six Chinese submarines, reports indicate that Pakistan has been in talks with Germany for several years over the acquisition of three nuclear-capable submarines. In this way, Pakistan would follow the same trajectory as Israel, whose German-built, Dolphin-class submarines are an integral dimension of its strategic force posture.

At the same time, Pakistan continues to develop its missile program, particularly in the field of cruise missiles. In the last year, Pakistan twice tested its newest cruise missile—the Babur—which it is also reconfiguring to have submarine-launch capabilities. With a range of 750 kilometers, the Babur could evade India's nascent missile defense systems, and would signal a significant step forward in the sophistication of Pakistan's delivery systems.

Pakistan may be able to reestablish strategic equilibrium vis-à-vis India by acquiring a new fleet of conventional submarines, but this would take time.

While conventional submarines lack the prestigious cachet of SSBNs and their ability to remain submerged for extended periods of time, they are much less expensive to build and maintain than their nuclear-powered counterparts. Islamabad will first need to make tough choices about its force posture, delivery systems, and the financial price it is willing to pay to narrow the strategic gap it will have with India on the high seas. How Pakistan responds to the forthcoming induction of India's strategic submarines over the next decade will have repercussions for both regional and international security.

INDIA AND PAKISTAN NUCLEAR

When the British withdrew from the Indian subcontinent after the second world war, it was divided, primarily on religious grounds, into the two states of India and Pakistan. At that time Kashmir was included in India, but the issue of which state it should belong to has been contested ever since, largely because Kashmir's population is predominantly Muslim. In 1947 a United Nations resolution called for a referendum in Kashmir to settle the issue on the basis of what the people wanted. It was, however never carried out and it is generally assumed that the reason for this is because the Indian government feared the popular vote would support unification with Pakistan on religious grounds. Many in Kashmir campaign for independence, a position that neither India nor Pakistan supports. Around 30,000 people have died in Kashmir in the last 11 years. What happens in Kashmir is at the heart of the continuing tension between India and Pakistan. The possibility of the world's first direct war between two nuclear-armed states occurring is very real. The history of the conflict over Kashmir is well documented with three India/Pakistan wars taking place since 1947. But this time it would be with both sides having access to nuclear weapons.

Since the attack on the Indian Parliament building in December 2001, the tension and rhetoric have grown considerably. India accused Pakistan of supporting terrorist groups. Pakistan, in turn, pledges its support for Kashmiri freedom fighters. One state's terrorist is another's freedom fighter. Since the attack in December, Pakistan has arrested around 1500 'militants' and banned five groups, two said to be sectarian, one pro-Taliban and two who have been fighting Indian rule in Kashmir. However, Gen Musharraf has pledged continued support for Kashmir.

Many people living along the border close to Kashmir have fled the area due to the large military presence being built up by both sides. From the end of 2001 there were clashes virtually every night in that border region, with sometimes one or two people being shot. There are claims that large numbers of military silos have been destroyed.

In an atmosphere of increased tension and sabre-rattling rhetoric on both sides, this led to the situation in May 2002 where upwards of a million troops were gathered near the border. Any mistake or small incident runs the risk of setting off something far, far worse.

NUCLEAR NUMBERS

Estimates on actual warhead numbers vary wildly with reports that India has anywhere between 50-150 warheads and Pakistan 10-100. There is a bit more clarity, however, regarding the missile systems that would deliver them.

India

Agni (Intermediate Range Ballistic Missile), nuclear capable and tested. Range: 1,500 miles Could reach Karachi in about 14 minutes

Prithvi (Surface to Surface Missile), nuclear capable and deployed. Range: 90-220 miles. Could reach Islamabad or Lahore within three minutes

Trishul (Surface to Surface Missile), nuclear capable.

Range: 6 miles

Pakistan

Ghauri (Intermediate Range Ballistic Missile), nuclear capable in production. Range: 930 miles. Could reach Bombay in 10 minutes. One medium-range and one short-range missile, both nuclear capable, were tested in May 2002.

THE CURRENT SITUATION

All this, of course, is fuelled by the continuing rhetoric on both sides. Officials in both countries claimed that they would not use nuclear weapons first, but they seem remarkably keen to use them second. Given the proximity of the two states, it is clear that millions of their own people would die along with millions of their nearest neighbours. India has said that it would not use nuclear weapons first, while Pakistan has clearly stated that it would.

Whilst a 'no first use' policy is an important step towards disarmament, it is all too often used as an excuse to build a large 'second use' capacity. Eventually, of course, the 'second use' becomes indistinguishable from the 'first use'. As the tension mounts, the temptation grows to get your retaliation in first.

But what are the immediate reasons for the current increasing tension and the risk of war? India appears to be escalating events but its argument is that it is following the lead of the US and the west by zero tolerance of terrorist attacks. It has identified what it sees as terrorists being harboured by another state so it threatens military retaliation.

Both sides have had internal problems as well. In Pakistan, Musharraf has been promising a democratic election ever since the army took control, but there has been only a referendum. Though it was boycotted by many political parties, Musharraf claimed it as a mandate for him to continue. Meanwhile in India, the ruling BJP has lost every state election for over a year, so now uses the well-known tactic of uniting the country against an outside 'threat'. Whatever the reasons for the tensions, the crucial aim is to avoid the devastation of nuclear war.

The British Prime Minister, Tony Blair, visited the region in January 2002 to try to persuade both sides that a war was not a good idea. This took place against the background of the bombing in Afghanistan, in which Britain was an enthusiastic participant. His approach raised concerns about Western hypocrisy, as if war is fine for some countries but not others.

The sincerity of Blair's mission was also in question after it transpired that his plea for peace preceded two British trade missions to Delhi in February, both designed to sell weapons to India. Defexpo is an arms fair whose promotional material pushes the weaponry on sale, with everything from small arms to missile systems. India and Pakistan have long been valuable markets for British arms manufacturers. So this arms fair, combined with the resumption of arms sales to Pakistan, as a result of its support for the war in Afghanistan, means that Britain will be arming both sides in any future war. This is, of course, not unique. A similar thing happened during the Iraq-Iran war.

So, what's the answer? The situation in south Asia shows the importance of nuclear disarmament. A war even with conventional weapons would be an appalling waste of life. But this would be turned into a complete disaster on an unimaginable scale if nuclear weapons were used. In the short term there must be more diplomatic language and there must be proper international negotiations at the UN to resolve the problem of Kashmir. Our own politicians could do more to help. How can the British Government's attempts to calm the situation be taken seriously when the Defence Minister, Geoff Hoon, appears on television saying that he would use nuclear weapons against any state if necessary?

In the long term, the declared nuclear weapon states (NWS)-US, UK, France, Russia and China-must carry out their obligations under the nuclear Non-Proliferation Treaty (NPT) and get rid of their nuclear weapons. The NPT was drawn up in 1968, giving the definition of a NWS as one that tested nuclear weapons before then. Because India was preparing its nuclear programme at that time, it would not sign. Because India would not sign, neither would Pakistan. Therefore, they cannot sign the NPT as NWS and, since the nuclear testing by both sides in 1998, they cannot sign as non-nuclear weapon states. The NWS made statements at the time of the tests saying how appalled they were at this development. But after 11 September, the US lifted sanctions imposed on both sides, in order to boost its coalition in the 'War on Terrorism'.

If the NWS put the words of the NPT into action, they would be in a position to push India and Pakistan to sign the NPT themselves. After all, part of the excuse given by India and Pakistan for the 1998 nuclear tests was that those nuclear weapon states had done nothing about their NPT commitments, so if nuclear weapons were good enough for them......

Both sides need to be persuaded that nuclear weapons make the world a more dangerous, not a safer, place and to take a step back and realise that peaceful resolutions to conflict are the best way forward. This should happen through the UN. But the UN also needs to look at the continuing nuclear policies of the NWS. There are peace activists in both India and Pakistan working hard to get their views across. Their work has been particularly difficult since the nuclear tests carried out by both countries in 1998. They have the entire might of the government and military propaganda machine ranged against them. We should do all we can to support them.

INDIA'S NUCLEAR DOCTRINE: STIRRINGS OF CHANGE

In the beginning of April 2014, at a conference initiated by the Indian government, Manmohan Singh casually urged the creation of a global convention to forswear thefirst use of nuclear weapons. Why the Indian prime minister chose to make this major policy declaration in the last hours of his term in office is a mystery.

To unravel this mystery, it is important to note the context. Singh was addressing a conference at the Institute for Defense Studies and Analyses (IDSA) titled "A Nuclear Weapon-Free World: From Conception to Reality." The IDSA is supported by the Indian Ministry of Defense and has been a favored venue for India's leadership to make important policy declarations on national security. The Indian bureaucracies that deal with foreign policy and security issues often use this forum to articulate their preferences on arms control, nonproliferation, and disarmament issues. It would be natural if these bureaucracies wished to commend the virtues of continuity in policy to the new Indian government headed by Prime Minister Narendra Modi, who took office in May 2014.

Following Singh's remarks, the then opposition Bharatiya Janata Party (BJP) instantly issued a rejoinder in its election manifesto, stating that the party "believes that the strategic gains acquired by India during the [earlier BJP-led] Atal Behari Vajpayee regime on the nuclear programme have been frittered away by [Singh's] Congress." Hence, the BJP pledged to "study in detail India's nuclear doctrine, and revise and update it, to make it relevant to [the] challenges of current times."

BJP spokespeople clarified that a review of India's no-first-use policy would be accorded priority if the party came to power. This evoked great concern in some quarters that the BJP would abandon no first use, which has been a central feature of India's nuclear doctrine since the country conducted a series of nuclear tests in 1998 and established itself as a nuclear weapons state. The BJP's Modi, campaigning for the 2014 election, subsequently declared that there would be "no compromise" on no first use, which reflected India's "cultural inheritance" (whatever that means). But as the respected *Economic and Political Weekly* commented in an editorial: "Given the BJP's naturally aggressive posture, such clarifications must be viewed with some scepticism and it is legitimate to explore what may be on the agenda."

All this rhetoric is par for the course in the heated atmosphere of the Indian electoral process. Disconcertingly, both the Congress party and the BJP have forgotten the historical record. India's no-first-use policy was originally declared by the BJP and the National Democratic Alliance government after it conducted the May 1998 nuclear tests. The prime minister at the time, Atal Behari Vajpayee, stated thereafter that India would pursue a policy of no first use of nuclear weapons vis-à-vis other nuclear-armed states and would not use these weapons against nonnuclear countries. This restraint was also embedded in the BJP's draft nuclear doctrine , declared in August 1999, which took several years to be finalized. It was finally endorsed by the Cabinet Committee on Security and officially promulgated in January 2003.

Consequently, India's no-first-use policy and its nuclear doctrine are BJP formulations. The Congress party adopted them and, with Singh's April speech, simply sought to extend no first use globally. This makes the BJP's concern with its own no-first-use policy and nuclear doctrine part of the mystery of Singh's proposal.

The Limitations of Nuclear Deterrence

There are valid grounds to revisit India's nuclear doctrine, as much has happened over the intervening years that challenges the assumptions made by the BJP. On the conceptual front, the limitations of nuclear deterrence have become apparent. In important ways, India's acquisition of nuclear weapons has not increased its security.

While nuclear weapons have obvious relevance for the external dimensions of national security, they cannot ameliorate threats to India's territorial integrity that arise from domestic discontent or from crossborder militancy and terrorism emanating from Pakistan. In other words, nuclear weapons cannot provide any defense against the subconventional threats to India's national security from extremist elements within its own territory or, especially, against those who receive moral and material assistance from across the border. As Singh repeatedly warned, the internal threats to India's national security are critical to its overall national security challenges. Nuclear weapons provide no defense against these dangers.

The evidence in this regard is overwhelming and discernible from continuing unrest in the state of Jammu and Kashmir and in northeast India and from Maoist violence in central and east India. Further, after Pakistan followed suit with its own nuclear tests in 1998, India's superiority in conventional forces was conspicuously eroded. This can be seen in India's fitful responses to incidents of crossborder terrorism from Pakistan and its thus far confused approach to the concept of Cold Start and delay in establishing the forces required to operationalize it.

Nuclear deterrence can only provide security against the use of nuclear weapons or a major conventional attack. This ineluctable reality evades India's strategic elites and its armed forces establishment. They find it hard to accept that nuclear weapons, unlike other weapon systems, are not designed for use and cannot achieve strategic objectives like gaining territory or dominating populations. Moreover, these weapons' immense destructive potential within very short time frames and their ability to cause genetic mutations over generations ensure that they are essentially meant to deter their use by an adversary. In other words, nuclear deterrence cannot accomplish any vital national security goals other than preventing an adversary from using nuclear weapons.

In a larger sense, no doubt, nuclear deterrence permits peaceful conditions to be established, a situation that is conducive to economic progress and the stimulation of regional trade and commerce. However, an entire spectrum of security threats also arises, ranging from border incursions to subconventional warfare and crossborder terrorism and militancy. Nuclear weapons provide no security against this range of existential security threats.

These fuller implications of the nuclear tests were not thought through before the tests were conducted in 1998. Perhaps these limitations surrounding nuclear deterrence were not knowable in advance. But this belief is questionable. It was known, for instance, that India would be subjected to punitive economic and technological sanctions that would affect its growth and poverty alleviation programs in response to the nuclear tests. Indeed, India's earlier experience after its so-called "peaceful nuclear explosion" in May 1974 was a forewarning that further nuclear tests would not enable India's entry into the Nuclear Non-Proliferation Treaty as a nuclear weapons state and that the imposition of more stringent sanctions was certain.

According to available evidence, the decision to conduct the nuclear tests in May 1998 was made by a very small coterie around Vajpayee. He and his advisers believed that India needed to go nuclear to meet the nuclear threats from Pakistan and China, elevate India in the comity of nations, and fulfill the pledge in the BJP's 1996 election manifesto to conduct nuclear tests if the party came to power. The rest is history: sanctions on India's civilian nuclear program were reinforced, severely impeding its progress—despite tall claims that the restrictions provided a fillip to indigenous research and development.

India's Atomic Energy Commission has traditionally argued that sanctions on importing nuclear technology, equipment, and materials from abroad did not hurt, since the commission could harness the human and technical resources available in the country to meet its requirements. This bravado was first expressed after India conducted its 1974 nuclear test. It is clear, however, that despite some limited success, India remained dependent on foreign assistance to establish its nuclear infrastructure. This fact was reflected in the United Progressive Alliance government's rationale for entering into the Indo-U.S. nuclear deal in 2008, namely to rescue India from its "nuclear pariah" status and open the way for imports of nuclear materials and technology.

The establishment of nuclear deterrence vis-à-vis Pakistan had only limited value for India's overall national security. It did not deter Pakistan's crossborder incursions in winter 1998 and spring 1999 into the Kargil sector of Jammu and Kashmir, which led to a short but intense conflict ending in the ouster of Pakistan's regular and irregular forces.

Pakistan had the advantage of surprise, but its intruders were no match for India's superior conventional forces, which were brought into the Kargil and neighboring sectors of the Line of Control. Yet despite India's overwhelming superiority in conventional arms, the effects of nuclear deterrence inhibited it from attacking Pakistan's lines of communications across the border or from enlarging the theater of conflict along the border to relieve pressure on the beleaguered Kargil sector.

Pakistan was disadvantaged by its need to maintain the fiction that militants had conducted these intrusions, and therefore it could not openly deploy its regular forces to defend them. Significantly, these operations revealed that a nuclearized Pakistan had constrained New Delhi from launching a counteroffensive elsewhere along the Line of Control or into Pakistan to relieve pressure on Indian forces in Kargil. New Delhi decided that it would exhibit restraint and not expand the theater of conflict. Political considerations were said to be at play, as India wished to establish that it was a responsible nuclear power by not escalating the conflict.

There was also a subliminal desire among Indian leaders to paint Pakistan into a corner by highlighting its irresponsible conduct in attacking across recognized borders without any provocation. In pursuance of this policy of restraint, the Indian Air Force was given strict orders not to attack Pakistani territory across the Line of Control or enter Pakistan's airspace. The ground forces were similarly prohibited from expanding the area of conflict along the Line of Control to relieve pressure on the Kargil sector. There is little doubt, however, that this restraint was also informed by New Delhi's awareness that an escalation of this border conflict could become uncontrollable and lead inexorably toward the nuclear threshold.

Pakistan Ups the Ante

A similar sequence of events inhibited India during its border confrontation crisis with Pakistan after an attack by Pakistan-based militants on the Indian parliament in mid-December 2001. India moved large elements of its armed forces to the India-Pakistan border, where they remained for almost one year. Unable to mount an attack into Pakistan, they returned without achieving anything worthwhile. Again, in November 2008, New Delhi found itself constrained in retaliating against brazen attacks by Pakistan-sponsored militants on several high-profile targets in Mumbai.

More generally, it would seem that Pakistan has acquired virtual impunity in launching terrorist attacks at will into India through organizations that enjoy its patronage, like Lashkar-e-Taiba and Jamaat-ud-Dawa. Admittedly, these groups operate in collaboration with local militants like the Indian Mujahideen, but leadership, funding, training, and sanctuary are provided by Pakistan. Despite grave provocation by these groups, India has been unable to undertake any punitive counterstrike but has sought redress by painting Pakistan into an ideological corner within the international system.

A more general argument against nuclear deterrence was made by the four horsemen, George Shultz, Henry Kissinger, Sam Nunn, and William Perry, in 2007 in the *Wall Street Journal*. "Nuclear weapons were essential to maintaining international security during the Cold War because they were a means of deterrence. The end of the Cold War made the doctrine... obsolete. Deterrence continues to be a relevant consideration for many states.... But reliance on nuclear weapons for this purpose is becoming increasingly hazardous and decreasingly effective."

Pakistan's decision to deploy tactical nuclear weapons in a battlefield mode along the India-Pakistan border can be surmised from a report by Hans M. Kristensen and Robert Norris of the Federation of American Scientists that identified Pakistan and China as either having or developing nonstrategic nuclear weapons. Pakistan had made clear, Kristensen told the *Times of India* , that it was developing its nuclear-capable Nasr (or Hatf IX) missile "for use against invading Indian troop formations that Pakistan doesn't have the conventional capabilities to defeat." These weapons, according to Indian experts, are meant to be used along the border in case of any skirmish with the Indian Army. The Nasr is described as "a 60-kilometer [37-mile] ballistic missile launched from a mobile twin-canister launcher." According to Pakistan's Inter Services Public Relations, the Nasr also has "shoot and scoot attributes" to serve as a quick response system to "add deterrence value" to Pakistan's strategic weapons development program "at shorter ranges... to deter evolving threats."

These developments have highlighted the insufficiency of India's no-first-use policy to deter Pakistan's destabilizing strategy. For one thing, this policy articulation frees Pakistan of the uncertainty and angst that India might contemplate the preemptive use of nuclear weapons to deal with terrorist attacks or limited conventional strikes by Pakistan. Pakistan could also go to the extent of deploying its short-range Nasr missile without being concerned that India would target it with its own nuclear missiles. For another, the determinism inherent in India's nuclear doctrine that any level of nuclear attack will invite massive retaliation is too extreme to gain much credibility. It defies logic to threaten an adversary with nuclear annihilation to deter or defend against a tactical nuclear strike on an advancing military formation.

Moreover, in an adversarial situation between two nuclear powers, recourse to massive retaliation by one side would surely trigger a similar counterattack. How would the mutual annihilation that would undoubtedly ensue serve the ends of national security? This is a question that must induce greater reflection on how to devise a more appropriate strategy to meet Pakistan's threat of using tactical nuclear weapons in crises along the India-Pakistan border.

Pakistan, for its part, has not countenanced a no-first-use policy on the grounds that the weaker conventionally armed power has to rely on nuclear weapons to ensure its security. However, conventional wisdom warns that deployment of nuclear weapons along the border makes these arms vulnerable to attack, which, in turn, could generate a "use or lose" mentality on the part of their possessor. A related danger that has not been sufficiently articulated is that nuclear missiles situated near the border could become vulnerable to targeting by long-range artillery, apart from special forces operations, highlighting the hair-trigger nature of such deployments. Pakistan argues that locating tactical nuclear weapons along the India-Pakistan border in a state of battle-readiness enables it to counter India's Cold Start strategy, which envisages positioning offensive, battle-ready forces along the India-Pakistan border to deter any crossborder attack.

In this fashion, according to one nuclear expert, "Pakistan has upped the nuclear ante in South Asia by choosing to adopt tactical nuclear weapons... because they lower the nuclear threshold, the point at which nuclear weapons are brought into use. As such, they are straining South Asia's deterrence stability, the idea that roughly equivalent nuclear capabilities will deter adversaries from using these weapons." Pakistan claims that deploying its tactical nuclear weapons would provide it with "full spectrum deterrence" against India. Rawalpindi would also be enabled to counter any offensive operations India might contemplate against Pakistan in response to another Mumbai-style terrorist attack.

The particular danger of this deployment pattern is that it creates pressures to delegate to field commanders the authority to use these missiles in a crisis situation. Pakistani authorities insist that no such delegation would be necessary. In the end, and especially with the fog of war intervening, whatever arrangements were thought to control such weapons could never be foolproof. The possibility of human error would have to be accepted. But, with nuclear weapons entering the calculus, such errors could have horrific consequences.

Adding to these uncertainties is the fact that the internal situation in Pakistan has been rapidly deteriorating over the last few years, with extremist and religious fundamentalist groups exercising control over growing areas in the country. Political differences between the military and civilian leaderships in Pakistan are also increasing, with the judiciary functioning not as an umpire but as a third leg in an unstable relationship between elements of the country's ruling elite. How this increasingly dysfunctional system can implement a responsible nuclear strategy is an open question. An impasse has now been reached that threatens the stability of India-Pakistan relations. It is arguable that India's commitment to a no-first-use posture has encouraged Pakistan to adopt its present adventurist strategy, secure in the belief that it could undertake provocative actions without the angst that India might contemplate a nuclear riposte. Its provocative actions would include promoting crossborder militancy and terrorism into India and even brazen actions like the attack on the Indian parliament in 2001 or the Mumbai attacks in 2008. Arguably, the adoption of a deliberately vague policy in regard to nuclear retaliation by India, instead of the certitude of a no-first-use declaration, might have better served India's overall strategic ends.

Apart from that, the no-first-use policy, which has been incorporated into India's nuclear doctrine, has several other infirmities.

An Inadequate Doctrine

The decision by the Cabinet Committee on Security to endorse India's nuclear doctrine makes clear that India will use nuclear weapons only to retaliate against a nuclear attack on its territories or on Indian forces anywhere; that nuclear weapons will not be used against nonnuclear states; but that, in the event of a major attack by biological or chemical weapons, India retains the option of retaliating with nuclear weapons. This enumeration of India's qualified no-first-use policy doctrine is flawed on several counts.

First, it does not address the possibility of an attack by nonstate actors, which is the present and imminent danger. Would the country hosting those nonstate actors be targeted following such an attack? And how would India address an attack by an international organization like al-Qaeda that is situated in several countries in the proximity of India?

Second, how would a "major attack" with biological or chemical weapons be identified? What is "major" and what is "minor" is debatable. This issue is significant since biological and chemical weapons are not truly weapons of mass *destruction*, but they are certainly weapons of mass *disruption*. Nonstate actors might favor these weapons due to the comparative ease of their manufacture, concealment, and transportation. Third, serious difficulties arise in any attempt to identify the perpetrator of a biological or chemical weapons attack that could be undertaken by state or nonstate actors or, not inconceivably, by a nonstate actor assisted by a state actor. This issue is ultimately a question of reliable forensics, which is at a rudimentary stage of development. The difficulty in identifying those guilty of chemical weapon attacks in Syria is instructive here.

India's no-first-use declaration cannot be separated from the country's overall nuclear doctrine as it has been articulated since 1999. Inadequate as it is, this doctrine deserves to be reviewed in the light of changes over the past fifteen years.

The current nuclear doctrine dictates that nuclear retaliation against a first strike would be "massive" and designed to inflict "unacceptable damage" upon the attacker. This is an unrealistic certitude because, ethically, punishing large numbers of noncombatants contravenes the laws of war. Besides, threatening massive retaliation against any level of nuclear attack, which would inevitably trigger assured nuclear annihilation in a binary adversarial situation, is hardly a credible option. No doubt, it raises a ticklish question: Would India then favor a counterforce or countercity strategy? India's stated adherence to an assured and massive second strike suggests the latter.

However, in addition to the other infirmities of a massive retaliation response, the uncomfortable reality is that the trade winds in May–September associated with the southwest monsoon blow from Pakistan into northern India. Consequently, secondary and tertiary radiation from a nuclear attack launched by India against Pakistan in these months would blow back into India's agriculturally rich Punjab and Haryana states and, indeed, into New Delhi. India therefore faces a huge time constraint to mount a massive nuclear attack into Pakistan. Operationally, too, destroying the territory in dispute is feckless.

In a nuclear adversarial situation, moreover, the inevitability of mutual destruction must also be considered. Is a counterforce attack on the adversary's military formations and assets the answer? The issue of uncontrollable escalation then arises, for which there is no reassuring answer. Leaving the problem of how India should retaliate to a nuclear first strike to the discretion of the prime minister would provide greater flexibility to mount the counterattack instead of threatening assured nuclear annihilation, which is just not credible.

India's present chain of command with respect to nuclear weapons functions under the rubric of a Nuclear Command Authority and a Strategic Forces Command. The prime minister has been designated as the "release authority." He has the unequivocal authority to decide whether, when, and how to use nuclear weapons. A Political Council headed by the prime minister constitutes the apex of this command structure. An Executive Council headed by the national security adviser serves the Political Council. Its composition includes the service chiefs and relevant government secretaries, including the scientific adviser to the prime minister.

The Strategic Forces Command is headed by a commander-in-chief; the incumbent comes from one of the three services of the Indian Armed Forces, on a rotating basis. The Strategic Forces Command is located within the Integrated Defense Headquarters in the Ministry of Defense. But it also functions under the Chiefs of Staff Committee. Its chairman is the most senior service chief, which ensures that the post rotates among the three services, without any fixed tenure. A conscious effort is evident, however, to assert the primacy of civilian control over the military at all levels of the nuclear command structure.

The element of doubt arising in this arrangement is that a tri-service command like the Strategic Forces Command should, logically, function under a single line of authority representing the three services, like a chief of defense staff, who would be a single-point adviser to the government on sensitive security issues. The proposal to establish a chief of defense staff, incidentally, is of ancient vintage and can be traced back to the Sino-Indian border conflict of 1962. The option of a chief of defense staff has been recommended by numerous inquiry committees, notably theArun Singh Committee on defense expenditure (in 1990) and, most recently, theNaresh Chandra Committee on national security.

But this proposal to appoint a chief of defense staff who could provide a unified service view to the government on sensitive issues continues to languish since it has been resolutely opposed by the Indian Navy and Air Force. The attitude of the Ministry of Defense and the Government of India, which could force through a decision, can at best be described as studied insouciance. It remains unclear in these circumstances whether, in a crisis situation, the strategic forces commander would report to the chairman of the Chiefs of Staff Committee, which would be an unsatisfactory arrangement as far as civilian control is concerned, or whether he would report directly to the national security adviser and the Executive Council, which is equally unsatisfactory from an interservice coordination perspective.

It is for these reasons that it makes more sense for the decision about whether, when, and how to retaliate against a nuclear attack to remain the prime minister's. Moreover, time would clearly be at a premium in a crisis situation. A committee system of decisionmaking is hardly suited to handle a fast-developing situation. Providing the "release authority" the greatest flexibility to decide how to mount the counterattack, according to the exigencies of the situation, provides a more workable solution to this problem.

The present doctrine fetishizes acquisition of a "credible minimum deterrent." But India is seeking a force structure that is no different from that established by the United States or the former Soviet Union. India seeks a strategic triad comprising land-based, airborne, and underwater nuclear weapon systems that will require increasing resources.

It is arguable whether India's strategic circumstances require a naval component for its deterrent or whether the country requires only a submarine-based deterrent, on the assumption that the nuclear deterrent posture ultimately rests on the survivability of the nuclear arsenal. Land-and air-based systems are more vulnerable to counterattack and destruction than submarine-based missiles are. That leads to the argument that taking the deterrent out to sea would ensure the acquisition of an invulnerable second strike capability. This question has not been seriously discussed in India, resulting in vociferous demands from the three services that the government concede some component of the nuclear deterrent to each of them.

Criticism is widespread that there is little transparency about the size and structure of India's nuclear forces and what its credible minimum deterrent comprises in terms of weapons systems. Instead of debating this issue, official spokesmen have argued that it is impossible to define what a credible minimum deterrent requires since there can be no "fixity" in this regard, which suggests that the contours of the credible minimum deterrent are a moving target. Incidentally, India's armed forces have been kept out of the nuclear decisionmaking process; hence, there is a touch of unreality about these declarations on nuclear force structures.

The survival of the chain of command also needs to be credibly ensured and made more transparent to provide leadership continuity in all eventualities. To achieve this objective, the Strategic Forces Command should be enjoined to maintain survivable, dispersed, and sheltered communications with multiple redundancies. Appropriate measures must be taken to ensure the safety and security of the nuclear stockpile at all times.

Conclusion

It should be emphasized that neither former Indian prime minister Manmohan Singh's last-ditch attempt to universalize India's qualified no-first-use policy nor the confusions created by BJP protagonists regarding their commitment to this policy are to be commended.

Clearly, none of the underlying issues that bedevil the nuclear doctrine allows for easy answers. For instance, the question of whether the retaliatory nuclear counterattack should pursue a counterforce or countercity strategy can be argued interminably.

However, a reasoned debate on this and other controversial issues is overdue. India's nuclear doctrine is not cast in tablets of stone. Circumstances change, making periodical reviews of the nuclear doctrine essential. India's nuclear doctrine has not been revisited for over a decade. The issues that suggest themselves for review are India's command-and-control arrangements, which require greater clarity; the threat held out of assured massive retaliation, which forebodes self-annihilation; imparting greater content to the objective of credible minimum deterrence; and revisiting or abandoning the no-first-use policy in light of its numerous deficiencies.

It would also be realistic to appreciate that India's major nuclear security problems arise not from the postulates of its nuclear doctrine but from the complexities of its geostrategic situation. India confronts two nuclear adversaries—Pakistan and China—that enjoy close relations with each other. It is clear that Pakistan's nuclear weapons are unequivocally directed against India and are under the command and control of the Pakistan Army. But the negotiation of nuclear issues and confidence-building measures has been left to Pakistan's civilian bureaucracy, which clearly lacks authority and functions under the close supervision of the army. How, then, should India negotiate?

There is a global consensus that the real danger from Pakistan's nuclear weapons emanates from militants gaining control over them. The impunity with which militants have attacked military installations and headquarters in Pakistan reveals the inability of the country's armed forces to defend themselves, as well as the likely existence of insider collusion with nonstate actors. Still, the Pakistani establishment chooses to externalize its difficulties by undertaking dangerous maneuvers like developing its short-range Nasr missile for a tactical role, which is universally condemned as highly destabilizing.

The recent debate in India on reviewing the country's no-first-use policy and its nuclear doctrine might only signify preelection rhetoric. But the essential problem that remains and will tax the government of Narendra Modi is how India plans to credibly engage Pakistan in the interests of nuclear stability in South Asia.

PAKISTAN'S BATTLEFIELD NUCLEAR WEAPONS AND THE LIMITS OF THE NATO ANALOGY

Pakistan announced the latest addition to its expanding nuclear arsenal. The short-range missile, known as the Nasr, potentially offers Islamabad the ability to deliver battlefield nuclear weapons against advancing Indian forces. Following another test in February of 2013, Pakistan declared that the Nasr was ready as a technology-demonstrative missile, a step below its gradual induction into the country's armed forces. Since then, prominent purveyors of Pakistani nuclear doctrine have labelled the Nasr as a counter to India's Cold Start limited war doctrine. Conceived by sections of the Indian Army and strategic community in 2004 (and still without the endorsement of New Delhi's leading policymakers), Cold Start supposedly envisions armored "integrated battle groups" making quick shallow penetrations into Pakistan and seizing territory in response to a terrorist strike involving Pakistani nationals. The seized terrain would then be used to negotiate the end of terrorist activity on Indian soil.

In addition, many proponents of the Nasr missile program often hark back to the Cold War era and compare Pakistan's current military posture vis-à-vis India with NATO's perceived military inferiority against the Warsaw Pact forces. As they see it, Pakistan's conventional forces are simply not strong enough to repel an Indian advance. Consequently, Pakistan should develop and induct battlefield nuclear weapons to prevent India from scoring a quick and relatively cheap victory with conventional forces alone. Staying with the Cold War theme, it's also perceived that the Nasr will provide Pakistan with enough 'flexible deterrence options' to implement a proportionate response [to Cold Start], rather than massive retaliation against India. Yet, while Islamabad is right to be concerned about India's growing military prowess, taking a leaf out of the old NATO copybook and deploying battlefield nuclear weapons is perhaps not the most appropriate counter-measure.

A trip back in time

As the most likely site of confrontation between NATO and the Warsaw Pact, West Germany was particularly concerned about the potential use of battlefield nuclear weapons. Writing in 1962, former Chancellor Helmut Schmidt argued that the introduction of these weapons into the European theater would destroy rather than defend Western interests. The then-West German defense minister supported this argument by claiming that "no one can prove that escalation would not take place. Everyone must assume that it could lead to thermonuclear bombardment within a few days." Moreover, "even if the use of tactical weapons did not lead to extremes of escalation, it would nevertheless lead to the most extensive devastation of Europe and to the extensive loss of life amongst its people.

And the peoples of Europe would not care whether it was tactical nuclear weapons or strategic missiles that brought about their extermination. It is utopian to hope for a mutually acceptable distinction between levels of nuclear conflict that would be sustained throughout a war."

Research emerging from a plethora of West German institutions also supported this position. In 1971, the German Max Planck Institute conducted large-scale surveys about the effects of nuclear war on Germany.

Its findings showed that using just 10 percent of NATO's tactical nuclear weapons while sparing the highly populated areas would result in the deaths of 10 million Germans. In addition, large parts of the country would have been affected by fall-out, with a radioactive belt along the East-West border of approximately 1000 rad. It was anticipated that West Germany's industrial capacity would decrease by 20 percent following the use of these weapons. Economic redevelopment and regeneration would only have been possible after a prolonged period of recovery and not without considerable external assistance.

According to the survey, increasing the amount of weapons expended to 20 percent, or the matching of NATOs ten percent by the Warsaw Pact, would lead to the "political annihilation" of Germany. The Federal Republic would have lost about 20 percent of its population, 50 percent of its industry and witnessed the near-total collapse of its critical infrastructure. Rejuvenating West Germany's industrial and agricultural sectors would have been impossible. With only a few survivors escaping the attack unscathed, the country's social structures would also have been damaged beyond repair.

Such reports propelled a strong sense of skepticism about the utility of battlefield nuclear weapons among the West German population and, indeed, its armed forces. In 1977 and 1982, the social science institute of the *Bundeswehr* surveyed West German military officers on the use and utility of battlefield nuclear weapons. Only 33 percent of the noncommissioned officers and 48 percent of commissioned officers gave their full agreement to the statement that "The Federal Republic must be defended even if nuclear weapons have to be used on her territory." By contrast, 73 percent of all West German enlisted personnel said that they agreed with the statement that "Nothing can justify a war in which weapons of mass destruction are used."

Back to the future?

These are undoubtedly lessons that Pakistan should take into account before the Nasr comes fully into service. Moreover, it has also been suggested that using just one of these weapons along the major axis of approach from India into Pakistan towards the cities of Lahore and Sialkot—major theaters of battle in the 1965 war—could lead to the deaths of thousands on both sides of the heavily populated border.

And while Pakistan's leaders might assume that the mere presence of the Nasr would act as a powerful deterrent against an Indian invasion thereby precluding its use, that logic might not find purchase in the minds of counterparts in New Delhi.

Indeed, senior Indian politicians have declared in the past that they would treat any use of nuclear weapons on the country's armed forces as a strategic nuclear attack. It remains to be seen how Pakistan would manage the challenges posed by escalation.

Finally, it is also important to note that Pakistan's current nuclear arsenal can easily be adapted for use as battlefield weapons. Missiles with longer ranges such as the Ghaznavi and Abdali can either be launched on a lofted trajectory or their boosters terminated earlier to reach locations near the India-Pakistani border where the Nasr might eventually be deployed.

In addition, Pakistan's current nuclear warheads can be made to explode in a fashion similar to battlefield low-yield nuclear weapons through pre-initiation, thereby precluding the need for the development of low-yield warheads.

Which begs the question: if the current Pakistani nuclear force is already inherently flexible enough to be deployed on the battlefield, then why is Islamabad expending precious resources on developing the Nasr? At the very least, Pakistan should desist from deploying this missile until there are clear indications that India's most senior politicians have endorsed the implementation of the Cold Start doctrine. Islamabad and New Delhi should also continue to jointly explore confidence building measures such as the redeployment of infantry forces and long-range high power artillery away from the most sensitive border areas. No need to ask what modern day Germany would recommend!

6

Myths and Realities of Nuclear Command and Control in India and Pakistan

THE POKHRAN AND CHAGAI TESTS, MAY 1998

The nuclear tests conducted by India and Pakistan in May 1998-Pakistan's tests being a predictable, direct response to those of its neighbour's-sent shock waves across the globe. The tests were quickly followed by both countries declaring themselves as nuclear-weapon states. The justifications put forth by them for their actions were anchored on the well-known virtues of the bomb as propagated by the the 'N-5' countries before them. The prime factor which motivated the tests in India were the domestic political ambitions of the Bharatiya Janata Party (BJP) government and pressure from the scientific community engaged in the nuclear weapons programme. The continued neglect by the nuclear-weapon states of Article VI of the Non-Proliferation Treaty (NPT) provided added justification.

The Pakistan-India Nuclear Equation: Some Genuine Concerns

The continuing adversarial relationship between the two countries has already resulted in three wars, and a limited war in Kargil in April-May 1999, barely a year after the nuclear tests. Some people in responsible positions, both in India and Pakistan, advocated the use of the nuclear weapons during the war in

Kargil. In view of this, and also the existing, rather primitive command and control facilities, genuine concerns have been expressed by many observers regarding the safe and proper management of nuclear weapons by both India and Pakistan. Dr. Shaun Gregory dismisses this view rather summarily by stating"*this analysis oversimplifies the situation, pays insufficient attention to balancing factors, and smuggles a number of unfounded assumptions."* He goes on, "*the point at issue is whether a stable nuclear relationship can be constructed in South Asia. Much of the answer to this question rests on whether robust command and control arrangements can be put in place to meet the requirements of stable deterrence."*

Stable Deterrence

'Stable deterrence' is but a mirage! This concept pre-supposes a mind-and technology-freeze by potential adversaries. It also assumes a halt to proliferation after a certain number of weapons and delivery systems have been reached. Unfortunately the quest for superior technology, combined with the desire to have an edge over the adversary, creates, if anything, a perpetually asymmetrical situation, leading to anything but stability.

Command and Control

As of now, there is simply no robust command, control, communications and intelligence systems (C3I) in place in either state. Given the economic and technological constraints, this is not likely to materialise for some time to come. All this makes the entire security environment in South Asia extremely dangerous and highly unstable.

The credit given by Dr. Gregory to both India and Pakistan for their 'reflection on the understanding' of the experience of the N-5 countries, is expressed as follows: "*...this reflection encompasses a rich understanding of nuclear deterrence, nuclear doctrine, strategy, posture, command and control arrangements and the role of arms control and confidence building measure..."*

This sounds reassuring, but in the view of many who have studied and worked in this field, it is, unfortunately, neither convincing nor backed up by the situation on the ground in both countries. To illustrate this point, it might be useful to briefly recount some recent incidents concerning 'command and control' and crisis management in India.

- The Purulia Incident (December 1995), where weapons were air-dropped by a civilian aircraft in the eastern part of India without any detection and/or interception of the said aircraft
- The shooting down of the Pakistan Navy's 'Atlantique' aircraft by the Indian Air Force in peacetime (August 1999)
- The hi-jacking of the Indian Airlines aircraft (December 1999) and the consequent lack of timely and efficient management of the situation
- The recent earthquake in Gujarat and the near total collapse of administrative machinery and rescue efforts
- The poor safety record in the nuclear power and mining industry

Given this kind of track-record, it is difficult to accept the reassurances regarding 'safety' and 'command and control' which have been provided from time to time by government agencies, their nuclear scientists, and also independent analysts. This is not to say that there is absolutely nothing in place by way of command and control systems, but the technologies to ensure safety and to prevent accidental deployment of nuclear weapons are still at an embryonic stage.

Dr. Gregory's suggestion that *"the imposition of high level control can be addressed by relatively low-tech procedural means such as the two-person rule (reinforced by command authority separation) and the expedient of keeping warheads and delivery systems separated until required"* merits further examination. What Dr. Gregory is suggesting is virtually the 'de-alerting' of weapons.

From my own standpoint, this is indeed an excellent idea, and a wonderful first step towards total nuclear disarmament. However, as far as 'command and control' is concerned, the two-person formula is fraught with danger unless there are matching technological interlocks in place. This holds true especially in the context of South Asia and also raises the question as to who will oversee this 'de-alerting' of nuclear weapons. The operationalising of nuclear weapons from a de-alerted state, given India's stated doctrine of 'no-first use', is unworkable because of the inordinate time delays this will impose on a second-strike response. This suggestion is therefore unlikely to be accepted or implemented, a sad fact which once again highlights the inadequacies of the 'command and control systems' currently available.

THE BILATERAL NUCLEAR RELATIONSHIP

Whilst sketching the historical development of nuclear capabilities of India and Pakistan, Dr. Gregory goes on to say that *"consequently both parties have already managed a functional bilateral nuclear relationship for more than a decade, and have steered this relationship through three important crises... Brasstacks in 1986/87... Zarb-e-Momin in 1990... and Kargil in 1999."*

The point to note about Brasstacks and Zarb-e-Momin is that these were major exercises conducted, by India and Pakistan respectively, after prior notification to each other. The question of adroit management of the nuclear environment was therefore not the real issue. Some analysts have given the 'crisis' label to these events. Whilst, no doubt, these exercises were closely followed by professionals on both sides, there was really no war hysteria prevalent at the time. Last but not least, delivery systems for the nuclear weapons were simply non-existent except for the air-dropping of nuclear bombs, procedures for which had not been perfected.

As for Kargil, we only managed to avert a catastrophe by the closest of margins, with some individuals in responsible positions in both countries advocating the use of nuclear weapons. This narrow escape was not due to any special nuclear relationship or understanding, but to heavy international pressure, especially that exerted by the United States. Such pressure worked in this case because the war was limited to Kargil and no international boundaries had been crossed.

War-Fighting Traits of India and Pakistan

Sundry points brought out by Dr. Gregory in this regard include the following:

- Intra-war escalation control
- Propensity to bilateral political and military dialogue to contain conflict
- Aversion to systematically attacking civilian targets
- Mutual assured destruction-of Islamabad, Lahore and Karachi in Pakistan, and of Delhi and Mumbai in India-as a powerful deterrent against nuclear risk-taking
- The continuing presence of Muslim populations in India in excess of those in Pakistan, as a restraining factor against attack on civilian targets
- The overarching dependence by Pakistan on the influence of the international community, especially the USA, in respect of its nuclear policy

As far as intra-war escalation control-the ability of political and military dialogue to contain conflict-is concerned, no such mechanism actually existed during any of the conflicts that have taken place.

Such dialogue usually either preceded or followed a conflict-be it 1948, 1965, or 1971. The only exception was when India asked Pakistan to surrender during the 1971 war in the erstwhile East Pakistan, which led to the creation of Bangladesh.

The effectiveness of 'mutually assured destruction' of major cities as a factor against nuclear risk taking would be a dangerous assumption. Should the two nations go to war with conventional weapons, and should one of Pakistan's major cities be directly threatened, it is quite on the cards that they may be tempted to carry out a first strike with nuclear weapons against Delhi or Bombay, or both. The deterrence factor is therefore most unlikely to work in this case. In such a case even international intervention is unlikely to avoid such a development.

Civil Military Interface

In India as of now, the military has not been fully integrated into the nuclear weapons control chain. In Pakistan on the other hand, the nuclear button is solely in the hands of the army. Neither of these situations are conducive to effective command and control.

Dyadic Coupling

The 'dyadic coupling' mentioned by Dr. Gregory for integrating the national nuclear command and control systems of both India and Pakistan is certainly a novel idea-but one that is perhaps still ahead of its time. Unless the two countries are able to resolve outstanding bilateral problems, including that of Jammu and Kashmir, any meaningful 'coupling' is totally unrealistic. This observation is based on the experience of numerous 'Track II' initiatives which have failed primarily because of the inability to integrate the 'techno-fix' with the political aspects which underpin India-Pakistan relations.

Fundamentalism and Terrorism

South Asia is also witnessing a trend of rising fundamentalism. India, Pakistan and Afghanistan each have their own brands of extremists. It will indeed be a frightening day should such groups gain access to nuclear weapons-a possibility which cannot be totally ruled out. Such groups do not work on the basis of conventional political logic or other norms of behaviour, and can therefore be totally unpredictable. A recent example was the open advocacy of 'jihad' or holy war as a legitimate means of defending a particular 'Vision of the Nation State', a view proffered by a former Chief of Army Staff and currently head of a well known Policy Research Institute in Pakistan.

NUCLEAR COMMAND AND CONTROL

Nuclear weapons are the most destructive and unrelenting instruments ever created by mankind. The whole world can be destroyed by less than 200 nuclear weapons within the space of a few days. Given the potentially disastrous complexities involved in nuclear force employment and contrasting control methods, building up a formidable command and control system has always remained a daunting and costly task for nuclear weapon states. Nuclear command and control systems are developed by states to ensure that nuclear weapons are used only when authorised by legitimate decision-makers, and that the possibility of accidental or unauthorised firing of nuclear weapons can be entirely ruled out. Thermonuclear weapons are so powerful that they can wipe out whole cities, killing tens of millions of people.

The unimaginable death and destruction that could result from the unauthorised use of a nuclear weapon has led the US, Russia and other nuclear powers to spend hefty amounts of money every year to develop a 'fail-safe' command and control system. A robust command and control system is also seen as an essential ingredient in the equation of deterrence between the two sides. US nuclear weapons laboratories — Lawrence Livermore, Sandia and Los Alamos — worked during the Cold War to make nuclear materials as safe as possible, using almost unlimited budgets. A strong command and control system for nuclear weapons involves hundreds of people working at different levels from top to bottom but the authority to take key decisions remains concentrated in the hands of a few individuals. At the heart of the complexity of this system lies a paradox. Governments try to ensure that weapons should always be ready for use when asked for by the authorised leader and a similar assurance that they will never be used unless commissioned by such authority. These apparently contradictory objectives become extremely important in the case of nuclear weapons because of the political and diplomatic utility they have acquired in addition to their enormous destructive power.

Some nuclear weapon states have developed a set of interlocked administrative and technological systems including combination locks aka Permissive Action Links (PALs), which can block unauthorised use of a nuclear weapon. Pakistan's nuclear security establishment also claims to have indigenously made coded locks that completely rule out the possibility of unauthorised use of nuclear weapons even if they fall into the hands of terrorists. However, there is no authentic information available about the nature of those combination locks. The standard 'two-man rule' is also believed to be in practice in Pakistan's command and control structure. This rule ensures that at every stage, from manufacturing to storage, at least two people capable of stopping unauthorised use remain present. Other procedural aspects include 'special safety design features' that reduce the risk of a warhead detonating if it catches fire or is otherwise damaged.

The strategic command organisations in all nuclear weapon states have evolved with the passage of time. During the Cold War, the US had a very loosely defined command and control structure and even nuclear weapons were dispersed in a number of European countries under the control of NATO forces. However, a number of crises, particularly the Cuban missile crisis of 1962, caused President Kennedy to take quick steps towards attaining higher standards of robustness in the command and control structure. President Kennedy, after consultations with leading experts at the Pentagon and the department of energy, ordered a review of the US's nuclear command and control, which led to the creation of a nuclear 'football'. The atomic football (also known as the president's emergency satchel, the black box, the button) is a briefcase that contains the information needed to enable the US president to authorise a nuclear attack while he is away from command centres such as the White House 'situation room'. The nuclear football works as 'a mobile hub' in the strategic defence system of the US and follows the president wherever he goes.

According to a Washington Post article, a military aide always accompanies the president, carrying the football in a black leather jacket. Bill Gulley, the former director of the White House military office, revealed in his famous book, Breaking Cover, that the contents of the football include: (a) the "black book" containing nuclear weapons' launch options, (b) a booklet outlining classified site locations, (c) a folder giving a description of the procedures for the 'emergency broadcast system', and (d) a three-by-five inch card with authentication codes. During their presidencies, Jimmy Carter and Ronald Reagan preferred to keep the launch codes in their pockets. According to some accounts, the football was immediately separated from President Reagan after the 1981 assassination attempt against him. Like the US, in most nuclear weapon states, only the highest political authorities are in a position to authorise the use of nuclear weapons. The possession of a nuclear weapon by military units does not give them the ability to use it.

In Pakistan, due to some serious imbalance between civil and military relations, the military enjoys absolute authority over the control and use of nuclear weapons. Unfortunately, the civilian prime ministers in our country do not even dare to ask the military authorities about the exact location of the nuclear arsenal — what to talk of any control over their use.

The unpredictability of integrated administrative procedures and technologies can sometimes result in major failures in command and control systems. One of the major threats associated with the event of a nuclear war is 'decapitation'. This involves a successful attack on a country's command and control system, which results in rendering its nuclear arsenal unusable. There are a number of steps that have been taken by nuclear weapon states to mitigate the possible loss of command. These include early warning of an impending attack by ground based radars, comprehensive planning to secure command centres, alternative command posts and establishment of multiple communication links between the decision makers and nuclear armed units that can survive an attack. However, these measures are extraordinarily costly and complex. Another alternative to avoid decapitation is to delegate the authority to use nuclear weapons to other officials but that increases the likelihood of unauthorised nuclear use.

COMMAND AND CONTROL OF NUCLEAR

Command and control of nuclear arsenals is a complex subject and involves many issues. There are different models, as we have seen in other countries, which are built on their doctrines, goals and type of adversary capabilities. There is a lot we can take from there and a lot we need not take from there. I would like to focus on what I consider to be a few central principles on which command and control of nuclear weapons should be established in India. It is not sufficient to say, let us take a little bit of this and a little bit of that and let us put it together in some form. Or even allow single Service ambitions or turf to be promoted unless it serves the larger purpose. The stakes are very high. This is not a business where failure at any level or in any form can be condoned or compensated by some other steps or organisations. It will be disastrous for this country if our system of command and control does not function the way it must function. How do we want it to function? To get the answer, we need to decide first what is the task we expect the system to perform.

Doctrine and Strategy

The core element is that the nuclear doctrine that we adopt will decide the nuclear strategy. Nuclear strategy in turn will decide the nature and substance of the command and control system which is going to execute the strategy in accordance with that doctrine. There is a linkage here-between the doctrine, strategy, and structure. If we are clear that our doctrine is going to be deterrence only, rather than fighting a nuclear war, the arsenal will have to be designed for that purpose and the command and control will have to correspond to that goal. Considering that nuclear threats to India are likely to emerge essentially from the immediate neighbourhood across the country's territorial boundaries, the very short time of flight due to the proximity factor will need to be catered for in the strategy.1 It is also clear that there is no conceivable political purpose which would require India to initiate a nuclear threat first, leave alone use of nuclear weapons first.2 The central elements and objectives of our doctrine should be:

(a) First, to deter nuclear threat and possible use by another state against us. This rules out deterrence of war as such (which would require inclusion of conventional forces into the spectrum of threats to be deterred) and an acceptance of the reality that nuclear weapons cannot deter each and every type of threat to national security (which may include transnational terrorism, for example). Deterrence of nuclear weapons could be achieved by adopting an offensive ordefensive strategy. In 1999, the National Security Advisory Board of the National Security Council (NSC) had proposed the defensive strategy and recommended a doctrine and strategy based on the principle that India would not be the first to use nuclear weapons. 3 The Indian political leadership had also affirmed, both before and after the nuclear tests, that India would not be the first to use nuclear weapons.

(b) Second, if deterrence fails (and an aggressor launches a nuclear strike against India or its forces), our nuclear forces should be able to immediately retaliate with adequate power to inflict an "unacceptable" level of punishment and destruction on the aggressor. Taken together, these two principles imply that India will not be the first to use nuclear weapons and, therefore, will also not be the first to threaten another country with nuclear weapons. With a defensive strategy of deterrence there would be no requirement of continuing control of nuclear forces during a nuclear exchange as was the case in the North Atlantic Treaty Organisation (NATO) strategy of flexible response.

(c) Third, the proposed strategy of "no-first-use" would require a single massive retaliatory punitive strike more in tune with what was the French strategy during the Cold War.4 A no-first-use strategy also means that our nuclear arsenal does not have to be maintained at hair-trigger alert of operationally deployed and instantly ready weapon systems like the two superpowers maintained during the Cold War. The command and control of nuclear forces, therefore, will have to be created and operated on that basis.

(d) Fourth, the nuclear strategy and posture must ensure a very high level of credibility and effectiveness that there will surely be a massive retaliatory punitive strike which would inflict unacceptable punishment. In the context of giving up the first strike option, this requires a very high degree of survivability of the nuclear arsenal, including its command and control system. This means that the command and control must be able to survive and continue functioning with high efficiency to achieve the political goals even after absorbing a first (attempted decapitation) strike. A high level of survivability has to be built on a combination of measures including:

   (i) High degree of mobility of assets, particularly the delivery means and warheads, separately as well as complete weapon systems. The greater the mobility of the arsenal, the greater would be its survivability. For example, a nuclear-powered submarine launched nuclear missile force would provide the greatest survivability and, hence, would require the smallest size of arsenal.

(ii) Extensive dispersal, including frequent moves and relocation of these assets along with an ability to operate from a myriad locations.

(iii) Extensive deception measures, including decoys and dummies. We are partly fortunate that overall Chinese surveillance capability (of course, Pakistan's is even less) to track in real-time or near real-time the position of the Indian nuclear arsenal in any form is not very strong. The Chinese capabilities will keep building in the coming years, but we must capitalise on the technological weaknesses of our neighbours to be able to execute a real decapitating strike. We need to build an arsenal of highly mobile delivery systems and high capability to match the delivery systems with nuclear warheads in a short period of time. The logic for the national planning parameter is that we need the capability to be able to launch a nuclear retaliatory strike within a very short time, say, 30 minutes, if the forces are already on a degree of alert, following a certain amount of tension or precautionary measures. If not, then within a maximum of one to two hours. The technical reasons of fusing/putting it together, putting on the warhead, aligning it, the process of loading it, should not exceed that, and the weapon systems must be launched within that time-frame. If it gets launched in two hours, it should be considered acceptable. But I think it is very important that we reduce this to a minimum credible period.

(iv) The fourth important element for command and control is the question: will India acquire battlefield nuclear weapons, or nuclear weapons for use in the battlefield scenario-in the conventional normal sense that we have understood use of weapons in the past? My answer is a categorical, absolute "NO" to tactical nuclear weapons. There are many reasons for this. Firstly, there is no tactical use of nuclear weapons of any size or yield which will not result in an impact that is not strategic. If that is so, then the linkage and its escalation into a full-fledged strategic exchange can be considered as almost inevitable and automatic (unless the adversary does not possess nuclear weapons). Even if it is argued that escalation may not take place or gets controlled, then you land up with a situation on the other side that the local exchange of nuclear weapons between the two armies gets delinked from the larger strategic equation. This implies fighting a war with nuclear weapons. I don't have to spell out the implications of that. It may well be the preferred option of some people and foreign governments at that stage, to try and stop such exchange at that point which most certainly implies not only a substantial loss of life, but also implicitly that India would lose that war.

Some Principles

The second set of issues here revolves around the question: what should be principles on which we should build our command and control system? There are accepted norms of command and control systems for military formations. Military power itself is an instrument for achieving political objectives and, hence, constitutes a political instrument of the state. Similarly, a nuclear weapon essentially exists as a political tool which must also, in the extreme case, be employed as a military weapon, although with little military utility as such. To maximise the political utility of nuclear weapons, therefore, the following must be kept in mind:

(a) First, firm political control over the nuclear arsenal. I will revert to that later.

(b) Second, a highly efficient and responsive military command and control system. With that I mean that decision-making must remain at the highest political level with the advice of the military and other experts, but essentially the operational command and control system as such must remain with the military forces for a series of reasons.

(c) The third principle is that there must be minimum disruption of well-tested existing organisations and procedures. Our goal should be to see where they need to take on additional responsibilities, with minimum modification. It would be a gross mistake of truly monumental dimensions to attempt an organisational revolution to manage a multiple set of things-fundamentally new type of weapons, new set of command and control systems and a new set of procedures to handle these. Any major experimenting or violation of basic principles of controlling military systems will lead to serious and irreversible problems for many years, perhaps decades, to come. Therefore, we must build on existing systems and procedures wherever they exist, and do so in an incremental form, review these constantly as we go along, and then at a future stage, if we still need to introduce significant changes, we should do so in an incremental, planned manner. A conservative approach will be well worth the effort. We are entering a stage where not enough thought has been given to the details of the circumstances and the way in which nuclear weapons are to be used. The military in particular has been kept out of most of the decision-making and examination of the implications in this process. The case of chemical weapons is symptomatic. Therefore, it is essential that we move into the nuclear weapons command and control through an incremental, evolutionary process built on existing capabilities, procedures and past experiences.

(d) The fourth principle is that costs must be minimised, otherwise we are likely to land up with an expensive system which may or may not work. Experimenting or rushing into something here is the last thing we should be thinking of. If that is so, do we have any models that exist at least partially, in which the military at least has handled similar tasks in the past? I would like to draw attention to the command and control of "Chiefs of Staff Committee (COSC) Targets" which have been effectively managed for more than four decades, in peace and war. The three Services, under the sanction and direction of their chiefs, have evolved the framework and procedures which authorise their staff to work out the targetting policy for a set of targets considered of central and strategic value, as the strategic targets to be released under the combined authority of the three chiefs of staff. Targetting and planning for this purpose has been maintained by the Indian Air Force (IAF) in all its details. The planned air effort takes into account the commitment for the COSC targets. The concept, in principle at least, is no different from targetting with nuclear weapons. Targetting with nuclear weapons needs additional factors to be considered, but lesser involvement of all three Services will be necessary if the delivery systems belong to one Service only. But the basic requirements and parameters of management are not very different, either in terms of organisational needs or management techniques. Secondly, the IAF has been undertaking, like air forces in other countries, strategic reconnaissance missions over the decades. The way command and control has been managed and the lessons derived from decades of highly successful operations would be extremely relevant to the issues related to command and control of strategic strike with the nuclear arsenal

(e) The fifth principle is that the bulk of the work related to effective management of the nuclear arsenal has to be done during peace-time. This involves scenario building and assessing the other country's postures, likely trends, changes that may take place, signalling of intent, etc. For example, what are the implications when the Chinese say during a crisis situation that "Los Angeles could burn?" Or if Pakistanis threaten grave destruction? How seriously should such pronouncements be taken? Do they constitute a firm form of escalation moving towards use of nuclear weapons or not?

(f) Last, but not the least, is the issue of assessment of what it will take to deter the other side under different sets of circumstances. This will remain a matter of judgement, but one derived from extensive and deep study of the cultural, socio-political and strategic factors affecting the likely response of a country to the threat and use of nuclear weapons. I am sure many more aspects and principles can be added to what the command and control system should be expected to do, and what it can do in the framework of a time horizon.

Having considered this and a few other factors, it is obvious that at the political level, command and control of nuclear weapons, in the ultimate analysis, must be exercised by the prime minister of India. Given our political constitutional system, it cannot be anybody else. This can change only if the constitutional basis of our governance changes. A concurrent issue is that there is a need for a consultative group or a decision-making group to assist the prime minister at that level of political leadership. This has two aspects. One relates to the chain of command to cater for a contingency if the prime minister is not available or is incapacitated. The Constitution lays down the succession process very clearly. But the process may be inadequate since it did not visualise the need to plan a response with nuclear weapons. So we have to evolve a suitable system of national command authority. Whatever system is evolved, the prime minister of India will have the prerogative to make changes to it. What is required is that each prime minister, at any one time, should have a well-defined system of national command authority for command and control of nuclear weapons. Which one it is, is not the point. It may also not be possible to formally declare the system, nor is it necessary, as long the operating formations that have to execute the orders are clear about the chain of command. In fact, there are strong reasons for not publicising the chain of command for obvious reasons besides the potential for domestic political difficulties of the type experienced often when a deputy prime minister was appointed. So let the prime minister decide who will be his successor. The prime minister, who selects his Cabinet ministers, will always have the prerogative to make even frequent changes to the chain of command; but he will have to ensure that the new person(s) concerned are briefed thoroughly and they understand the role fully.

At the same time, a decision-making-cum-planning body at the political-strategic level is needed which will then authorise the planning of targetting policy and the force development and deployment policies. If the NSC functions, then the Cabinet Committee would be the obvious organisation. Even in that case, there is a need to immediately resurrect the Defence Committee of the Cabinet (DCC) with the three chiefs in attendance, on a permanent basis, not just on invitation, which should start taking the planning process forward. Their attendance implies that they would not participate in the deliberations of the Cabinet, but will be available to answer queries and provide explanations where needed.

It may be recalled that when the higher defence organisation was reorganised in 1947, it was based on the experiences of the UK and the USA (the latter being a nuclear weapon power) during World War II. In fact, Lord Ismay, who planned the post-War higher defence organisation for the UK and the USA was also the person who planned the organisation for independent India. This was based on corporate decision-making at each level with a Defence Committee of the Cabinet at the apex, with a Defence Minister's Committee, the Chiefs of Staff Committee, Joint Planning Committee, a Joint Intelligence Board and another dozen committees of the government to take decisions concerning various aspects of defence below that within the governmental framework, located in the Cabinet Secretariat. Interestingly, the Joint Planning Committee was to be in permanent session with a permanent staff "in particular to prepare plans for the joint employment of the three armed forces." Unfortunately, the permanent staff was never set up. In 1986, the government established a joint Defence Planning Staff of the Chiefs of Staff Committee. However, its relationship with the Joint Planning Committee was never clear. The result was that the operations branch of the individual Services kept operating nearly autonomously. This, in turn, created numerous incidents that have tended to increase the gap of mutual understanding of roles and missions, especially between the army and the air force. Over the decades, the effort of the army and the navy then has been to try and bring as much of the air power as possible under their own control. But classic cases of failure of joint planning naturally arose out of the failure to establish the requisite structures for this purpose which in turn also adversely affected the development of a culture of jointness that is so much talked about but rarely practised these days.

There is a need to address the question of where the inputs to the DCC or the Cabinet Committee on National Security would come from. These inputs will be a mixture of the military elements and political-diplomatic implications of decisions. Thus, an increasing amount of military component gets introduced into the command and control system as we move down the ladder of national command and control of the nuclear arsenal. The logical locus of such component of the management system is the Ministry of Defence. Other ministries and departments like the Finance Ministry have an important role to play in the force planning though their role in force employment would perforce be limited. In my view, the Defence Minister's Committee (DMC) should be resurrected (with some modifications) at an early date with the clearly defined role of decision-making about strategic planning and force structure planning, including that for nuclear weapons. The DMC would naturally be chaired by the defence minister, and have as its members, the minister for state for defence, the three defence Services chiefs, the defence secretary, the foreign secretary, secretary Department of Atomic Energy, the home secretary, scientific adviser (SA) to the defence minister, the chairman Joint Intelligence Committee (JIC) and the finance secretary. The DMC should be logically served by a professional strategic planning staff under the defence minister (in the Ministry of Defence) which should be able to situate the nuclear strategy and policy within a broader strategic planning for defence.

The requirement shifts to more military-specific planning and direction-the nuts and bolts, so to say. This is really what should be treated as a task of what may be termed as the Nuclear Planning

Group which would work out the detailed targetting policy. This is the sort of function that the IAF has been undertaking for decades in respect of COSC targets. The Nuclear Planning Group should preferably be headed by the defence minister himself with the three chiefs of staff, SA to the defence minister, and the defence secretary as members. The Defence Planning Staff is really now in a position to perform the role of an integrated staff and provide staff support for the Nuclear Planning Group that will go into detailed planning in respect of targetting policy, dispersal policy, deception policy, survivability policy, communication policy, etc.

DETERRENCE, DISARMAMENT AND ARMS CONTROL

In an April 2009 speech in Prague US President Barack Obama spoke of a world free of nuclear weapons. Obama stated that the United States would maintain nuclear deterrence during the disarmament process. This presentation discusses the limitations and deficiencies of the traditional mutual nuclear deterrence and assesses why progress in nuclear disarmament since the end of the Cold War has fallen short of expectations. Comprehensive deterrence is more complicated than normally assumed. It covers not only nuclear weapons as such but consists of several categories of nuclear and conventional weapons that are related. Arms control issues are linked although they are dealt with in separate arms control fora. An arms control and disarmament approach has to be applied broadly and should cover all or most of them. Transparency and confidence-building measures cannot be improved unless they cover the interconnected arms and arms control issues including strategic, non-strategic, deployed, non-deployed and conventional weapons as well as missile defense.

MAD

The so-called four horsemen, Henry Kissinger, Bill Perry, Sam Nunn and George Shultz, have published several articles in the *Wall Street Journal* on how to reduce the significance of nuclear weapons. In their 2011 piece (Kissinger), they conclude that this is only possible if the strategy of Mutual Assured Destruction (MAD) will be replaced by a 'new and more stable form of deterrence with decreasing nuclear risks and increasing measure of assured security for all nations'.

Decreasing the significance of MAD will only be successful if reliance on nuclear weapons and their hazardous consequences is addressed. The concept of deterrence as a war fighting strategy is ineffective.

What is MAD? It is the capacity to inflict maximum damage on an adversary. What does nuclear deterrence mean? It is the capability to retaliate if attacked or threatened with attack by a nuclear weapon power. Although MAD implies that the ability to eliminate the enemy once would be sufficient, the deterrence strategy of the Cold War resulted in a nuclear arsenal that could destroy the world 50 times.

Why did this happen? Mutual deterrence was not simply the threat with mutual destruction, it was destruction organized in a certain sophisticated way. Nuclear weapons became smaller and were equipped with a single warhead to cause limited damage. The idea was that after a first nuclear strike the enemy would blink and withdraw. Yet it goes without saying that there was no guarantee how the other side would react. Therefore, several strategies were developed to control a possible escalation. NATO adopted 'flexible response': small tactical nukes should be used against a conventional attack by the Warsaw Pact; retaliation could escalate by several steps (intermediate, strategic). The aim was to achieve escalation dominance – not only to be capable of striking first, but also striking last. Missiles with multiple warheads (MIRVs – multiple independently targetable reentry vehicles), deeply buried in silos and transportable on tracks, were expected to make this possible. Again, there was no guarantee that one side could ever reach this aim. Missile defense was seen as dangerous because it would invalidate deterrence by preventing retaliation. Anti-ballistic-missile (ABM) systems were prohibited by a 1972 Treaty (which was abandoned by the Bush Administration in 2002).

But there was also an autistic dimension (Senghaas, 1981) to these arms race dynamics. Arms-planning was based more on anticipation of what an enemy might plan than on what it had already produced. Technology was another driving force. Metaphorically one could argue that if one side disappeared but the other side did not know, then the arms race would continue. In the end, the legacy of the Cold War was nuclear arsenals that could annihilate the world half a hundred times.

Deterrence requires specific targeting. Push and pull factors determine nuclear planning. This would not be changed by political decisions. This observation is based on the 'Nuclear Posture Review' (NPR) of George W. Bush that was capabilities-based rather than threat-based, which means that it was not based on a threat analysis but on all kind of contingencies and cases. The current US Operations Plan (OPLAN) 8010 of February 2009 is based on Bush administration guidance and target lists (Kristensen, 2010; Kristensen and Norris, 2011). Without abandoning the concept of deterrence immediately, first steps could be reductions in the number of targets, missions and categories of targets. Targeting in this type of nuclear planning is a driving force for modernization of nuclear weapons. It goes without saying that for all these weapons to be effective, targets had to be identified. Together with an increasing number of nuclear weapons, the number and categories of targets grew throughout the Cold War as well. Strike options multiplied. Nuclear infrastructure, the political and military leadership and all kinds of forces were targeted. During the 1970s, MAD slowly moved from counter-value (the destruction of cities and population centers) to counter-force (force on force) planning. The result was a further expansion of targeted weapons and strategic assets. In turn, missions against the adversary's country became broader, and they also included territories of allies in case they would be occupied. With the end of the Cold War, the target lists were not reduced. On the contrary, more targets and target categories have been added, such as weapons of mass destruction (WMD) and terrorist groups, which have been defined very generally.

Nuclear Arms Control and Non-Proliferation Are Not Disarmament

There have been several attempts to control this process of arms built up. Arms control negotiations during the East-West conflicts were not disarmament, however. The 'Strategic Arms Limitation Talks' (SALT) and 'Strategic Arms Reduction Talks' (START) negotiations and agreements were a controlled or managed arms race, without even arms limitations. The negotiations on a 'Fissile Material Cut Off Treaty' (FMCT) were never intended to reduce stocks of fissile material but at best to decrease its production. Only one agreement, the 1987 'Intermediate-range Nuclear Forces' (INF) Treaty, eliminated a category of weapons, and this was only possible because they could be compensated for by deploying technologically advanced sea-based missiles. First the European NATO members had thought that the US-Pershing II and Cruise Missiles would deter the Soviet SS-20 because they did not trust the United States to use their strategic weapons. Then they eventually resisted the deployment of the INF because they were the primary targets of a nuclear exchange that could be limited to the European theater and would spare the superpowers themselves.

The administration of George W. Bush in the aftermath of 9/11 was strong on non-and counter-proliferation. It started several initiatives in these areas, including the 'Global Initiative to Combat Nuclear Terrorism' and the 'Proliferation Security Initiative' (PSI), which was a series of bilateral agreements that allowed interdiction of suspicious shipments, and it sponsored UN Security Council Resolution 1540 prohibiting transfer of WMD and related materials to non-state actors. However, the Bush administration ignored and even despised arms control and disarmament.

By contrast, President Barack Obama spoke of 'a world free of nuclear weapons' and also of disarmament of the nuclear weapon states in an April 2009 speech in Prague. What he suggested was not disarmament but arms control measures: a follow-up treaty to START, ratification of the 'Comprehensive Nuclear Test Ban Treaty' (CTBT), achievement of the Fissile Material Cut-off Treaty and a fuel bank to secure vulnerable loose nuclear material. Obama's proposals all fall within the concept of mutual deterrence. His 2010 'Nuclear Posture Review' stresses the 'fundamental role' and not the 'sole purpose' of nuclear weapons for deterrence. The approval of the New START-Treaty in the Senate in 2010 was only possible in combination with a US$85 billion modernization of the nuclear weapons complex. President Obama also continues to support a non-proliferation policy. After Obama's initial period in office, it became clear that arms control plus non-proliferation – although helpful – does not automatically lead to disarmament.

Space and missile proliferation are two other separate but related topics. They do overlap in a broader way in the context of emerging threats and challenges. On the one hand there are the missile proliferation and the emerging missile threats from new and potentially new nuclear powers. Missiles become really dangerous if they are connected with WMD, however. On the other hand there is the question on how to prevent the potential use of space for military purposes. A special challenge is the dual use of delivery systems and space technology.

There is an inter-connection because there is a link between space-launch vehicle programs and ballistic missile programs, several regimes address both of them. There is the 'Hague "Code of Conduct against Ballistic Missile Proliferation" ' (HCOC), also known as the 'International Code of Conduct against Ballistic Missile Proliferation'. Its norms and standards are not binding, but the regime encompasses both ballistic missiles and space programs. On the one hand, there are measures against the proliferation of ballistic missiles and delivery systems, and on the other hand it addresses space-launch vehicle programs. Then there is 'Missile Technology Control Regime' (MTCR) with an overlapping agenda with the HCOC. The 'Outer Space Treaty' does not include ballistic missiles. There is also the well-known Russian-Chinese CD (Conference on Disarmament) Working Paper to prevent an arms race in outer space with the acronym PAROS.

Concerning space and the EU, the European draft of the 'International Code of Conduct for Outer Space Activities', which is also not legally binding, tries to map out guidelines to create and maintain sustainability, safety and security in space. But it is not only a European issue. In the United States there is a debate about whether to join this agreement because there are fears that the agreement could restrict missile defense program of the United States and their national security. The United States also never excluded that some components of a missile defense system might be deployed in orbit. So there is another link between missiles and space.

Linked Issues and First use Scenarios

Arms and arms control issues are linked although they are dealt with in separate arms control fora. Strategic and non-strategic nuclear weapons, missile defense systems, global prompt strike forces, conventional forces in Europe, space and even cyber-security are complex, and related topics (Browne *et al*, 2013). An arms control and disarmament approach has to be applied broadly and should cover all or most of them. Transparency and confidence-building measures cannot be improved unless they cover the interconnected arms and arms control issues including strategic, non-strategic, deployed, non-deployed and conventional weapons as well as missile defense.

Nuclear weapons possessing states cite real or perceived imbalances in conventional weapons as reasons why their own nuclear arsenal need to be maintained. Non-strategic, tactical nuclear weapons have not been addressed by the bilateral US-Russian arms control negotiations and agreements. For NATO they have been the rational to counter superior conventional Warsaw Pact forces during the Cold War. Now NATO does not consider Russia as its adversary. However, Russia sees its tactical nuclear forces to counterbalance NATO's superior conventional forces in Europe which means it would keep the option open to use them first if there is the risk to lose them in a conventional war. In turn, some NATO members see the Russian tactical nuclear weapons as threatening. In total Russia is supposed to possess 5-10 times more of them than NATO's 200 warheads. That is why the Republicans in the US-Congress requested from President Obama to begin talks about these weapons as one condition for the ratification of the New START-Treaty. Some argue that because of this numerical imbalance strategic and non-strategic nuclear weapons should be addressed together. It goes without saying that conventional weapons in Europe will have to be part of the equation as well. Furthermore, there is not only a link between large conventional forces and non-strategic nuclear weapons but also between these two and strategic nuclear weapons. A large-scale conventional attack always can escalate to the strategic level unless all sides renounce a first use of nuclear weapons. A limited first nuclear strike against a large-scale conventional attack is only credible if it is backed up by strategic nuclear forces. No side can ever be sure that deterrence works and remains stable, however (Sokov, 2013). The other side could always retaliate with a second strike on the next higher level of nuclear weapons.

Obama's NPR maintains strategic deterrence at reduced nuclear force levels. The 'fundamental role' of nuclear weapons is not to be war-fighting weapons but to deter a nuclear attack as long as nuclear weapons exist. The NPR declares that the United States will not use or threaten to use nuclear weapons against non-nuclear weapons states that are party to the NPT and in compliance with their nuclear non-proliferation obligations. The NPR shields away from the political and diplomatic consequences associated with a 'no-first-use' pledge. According to the NPR, the United States is not prepared at the present time to adopt a universal policy that deterring nuclear attack is the 'sole purpose' of nuclear weapons, but will work to establish conditions under which such a policy could be safely adopted. This means that the United States reserves both the option of using nuclear weapons first in response to massive non-nuclear aggression for example with conventional weapons and a preemptive first strike against the adversary's nuclear forces in 'extreme circumstances'. However, the most likely scenario in which the United States would use nuclear weapons first is a conventional war that was escalating to a point when the United States assumes that the adversary is about to use nuclear weapons. In this case the United States would try to preempt such an escalation by using small nuclear weapons against the adversary's conventional and/or nuclear weapons (Perkovich, 2013).

Since President Obama and Russian President Dmitry Medvedev signed the New START-Treaty in April 2010, the US administration has repeatedly stressed that the treaty does not limit or constrain US options for deploying missile defenses. The preamble of the New START-Treaty recognizes that offensive and defensive strategic arms are interrelated, however. This was the logic behind the 1972 Anti-Ballistic Missile (ABM) Treaty that George W. Bush scrapped in 2002. The official US position remains that the limitation of the number of strategic warheads (New START) is independent of missile defense. If the New START-Treaty had included an explicit link between offensive and defensive weapons, it would have jeopardized ratification by the Senate.

If the United States is going to follow a policy of deterrence, it cannot rely on strategic missile defense to intercept large numbers of long-range missiles. The efficacy of deterrence can be reduced by a strategic missile defense system. There has been a connection between offensive and defensive weapons since the invention of the sword and the shield. It will become more important as strategic nuclear arms are reduced. The strategic missile defense can be a driving force for new offensive weapons. Whether strategic missile defense actually works will always remain uncertain, so it cannot replace deterrence. Russia still has reservations about US missile defense plans in the Middle East and in South East Europe. However, tactical missile defense on an operational and non-strategic level should not be a danger for Russia. In March 2013 the United States has canceled the final phase of the European-based missile that was considered to be a major obstacle to further nuclear arms reductions which appears not to be sufficient for Russia to drop its suspicion so far.

Since China's nuclear forces are believed much smaller than those of the United States or Russia, it would be unable to retaliate to a first strike and could be tempted to a preemptive attack (Arbatov and Dvorkin, 2013a). This Chinese perception might be reinforced by the missile defense systems of the United States and Russia (Arbatov *et al*, 2013b). In China's view they would undermine its deterrence capabilities since they could intercept Chinese remaining strategic missiles after a first strike. Also, China might conclude that the United States was about to attack its nuclear arsenal with conventional weapons and a nuclear retaliation would be prevented by missile defenses; so China might use nuclear weapons first, because they do not want to lose them. Not surprisingly, the 2013 Chinese white paper on defense (2013) omits for the first time its 'no-first use pledge' that was explicitly and unconditionally included in each of China's previous defense white papers (*New York Times,* 2013).

There is another fairly new issue that will have an impact on the global balance of forces. The conventional global prompt-strike weapons, when deployed, would provide the capabilities to hit targets worldwide within minutes. The US advantage in this area could do both replace some nuclear ICBMs and give NATO the opportunity to reduce conventional weapons that are deployed in Europe.

However, Russia tries hard to succeed in enhancing its prompt strike precision-guided conventional capability (Sokov, 2013). The development, deployment and employment of prompt-strike capabilities could have two opposing consequences: Either they can replace gradually strategic nuclear weapons with long-range conventional systems. Or, states which fear that they could be a target of an attack would all the more rely on nuclear weapons.

Arms and arms control issues are related in manifold ways:

- The number of nuclear warheads includes strategic, non-strategic, deployed, non-deployed weapons.
- Non-strategic weapons are seen as counterbalance to conventional weapons in Europe (includes first use).
- An escalation of a large-scale conventional attack to the strategic level is possible (unless there is a non-first-use policy).
- A limited first nuclear strike requires escalation dominance up to the strategic level or a stable deterrence.
- The United States and Russia keep the option of a preemptive use of nuclear open when a conventional war is likely to escalate to the nuclear level.
- Missile defense systems might be an obstacle for drastic reductions of the number of strategic nuclear warheads and even provoke an arms race. Mutual nuclear deterrence prevents the development of a full-scale missile defense system.

- China might be afraid to lose its second strike capability through a nuclear and/or first strike and the missile defense system and might use nuclear weapons first.
- Global prompt-strike weapons could either replace strategic nuclear dipped missiles or reinforce the will to keep nuclear weapons in potential target countries.

How could this arms-menu be addressed with arms control or disarmament talks?

- Any further reductions must include non-deployed warheads that are held in reserve, and deployed strategic as well as non-strategic warheads.
- A discussion of non-strategic warheads postures must involve the link to conventional weapons (Seay III, 2013) since there are asymmetric relationships in both categories. There also can be a link to strategic nuclear weapons, however.
- Lesser steps such as transparency and confidence-building might be useful but not sufficient.
- Once the concept of mutual deterrence is abandoned missile defense can be powerful instrument against new nuclear weapon states. Until then the United States, NATO and Russia could provide written political commitments not to deploy their missile defense systems in ways it would undermine their strategic deterrence (Browne *et al*, 2013).
- Global prompt-strike weapons must be brought into the equation of strategic and conventional weapons.
- Deterring states of concern from using nuclear weapons is better achieved by conventional weapons and other non-nuclear options (for example, damaging telecommunication networks). Tailored conventional strikes involving less firepower are a more credible and useful alternative to Cold War-era strategic nuclear deterrence. Militarily they can be more effective and they drastically reduce unintended casualties.

This grand agenda of arms control and disarmament might be too complex to negotiate (Ingram, 2013). No legally binding treaty can cover all the issues. Treaties can limit and cut what all sides see as unnecessary forces for their deterrence. Until deterrence as such will be questioned the other issues will have to be treated with political commitments and enlightened self-restraint. Why should states want to do this? If states act according to the principle of 'relative gains' they would always want to have more advantages than the others. If states apply the principle of 'absolute gains' they appreciate the net advantages they get in on area even though they have to make some net sacrifices.

Deterrence

Obama wants to be on the safe side: he wants to retain a deterrent capability as long as nuclear weapons exist even though no one knows whether deterrence actually works. Realists like Kenneth Waltz strongly believe it does work because there was no nuclear war between the United States and the Soviet Union. But in reality we do not know if this is true since you can't prove the negative – why something did not happen. The avoidance of nuclear war between the two Cold War superpowers probably resulted from a combination of political and military factors, such as arms control negotiations, confidence-building measures and cooperation in the Conference on Security and Co-operation in Europe (CSCE) and in other regimes and institutions.

Deterrence is a combination of two strategies: avoiding war and winning a war in the case the first option fails (Betts, 2013). In order to be credible as a 'peace-keeping strategy' it also has to be a 'war-fighting strategy'. This contradiction is in many ways not reconcilable. Therefore, the lessons of mutual nuclear deterrence, in both theory and practice, demonstrate that deterrence has several problems :

- Nuclear deterrence is only credible if the adversaries permanently demonstrate that they are serious about using nuclear weapons. This in turn threatens them with self-destruction.
- Deterrence does not prevent conventional wars. Nuclear powers were involved in conventional wars. In Korea the Chinese, in Vietnam the Vietcong, and the insurgents in

Afghanistan and Iraq did not care about the American nuclear bomb. In the Falkland war Argentina was not afraid of the British one. Arab states attacked Israel in 1973 that had already nuclear weapons. Two nuclear powers, India and Pakistan, went to war in 1999 and Pakistan probably was behind the terrorist attacks on the Parliament of the nuclear armed India in 2001. Moreover, possession of nuclear weapons could encourage conventional provocation or backing for terrorist groups.

- The concept of deterrence only works with rational actors. It requires adversaries to rely on each other to respect deterrence and adhere to its principles. Furthermore, they have to communicate with each other and understand each other's signals.
- Deterrence promotes hostility and mistrust when adversaries permanently threaten each other.
- Reliance on mutual deterrence causes nuclear proliferation and arms races. This was evident during the Cold War, but it is also true for regional conflicts, such as India-Pakistan. Deterrence is North Korea's rationale for possessing nuclear weapons, and it could lead to an arms race in the Middle East. Indeed, mutual deterrence and disarmament are opposing concepts.
- Deterrence can create instability and dangerous situations through miscalculations, miscommunication and technical accidents. The film classic 'Dr Strangelove' shows how just such a possibility could occur. The dissolution of the bipolar world and the potential emergence of new nuclear powers might lead to a 'multinuclear world' that would multiply such risks and uncertainties.
- The threat of nuclear retaliation is useless against terrorists.
- Deterrence is a weak tool against cyber-attacks, because it is extremely difficult to identify the attacker (Betts, 2013).
- The United States and NATO want to build a missile defense system against missiles from the Middle East, but Russia opposes it. As a result, missile defense has become the major stumbling block to further arms reductions. However,

missile defense below the strategic level should not be a threat to Russia. Yet if the United States and NATO keep open the option to upgrade missile defense, they can no longer rely on effective deterrence. Missile defense only works properly outside a system of deterrence.

- The announced intention to annihilate large parts of humanity is both unlawful and immoral. The International Court of Justice ruled that 'the threat or use of nuclear weapons would generally be contrary to the rules of international law applicable in armed conflict, and in particular the principles and rules of humanitarian law'. The pope regularly encourages the international community to work toward the elimination of nuclear weapons.
- Mutual deterrence is expensive because it requires continuous modernization and the development and production of new weapons to close real and assumed loopholes in the system.
- If deterrence failed, it would be a global disaster.

Beyond Mutual Nuclear Deterrence

What can be done to reverse the negative trends caused by nuclear deterrence?

- A true 'no first use' doctrine would remove conventional, chemical and biological weapons from the target list. Nuclear weapons should be seen as strictly for retaliation against a nuclear attack. They are not necessary for any offensive or preventive purpose, nor are they useful for defense, except as a deterrent to an intentional nuclear attack. The notion that nuclear arms are essentially no different than conventional weapons should be abandoned. Nuclear weapons should be retained only for a second strike.
- An unconditional commitment by nuclear weapon states to 'negative security assurances' would remove all non-nuclear weapon states from the target list. Nuclear weapon states should commit themselves to 'negative security

assurances'. This is the guarantee not to use nuclear weapons against non-nuclear weapon states.

- The creation of 'Nuclear Weapon Free Zones' must be combined with 'negative security assurances.'
- The list of countries that are targeted for US nuclear strikes is outdated and can be reduced. Bush's classified NPR and OPLAN 8010 both target China, Russia, North Korea, Iran, Syria, Cuba (only in the NPR) and an unnamed country that hosts terrorists (supposedly Pakistan).
- General target categories like WMD, non-state actors, war supporting infrastructure and military-political leadership are too sweeping and should be redefined and minimized.
- Counter-force planning associated with preemption, launch on warning and all kinds of military targets should be abandoned.
- The use of small nuclear weapons to control and limit damage is not feasible and produces unrealistic expectations.
- Similarly, expectations that damage can be regulated and making distinctions between 100 per cent, 80 per cent, 'light', 'moderate' or 'severe' destruction are absurd. There is no difference between rubble, gravel or dust after a bombardment.

7

India and Pakistan: On the Nuclear Threshold

This briefing book contains material from the National Security Archive's project on U.S. policy toward South Asia, which is documenting nuclear developments in India and Pakistan from the 1950s to the present. The archive is collecting U.S. government records that illustrate American policies and perspectives. Information is being collected from the National Archives and the presidential libraries, and through Freedom of Information Act (FOIA) and Mandatory Review requests, used to obtain the declassification of now-secret materials. A selective and focused collection of documents will be made available to researchers.

The project is creating a comprehensive history of nuclear developments in South Asia, including weapons programs in India and Pakistan, as well as international efforts to curtail proliferation in the region. Information about factors that influenced nuclear issues, such as the unresolved enmity between India and Pakistan, and India's perception of China as a security threat, will also be incorporated. The U.S. has generally opposed nuclear proliferation in South Asia, while seeking to preserve good relations with both India and Pakistan. At times, however, its commitment has been questioned, because it has seemed to subordinate nonproliferation policy to other concerns. During the Soviet occupation of Afghanistan, for instance, the U.S. provided massive levels of economic and military aid to its ally, Pakistan. The assistance was widely criticized, because Pakistan was demonstrably importing nuclear-related material, from China and other nations. Few doubted that it was engaged in an active nuclear weapons development program.

China's role as a leading provider of sensitive technology to Pakistan has repeatedly strained U.S.-China relations, and has complicated efforts to expand U.S.-China trade. The Archive's South Asia project is using the FOIA to seek the declassification of documents discussing this issue, and other contemporary and controversial topics. Materials collected for this project will, of course, reflect a U.S. perspective. As noted, nonproliferation policy is influenced by other concerns, including competition among the major powers. The Archive's efforts are directed toward enhancing understanding of U.S. decisions and the issues that influenced policy formulation. The analyst for the South Asia nuclear project is Joyce Battle, who prepared this briefing book. She is also the analyst for the Archive's documentation projects on the Persian Gulf and U.S. policy toward Iraq. Materials collected for the latter project were published in a document set, Iraqgate: Saddam Hussein, U.S. Policy and the Prelude to the Persian Gulf War, 1980-1994.

BRIEFING BOOK DOCUMENTS

The documents in the briefing book date from 1961 to 1983. In 1961, India had an advanced civilian nuclear program, while Pakistan's was in its early stages. In 1983, nine years had elapsed since India's explosion of a nuclear device, and Pakistan's nuclear weapons program was well under way. During the early 1960s, India under Prime Minister Jawaharlal Nehru strongly advocated global disarmament, but was apprehensive about China's nuclear weapons program. India's concern increased following its October 1962 territorial war with China. The stakes were raised by China's first nuclear weapons test in October 1964. Many observers thought it increasingly likely that India would respond to China's actions by seeking its own weapons capability. War with Pakistan in 1965 further alarmed India: it was angered by China's outspoken support for Pakistan during the conflict, and disappointed by what it viewed as insufficient Western attention to its security needs. The

U.S. considered various options that might dissuade India from developing nuclear weapons, including scientific cooperation aimed at enhancing India's national prestige. It also joined in cooperative arrangements with both India and Pakistan to monitor nuclear and missile developments in China and the Soviet Union. India, for its part, launched a campaign seeking security guarantees to shield it from Chinese nuclear attack, arguing that such assurances might make a nuclear weapons program of its own unnecessary. Various options were proposed: U.S. guarantees, joint U.S.-Soviet guarantees, guarantees from all the nuclear states, British guarantees, or guarantees in conjunction with the nuclear nonproliferation treaty, then being negotiated. U.S. policy makers seriously considered these proposals, although some doubted that they would deter India from developing a bomb.

The Embassy in New Delhi viewed India's overtures sympathetically, while the Defence Department opposed any commitment to India that would alienate Pakistan, a U.S. military ally. In 1967, both President Lyndon Johnson and Defence Secretary Robert McNamara supported the concept of guarantees during meetings with a visiting Indian representative. Later that year, U.S. and Soviet officials were still discussing security guarantees, hoping to induce India to sign the nuclear nonproliferation treaty. No agreement was ever reached, however, in part because India itself concluded that such commitments would not guarantee its security in the event of actual nuclear conflict. In May 1974, India tested a nuclear device, although it called the event a "peaceful nuclear explosion."

Its terminology did not forestall censure, both within the international community and from domestic critics. The test had serious consequences: India lost much of the foreign technical assistance that had till then sustained its civilian nuclear program. A Pakistani reaction to India's test of a nuclear explosive was predicted, and confirmed within a few years. By the mid-1970s, intelligence reports indicated that Pakistan had an active nuclear weapons program, and in 1983 the State Department noted that it had "unambiguous evidence" of this fact. Documents in this briefing book illuminate aspects of the internal debate among U.S.

officials, as they attempted to formulate effective policies toward nuclear proliferation in South Asia while protecting sometimes conflicting interests and objectives.

INDIA'S PROPAGANDA AGAINST PAKISTAN AND CHINA

Although Indian officials and media have always implicated Pakistan and China on various issues, now with the help of American media, they have started a new phase of propaganda against these two countries in respect of Gilgit-Baltistan. In this respect, Indian writer B. Raman has already been maligning both Beijing and Islamabad, while Selig Harrison, former correspondent of the "Washington Post" in New Delhi has left no stone unturned in this regard.

On August 27, 2010, the "New York Times" carried an article by Selig Harrison who wrote, "While the world focuses on the flood-ravaged Indus River valley, a quiet geopolitical crisis is unfolding in the Himalayan borderlands of northern Pakistan, where Islamabad is handing over de facto control of the strategic Gilgit-Baltistan region in the northwest corner of disputed Kashmir to China. The entire Pakistan-occupied western portion of Kashmir stretching from Gilgit in the north to Azad (Free) Kashmir in the south is closed to the world...but reports from a variety of foreign intelligence sources reveal, "two important new developments in Gilgit-Baltistan: a simmering rebellion against Pakistani rule and the influx of an estimated 7,000 to 11,000 soldiers of the People's Liberation Army."

The report caused considerable sensation in India. The Government of India, while expressing its concern, ordered a verification of it by its agencies. A strong denial of the report came from the Pakistani Embassy in Beijing. "A senior Pakistani official on August 31 denied recent reports that Chinese troops are stationed in the area of Pakistan-controlled Kashmir to build a high-speed rail and road there. Masood Khan, ambassador of Pakistan to China told the Global Times, "The story is not true," and "It is totally fabricated." On the other hand, Chinese Government officials and journalists describe Jammu and Kashmir as "Indian-controlled Kashmir." On the September 1, 2010, the Government-controlled Xinhua news agency disseminated the report: "China rejected reports of the presence of over 11,000 Chinese troops in northern Pakistan, saying that such "groundless reports" were made with "ulterior motives." Chinese Foreign Ministry spokesperson Jiang Yu remarked, "We believe the attempts of some people to fabricate stories to provoke China-Pakistan are doomed to fail." The comment came in response to recent reports of some American and Indian press that China had deployed more than 10,000 troops in the Gilgit-Baltistan region of Pakistan. The next day, during the regular briefing of Bejing-based journalists including some from India, Jiang Yu reportedly used the expression "northern Pakistan" while referring to Gilgit-Baltistan in context of the chapter of Selig Harrison.

As Pakistan's close neighbour and all-weather friend, China has been helping Pakistan for its severe natural disaster. The Chinese Government has offered several instalments of humanitarian relief supplies worth more than RMB 100 million. An international relief team sent by the Chinese Government has arrived in the hardest-hit southern part of Pakistan and set up a mobile hospital which is in operation now. Beijing has provided sincere and timely assistance to Pakistan without any strings attached. According to reliable sources, China recently refused to grant a visa to Lieutenant General Jaswal, head of Indian Army's Northern Command, and the Indian side said that the refusal was about the Kashmir issue. China's visa policy towards the residents of Indian-held Kashmir is consistent and remains unchanged. Unlike the western countries, Beijing more strongly holds that the Kashmir issue should be properly handled through dialogue and consultation between India and Pakistan.

The fact of the matter is that the Chinese reference to northern Pakistan could have been the result of the use of a similar expression by Selig Harrison who has referred to Gilgit-Baltistan as "Himalayan borderlands of northern Pakistan." Nevertheless, it is evident that the Chinese, while sticking to the decisions to issue stapled visas to residents of Jummu and Kashmir and to assist Pakistan in the development of its infrastructure in Gilgit-Baltistan have irked the Indian eyes—whose high officials and journalists have misperceived the close ties of Beijing with Islamabad.

As regards Beijing's contention that their troops were present in the Gilgit-Baltistan region only for humanitarian relief work, the Chinese have made two humanitarian interventions in the area this year. The first was in January last. On January 4, a landslide created a huge artificial lake in the Hunza area, which subsequently burst submerging a large number of villages in the Gojal Tehsil. About 22 KMs of the Karakoram Highway were submerged under water totally disrupting road communications with Xinjiang in China and with the rest of Gilgit-Baltistan. The Pakistan Army was able to go to the assistance of the affected villages only in the downstream area. It was not able to reach the affected villages in the upstream area for want of helicopters. The Pakistan Government appealed to the Chinese for assistance. Workers of the Chinese Red Cross and engineers of the People's Liberation Army entered the Hunza area for relief.

In that connection, The Xinhua reported: "On January 19, at the request of the Pakistani government, the Chinese side made special arrangements to open the Kunjirap border and facilitate the purchase of relief goods from China and its clearance. The second humanitarian intervention at the request of Islamabad was made after the recent floods.

It is mentionable that during the visit of President Zardari, under Memorandum of Understanding (MoU) officials of the two Governments signed—that China will build the 165-km long Jaglot-Skardu road and the 135-km long Thakot-Sazin road. Under another MoU to be jointly executed by Chinese company Datang and Norwegian company EBT—500 MW electricity would be produced through wind power.

China and Pakistan plan on building a rail link, which would pass through Gilgit-Baltistan near the Karakoram Highway. This has sparked a debate in India. In this regard, Indian Minister of State for Defence M M Pallam Raju said, "It is definitely a matter of concern." Besides, the two leaders of Pakistan and China discussed a host of issues relating to strategic partnership. The most prominent area of this bolstering of ties—especially for the world is the Sino-Pak civilian nuclear deal which is now beginning to see complete formalisation and initiation. It is unfortunate that the US and India have expressed their concerns about this deal, where the main goal is to address the acute power crisis in Pakistan. While rejecting particularly US objections, China has once again clarified that it will supply two nuclear reactors to Pakistan under the old nuclear deal.

It is also regrettable that, until now, we have been denied the same right to civil nuclear technology that India was granted by the US in 2008. It provides the precedent, and in fact, has opened the door for any similar sort of nuclear deal in the future. Indeed, after setting precedent by themselves, both India and the US have no legal and moral grounds to challenge the legality of the Pak-China nuclear deal. In fact, Pakistan's province, Balochistan where China has invested billion of dollars to develop Gwadar seaport that could link Central Asian trade with rest of the world, irritates both Washington and New Delhi. It has even shifted the central gravity of the Great Game to Pakistan.

Returning to our earlier discussion, Selig Harrison's information about the presence of Chinese troops in Pakistan has not independently be confirmed as it is part of a new propaganda game against China and Pakistan. —Opinion-Maker

OBAMA & AMERICA'S CONTINUING AFGHAN MUDDLE

The latest, released earlier this week, is Obama's Wars by Bob Woodward, one of the two journalists who exposed the Watergate scandal. The earlier one published in May is The Promise by Jonathan Alter, which reviewed the first year of the Obama Presidency. The descriptions in these books – based on briefings by White House officials and interviews including with the President himself – of how decisions on Afghanistan were made last year reveal intense policy rifts and personality clashes within the Administration over the course to follow in what is now America's longest war. They offer instructive insights into the tensions that continue to afflict the US approach. Both books confirm the deep divisions within the US government over how to handle Afghanistan. The most protracted Presidential consideration of a national security decision since the 1962 Cuban missile crisis – which led up to President Barack Obama's announcement of a military surge last December.

Woodward's book focuses on the Afghan war and the internal 'wars' over it by recounting what happened in the strategy discussions. Both books depict Obama as having doubts about investing more deeply in the Afghan conflict and who felt that his military advisers were trying to manoeuvre him into a decision of escalation that he was uneasy with, recognising as he did its risks and the political and economic costs of prosecuting an open-ended war. From the coverage and extracts of Obama's Wars, it seems the US President was deeply conflicted about expanding the war as was his national security team. Obama is left in Woodward's book with the realisation that the policy review process did not yield a clear solution.

Accounts in both books show Vice President Joe Biden advocating a narrow counterterrorism mission in Afghanistan with a lighter footprint and greater reliance on drones and Special Forces and opposing the large-scale counterinsurgency campaign proposed by the military and the Pentagon. "Obama and his senior staff", writes Alter, "believed (Admiral) Mullen and (General) Petraeus were using McChrystal to jam the President, box him, manipulate him, game him" into a policy of extending the war by an unlimited commitment lasting ten years or more.

Woodward's book depicts an exasperated Obama asking his commanders for an exit plan. What he gets instead is military advisers "steering him towards one option and thwarting his search for an exit plan." In response he writes a six-page "terms sheet" that spells out the conditions for the surge so as to prevent any mission creep. Reports of the book cite Obama telling Defence Secretary Robert Gates and Secretary of State Hilary Clinton in an October 2009 meeting: "I'm not doing 10 years – I am not doing long-term nation building – I am not spending a trillion dollars (in Afghanistan)." In confronting the choice between the Biden plan and the one presented by Generals McChrystal and Petraeus, President Obama opts for a middle path, combining elements of both. He gives the military substantially what they wanted but imposes resource and time limits. Most importantly, he announces a date, July 2011, when a withdrawal of American forces would begin from Afghanistan. This surge-and-exit approach was designed to give something to both supporters and opponents of the war. As he tells a senator in Woodward's book: "I can't let this be a war without end and I can't lose the whole Democratic Party."

These anecdotal details about the crafting of Obama's Afghan strategy raise a number of questions. Have the fierce policy differences been reconciled behind an approach that has strategic clarity? Did the "hybrid" plan promote a consensus or leave differences to persist? Has this compromise injected insoluble tensions in US strategy? Does July 2011 reflect a political position rather than a firm deadline in a coherent strategy? Does the date signal a desire to exit but without having a credible exit plan? Answers to these questions go to the very heart of where the US-led mission stands at present and its prospects. While US thinking has evolved since the intense policy battles last year it is not yet clear whether the different elements of its approach have been aligned in terms of timelines, capacity and goals.

Year 2010 has so for been a grim year for coalition forces, with record casualties, falling public support for the war and a Taliban movement that is at its strongest since 2001. There is little consensus between or within coalition countries on how to deal with or even define the approaching Afghan endgame.

The strategic flaw in the US policy is that military action continues to define ongoing coalition efforts rather than a political strategy. There is still an aversion to negotiating with the Taliban even though virtually everyone agrees this will have to take place in order to bring an unwinnable war to an end. The belief that a political strategy can or will emerge from a change in the military balance on the battlefield is questionable on many counts but most importantly because it assumes that the surge can bring about a game changing outcome which in turn will strengthen the hand for negotiations later with the Taliban.

The Obama administration's dithering over a decision to shift gear from a military to a political strategy of accommodation with the Taliban may be explained by the compelling consideration to avoid an impression of defeat. But persisting with a failed policy does not address this dilemma. The administration may also want to avoid exposing itself to attacks from the Republicans and the right-wing ahead of critical mid-term Congressional elections in November.

This places the Obama administration in an untenable position where it knows it cannot fight indefinitely but lacks the political courage to negotiate. The only way it can extricate itself from this predicament and pave the way for an orderly withdrawal of Western forces is to pursue a negotiated political settlement and bring Afghanistan's neighbours on board to endorse such a deal. The reluctance to open a dialogue with the Taliban not only delays the inevitable but heightens the risk of a less than tidy or 'dignified' exit. The pursuit of an 'outcome' to avert an impression of defeat can lead to the very mission expansion and goal multiplication that Obama has been rightly determined to avoid. —KT

KASHMIR CONFLICT: THE EXPANDING OWNERSHIP!

IT is interesting to observe that ownership of Kashmir conflict is expanding, the stakeholders are far greater that can be visualised. Now even the non-Muslim Kashmiris are also getting on board. Kashmiri youth has taken the lead and assumed the responsibility of carrying forth the struggle to its logical conclusion. Old guard Kashmiri leaders and veterans of first generation struggle are extending full support to the youngsters. Its like a change of leadership that is in its transitional phase. Entire IOK is in a state of defiance. With death tolls exceeding psychological number of 100, the struggle sees to have entered in an irreversible phase. Secretary Generals of UN and OIC have expressed their concern over the brutalities being committed by Indian security apparatus in Kashmir.

Unable to sustain a protracted state of denial, India has, yet once again, acknowledged the disputed status of the territory. Recently, Prime Minister Singh held an emergency APC in New Delhi, which decided to send a 37-member delegation to occupied Kashmir to talk to local politicians and business groups in an effort to ease tensions. Though it was a lacklustre 'All Parties Conference', it has kick-started a fresh political initiative by the Indian bi-partisan political leadership. While at the same time, erratic statement of Indian foreign minister in New York UN has demonstrated Indian's Machiavellian approach to the issue. Indian initiative may however be a non-starter due to the condition that talks should be held within the framework of the Indian constitution, whereas first assertion of the Kashmiri leadership is that Jammu and Kashmir is a disputed territory as such Indian Constitution does not apply here; and that India has made several promises at the international level, which ought to be fulfilled.

To coincide with the arrival of the Indian fact-finding mission in Srinagar, identical resolutions were adopted unanimously by the National Assembly and the Senate of Pakistan, condemning "state terrorism" in the region and reaffirming Pakistan's "diplomatic, political and moral support" for Kashmiris in their struggle.

Resolution adopted by the assembly expressed "grave concern on the situation in occupied Kashmir", condemned "India's state terrorism" and demanded that India "stop murder and plunder", withdraw occupying forces from the "state/urban population, cancel black laws, lift curfew, end media blackout, release Kashmiri leaders and thousands of imprisoned youth, refrain from obstructing the performance of religious duties and locking mosques and allow international human rights organisations to come to occupied Kashmir". It emphasized that Kashmiris were engaged in a "peaceful struggle for their right of self-determination in accordance with the United Nations Charter, UN resolutions, the Universal Declaration for Human Rights and resolutions of the Non-Aligned Movement as their basic right". It appealed to world nations "not to remain silent spectators of the Kashmir situation and compel India to stop injustice and repression on Kashmiris and resolve the Kashmir issue, and take practical steps for the implementation of (relevant) UN Security Council resolutions."

Kashmiri peoples' and political leadership's response to Indian parliamentary delegation clearly indicates that its not just a huge trust deficit between New Delhi and freedom fighters but a complete rejection of Indian hegemony over Kashmir. Main stream political leadership of IOK decided to abstain from directly interacting with the parliamentary delegation because they are now wary of such visits as these represent only an effort at short-term crisis management and that there is neither any clear commitment towards effective resolution of the issue nor any path finding effort for addressing the aspirations and interests of the IOK masses.

However, a memorandum was addresses by the IOK political leadership to the visiting delegation, recommending a negotiation based plan of action for resolving the dispute.

Kashmiri political leadership is right in following this approach because Kashmiris have repeatedly seen in the past that it is only when a major crisis erupts that visible efforts are made by India to engage and understand peoples' aspirations; and as soon as the immediate crisis subsides, inherent political complacency and negligence is restored.

IOK political leadership has made it a point to not to ask for unilateral political concessions, rather they are pursuing for a joint commitment to a meaningful process that guarantees results. They are of the opinion that this is possible only if serious efforts are made to create a conducive environment for dialogue by removal of the harsh and repressive measures, like Armed Forces Special Powers Act (AFPSA), which are in force in IOK, to suppress aspirations and fundamental democratic rights of Kashmiris.

IOK leadership has suggested that to begin with, resolution of the Kashmir dispute in accordance with aspirations of the people of Jammu and Kashmir should become a 'Common Minimum Programme' shared by all political parties in India and in Pakistan, so that such a process is transparent and is designed to deliver a negotiated solution to the Kashmir issue that is mutually worked towards by and is acceptable to all parties concerned.

Making a fresh demand for a result-oriented dialogue, the moderate faction of the All Parties Hurriyat Conference (APHC) and Jammu and Kashmir Liberation Front (JKLF) have demanded setting up of Kashmir committees in India and Pakistan to find an everlasting solution to the Kashmir issue. "We look forward to entering into a dialogue based on shared commitments... Let the Government of India establish and empower an official body, a Kashmir Committee, consisting of senior representatives of major political parties to develop and enter into a process of engagement with representatives of the people of Jammu and Kashmir," the Chairman of APHC Mirwaiz Umar Farooq and JKLF Chairman Muhammad Yasin Malik said in a joint memorandum. "We believe that a similar Kashmir Committee, bringing together all political forces, should also be established in Pakistan. We will suggest to political parties in Pakistan that this be done."

The memorandum further said, "This (setting up of Kashmir committees) will ensure that all major political forces in India and Pakistan are on board with the peace process and it will help institutionalise and sustain the process to resolve the Kashmir problem.

"On our part we are ready and willing to engage and sustain a meaningful and irreversible process of dialogue designed to avoid the failures of the past and to jointly develop and implement a solution to the Kashmir dispute that is acceptable to all sides – India, Pakistan and above all the people of the State," the memorandum said.

It is unwavering determination of the people of Kashmir that has sustained the freedom struggle against the barbarity of India and its occupation forces in the face of the placatory silence of the international community, for example President Obama conveniently skipped the issue during his recent address to UNGA. It is disappointing to see what has become of 'candidate Obama' who was an ardent supporter of the cause of Kashmiris. It is UN Secretary General's legal obligation to stand for Kashmiris against Indian homicide in occupied Kashmir since the Kashmir dispute is on the agenda of UN Security Council. Moreover, being a depository of all resolutions on Kashmir dispute, UN is the rightful sponsor for undertaking a concerted campaign to throw up a viable solution to the dispute. Time has come for the UN to own the conflict, dust off archives and jump-start the process. Let's go beyond rhetoric!

INDIAN DEFENCE MODERNISATION CHALLENGES AND STRATEGIES

Military technological differential is the key to competitive advantage in wars of today and tomorrow. And whoever controls superior military technology in the 21st century would dominate in war and peace, on the battlefield and in the market. Force multiplication is no substitute for force where technological differential become low. Defence modernisation is one area where trends in weapons manufacture and markets abroad have a major influence on not only costs and technology, but also access to them. We had relied heavily on Soviet weapons and equipment since the mid-1960s, and the European industry provided an alternative, supplying one-fifth of our total needs.

We have had negligible access to American weapons systems and military technology over the decades. But things are changing and it is necessary to look at them carefully to work out our defence modernisation strategies. The end of the Cold War resulted in contraction of defence industry worldwide.

Smaller production runs increased the unit costs of weapon systems; and rapid advances in technology have pushed costs further. Defence establishments worldwide have resorted to upgrades to enhance the operational capabilities as a via media to replacements. But this remains a partial solution in modernisation strategies. Meanwhile, collaborations and mergers became the norm in defence manufacturing, with an obvious strengthening of American hold over military industry worldwide. While some access to American weapons systems has opened with the sale of the artillery Firefinder radars to India, this process still could only amount to a marginal opening of a small window. The European option for weapons acquisitions remains.

But the European defence industry is in a difficult situation for a variety of reasons that we need not go into detail here. Its consolidation has resulted in deeper linkages to US industry. We faced its implications after the 1998 sanctions, when naval aircraft and helicopters which we had purchased from the UK were held back while being overhauled at the manufacturers. It took a couple of years before the problem could be resolved, and the costs obviously went up. The disintegration and collapse of the Soviet Union, which has been our primary source of defence equipment since the mid-1960, resulted in serious disruption and decline in the output of the former Soviet defence industry. What Russia retained in reasonably good shape were the Soviet Union's outstanding design bureaus. We must also note that the comprehensive self-reliance model put into place during Prime Minister Jawaharlal Nehru's time underwent change since the 1960s.

This was based on three parallel tracks: Buy weapons, licence manufacture as much as possible, and undertake design and development (with foreign collaboration to build our own expertise). Unfortunately, as licence manufacture increased, providing significant indigenous capabilities and a degree of independence from imports, this also led to a sort of strategic complacency in that the key area of our needs for future modernisation, design and development of weapon systems, started to suffer. Notable examples are combat aircraft where the LCA design was started 30 years after we had undertaken the design and development of an excellent multi-role combat aircraft, the HF-24 Marut, while technology galloped! Similarly, the design and development of the Mainbattle Tank, Arjun, started just after the 1971 War, has yet to enter operational service. Meanwhile techno-operational environment has changed substantively forcing us to buy the T-90 tanks.

The Indian Navy has fared better, although resource crunch delayed its shipbuilding programmes, forcing us to now buy the Gorshkov aircraft carrier when the indigenous Air Defence Ship should have been in service by now. Other examples abound. But the point that we need to note is that a comprehensive strategy for modernisation has been practically absent since the 1970s.

Our weakness since then actually lies in design and development of weapons systems. The DRDO has made valiant attempts, but seems to have shied away from collaborative projects. Scientific professional pride decried collaboration on grounds that it would hamper indigenous development; politically, foreign collaboration aroused negative passions; and the defence establishment was looking to immediate needs rather than long-term capacity building in defence industrial capability. Acquisition of military technology, therefore, has been localised to import of production technology rather than building design capabilities.

It is in this context that a unique historical opportunity opened up just at the time the most severe crisis for defence modernisation occurred with the collapse of the Soviet Union. The former Soviet Union looked for collaboration in design and development of military systems.

The West plugged in where it suited them. But it was China, not India, which took advantage of the situation. By mid-1990s over 3,000 Russian engineers and engineers were reported to be working in Chinese defence industry, upgrading and working on design and development of numerous systems which China had not been able to achieve for decades. China is investing in military R&D programmes in Russian institutions and in collaborative programmes where our recent attempts at joint development of the Brahmos missile pale in comparison.

It is still not too late to plug into Russian design base and capabilities, although as it picks up economic strength it may seek to apply tougher terms. Similarly, we have been the largest customer of British Aerospace's weapons and equipment for five decades. But there is little in the country in the shape of joint production, leave alone joint design and development programmes. Regardless of the level of budget being allocated in any particular year, the backlog of modernisation and the needs of future high-technology weapons systems would require investment of the order of $20 billion over the next decade. And that is why most of the global arms manufacturers are setting up shop in India in the hope of selling arms. But this also provides us with a powerful bargaining chip to build indigenous design, development, manufacturing and export capabilities through joint collaborative programmes. What we need is to be clear on our strategy for modernisation that goes beyond mere procurement and licence production. This is also where the private sector can play a crucial role.

In a developing country like ours, there are additional complicating factors in the modernisation processes. First, a large proportion of our defence equipment is still purchased from abroad. Our traditional supplier, the former Soviet Union, disintegrated and landed up in serious socio-economic crisis. Bilateral trade also suffered heavily.

The negative impact on supplies of weapons equipment and spares created additional complications for us. Also, many inefficiencies and complexities had crept into our procurement system and decision making for modernisation. Some of these have been sorted out by implementing the decisions of the Group of Ministers taken three years ago to improve the management of national security. But the result has been that with a system that allocates funds on an annual basis, with a review half-way down, large amounts of funds budgeted for defence and modernisation have been lapsing at the end of the financial year for the past few years.

For example, for the three-year period ending March 2003, a total of Rs 25,699 crore remained unspent out of the total budgeted figure of Rs 1,85,587 crore. The effect has been that while defence modernisation had suffered earlier due to lack of resources, now the inability to spend available resources within the stipulated financial year has adversely affected defence preparedness.

Establishing a DMF of Rs 25,000 crore would go a long way in assuring that modernisation processes do not suffer due to procedural delays and other unavoidable reasons. Both the National Security Advisory Board and the bipartisan Standing Committee on Defence of Parliament have been pressing the issue for years.

The actual functioning of the DMF, of course, must be evaluated carefully over the coming years, since this is a deviation from the traditional budgetary approach. Its utility may remain less than optimal if the five year plans are not finalised well before the Plan period commences.

Also, we need to redefine the budget heads to clearly indicate the resource allocation and utilisation under three functionally different heads of modernisation, maintenance and operating costs of the defence forces separately rather than the current system that does not indicate functional segments of a large amount of the tax-payers' money in an area so crucial to our security and defence.

INDIA'S MILITARY PREPAREDNESS

India has a penchant for blacklisting foreign arms producers without considering negative effects it has on India's military preparedness. This is the reasons why recent reports of irregularities in the procurement of seven Barak anti-missile defense systems and 200 missiles from Israel Aircraft Industries Ltd (IAI) have caused serious concern to the Indian armed forces. They fear that the Government may get forced to blacklist IAI as per the provisions of defence procurement procedure. Should that happen, India's defence modernisation plan would suffer irretrievable damage.

Having seen the adverse effects of banning Bofors, HDW and Denel, they dread a similar fate for a large number of ambitious plans under implementation. IAI is deeply involved in most of the major modernisation plans of the three services. In addition to the upgradation of fighter aircraft (Jaguar, MIG-21, MIG-29 and Mirage-2000), transport aircraft (AN-32) and all helicopters of MI series, it is supplying three Airborne Early Warning and Control System (AWACS) systems to India. It is also the prime supplier of unmanned aerial vehicles to the three services. Most importantly, IAI is involved in a number of developmental projects. India simply cannot afford to cut off all dealings with it. The saga of banning Bofors, HDW and Denel cannot be repeated.

Bofors

After carrying out trials of various guns on offer, India opted for Bofors 155 mm FH-77B towed artillery system. A contract for 410 systems was signed with the Swedish firm in 1986 for Rs1437.72 crore. The contract included transfer of technology for subsequent manufacture of guns in India. India had planned to produce 1,840 pieces within the country to equip 92 artillery regiments. However, with the exposure of kickbacks, the Government banned Bofors for all future dealings. It had the following effect:-

- Although India had paid for transfer of technology, it failed to utilise it. India lost an opportunity to create a base for further development of artillery weapon systems. As a result, indigenous competence to manufacture and maintain guns remained stunted.

- As spares could not be procured from Bofors, middlemen thrived making huge profits. In the absence of adequate spares, the Army had to cannibalise parts from some guns to keep other guns functional. Essential maintenance also suffered.
- Without help from Bofors, India is struggling to carry out overhauling of guns in the stipulated time frame. It is feared that delay in overhaul will adversely affect extension of useful life of the gun systems. Indigenous capacity installed with a Base Repair Workshop is far too less and it will take unacceptably long to overhaul the complete inventory.
- The Navy was already using Bofors guns on some ships and they faced difficulties in ensuring regular supply of spares.
- Indian inventory of 84 mm Carl Gustav Rocket Launchers suffered as Carl Gustav subsequently became a subsidiary of Bofors and thus, came under the ban.

Denel

Discussions were in final stages with Denel of South Africa for 155 mm howitzers (both towed and self-propelled) when it emerged that Denel had employed unacceptable means to grab contract for the supply of NTW-20 Anti-Material Rifle. It was alleged that Denel had engaged middlemen to offer bribes to obtain sensitive information about the internal proceedings of the Commercial Negotiation Committee. The Government decided to blacklist Denel in 2005 and cancel all orders placed on it. The development was highly unfortunate. Bhim project was almost concluded with Denel's T-6 155mm turret from the G-6 being mounted on Arjun hull.

An initial order had also been placed on a public sector undertaking. With the blacklisting of Denel, Indian Army's Field Artillery Rationalisation Plan suffered a crippling blow. The total requirement envisaged by 2025 is 3600 artillery guns of 155mm/ 52 calibre. The current inventory is of 410 Bofors guns only. Therefore, India desperately wants to procure 400 additional gun systems (220 wheeled and 180 tracked) on priority to meet inescapable minimum requirement.

Field trials in respect of wheeled systems were carried out in 2003 to ascertain compliance of Services Qualitative Requirements. Three competitors participated-Denel, Soltam Atmos 2000 and FH77 of SWS Defence. All the three systems failed to meet specified standards. Retrials of duly improved versions were held in 2004. With the blacklisting of Denel, the choice got limited to Soltam and FH77. As per the press reports, FH77 emerged far superior to Soltam and was the choice of the Army. However, due to politically sensitive reasons, the Government incorrectly termed the case as a single vendor situation and decided to float fresh tender enquiries with reformulated Qualitative Requirements. Tender for wheeled guns was floated in March 2007 and the second tender for tracked guns followed soon thereafter. It is learnt that 12 producers of guns have been invited.

Nearly 20 years have passed since the induction of Bofor guns; no new gun system has been procured. Due to ban on Bofors and Denel, India has shut doors on two major producers of guns and thereby limited its choice. Continued shortage of suitable 155mm/ 52 calibre gun systems implies major gaps in India's defence preparedness. Additionally, India's quest for indigenous production of 155 mm ammunition also suffered a major blow. Work on a new ordnance factory in Nalanda to manufacture 155mm ammunition for Bofors guns has got stalled, as Denel was to provide technical know-how. Hundreds of crores of rupees have also gone down the drain.

HDW

The case of HDW makes instructive reading. A contract was signed with the German firm in December 1981. India was to get two HDW 209 class fully built submarines and sub-assemblies and components for assembling two other submarines in India. HDW was also to provide required training to Indian personnel.

HDW delivered two submarines in 1987 and two more were assembled in India in due course. As allegations of bribery and kickbacks became public, the Government decided to blacklist the company. It was also decided not to build any more submarines of the same class. Marlog, a company jointly owned by HDW and Ferrostal, took over the responsibility to fulfil all contractual obligations.

There are just a handful of competent submarine manufacturers in the world. By blacklisting HDW, India antagonized one of the leading producers and thereby deprived itself of the benefits of latest technological advancements. HDW is the world leader with the most advanced air-independent propulsion system. Continued collaboration would have given a boost to indigenous submarine building competence. Additionally, India would have acquired wherewithal as regards maintenance, overhaul and repair support.

As India had not received the complete drawings and NATO identification numbers for all spare parts of the submarines, it faced immense problems in procuring them from other sources. Middlemen made huge profits. The Navy wanted to increase the offensive punch of the submarines by mounting Exocet missiles on it. As HDW could not be engaged, others laid unacceptably harsh conditions. Indian plans for the upgradation of the submarine entailed an increase in their length and that could be done only by HDW. To sum up, by blacklisting HDW India deprived itself of maintenance support, upgradation opportunities and development of indigenous skills.

DEFENCE PROCUREMENT PROCEDURE

Defence Procurement Procedure-2008 (DPP-2008) has laid down clear guidelines for all foreign vendors. They are warned not to resort to any unethical practice to influence the decision makers. A 'Pre-Contract Integrity Pact' has been made mandatory for all schemes exceeding Rupees 100 crores. The vendors are required to sign and submit it separately along with the technical and commercial offers. It is a binding agreement in which the procurement agency promises that it will not accept bribes during the procurement process and bidders promise that they will not offer bribes. It also includes an undertaking by each bidder to disclose all payments made in connection with the contract in question to anybody (including agents and other middlemen as well as family members of officials).

The Government can enforce the following sanctions for any violation by a bidder of its commitments or undertakings:-

- Denial or loss of contract.
- Forfeiture of bid security and performance bond.
- Liability for damages to the principal and the competing bidders.
- Finally, debarment of the violator by the principal for an appropriate period of time.

While signing the final contract, every vendor (irrespective of the contract value) is required to give an undertaking that he has not given, offered or promised to give, directly or indirectly any gift, consideration, reward, commission, fees, brokerage or inducement to procure the contract. Any breach of the aforesaid undertaking by the seller or any one employed by him shall entitle the buyer to cancel the contract and all or any other contracts with the seller and recover the loss arising from such cancellation. Should the Government desire to ascertain if any unauthorized payments have been made, a vendor has to allow inspection of his account books.

It will be seen that debarment of a vendor is the last resort and has to be taken only in extreme cases.

Appraisal of the Issue

Before initiating any action against a company, the Government must weigh pros and cons of all alternatives open to it. While punishing a defaulting vendor, own interests must be fully safeguarded. India must consider the following points while taking decision on blacklisting foreign vendors:-

- There are limited manufacturers of major high-tech defence systems in the world. Additionally, world defence trade is circumscribed by embargoes on technology export. Thus, there are very few manufacturers who possess and are willing to offer advanced weaponry to India.
- To develop indigenous defence industry, India needs imported technology and reliable foreign partners with long term commitment. Blacklisting nullifies all transfer of technology agreements, even if paid for.

- India needs to modernize its armed forces expeditiously and its shopping list spans a vast canvas, including all major systems. As most major defence companies produce a large array of equipment, blacklisting in one contract will have a ripple effect on all other purchases as well.
- India possesses a huge inventory of weapon platforms which are in need of immediate upgradation to increase their useful life. This task can be undertaken by a handful of companies. Banning any will reduce own options.
- No company produces a complete defence system. Most major producers are in fact mere integrators. They outsource major assemblies from varied sources. Blacklisting of an assembly supplier can also jeopardize major acquisition proposals.
- One of the stated aims of DPP-2008 is to 'demonstrate the highest degree of probity and public accountability, transparency in operations, free competition and impartiality'. Blacklisting of vendors reduces competition and forces the Government to resort to single vendor procurements with related cost penalty. This is also contrary to Government's declared policy.
- Every time a finalised contract is suspended, the earmarked funds remain unexpended resulting in their surrender.
- Most importantly, the services get deprived of the essential equipment. It may have critical effect on nation's war preparedness. Fresh floating of tenders entails major delays and cost overruns.

In every irregular transaction, there are always two parties- the bribe giver and the bribe taker. Action must be taken against both and in equal proportion. It is unfair to apportion the entire blame to bribe givers and take no action against those who demand and extract bribes. It conveys an impression that the Government is reconciled to the fact that procurement functionaries are bound to fall prey to temptations, if offered to them. It amounts to a tacit admission by the Government of its inability to find officials with unimpeachable integrity and to exercise control over them. The Government thus, feels that the onus of keeping all transactions clean is entirely on the vendors-they should decline to pay bribes even if demanded by the decision makers. This is a strange logic. Instead of putting its own house in order, India holds foreign vendors accountable for all wrong-doings.

The Way Forward

The Government must have conclusive proof that a major breach of probity provisions has taken place. Media reports and rumours cannot be the sole basis. As has been seen, a majority of media reports are subjective, biased and even planted to sabotage a deal. This could be done either by a losing vendor or even by entities inimical to India's interests. As has been seen earlier, every blacklisting of a foreign vendor puts back India's defence modernisation plans by decades. Undoubtedly, it is the most cost effective option available to adversaries to impede India's defence preparedness.

Retaliatory action must always be well considered and commensurate with the degree of misdemeanor. It does not have to be blacklisting at the outset. It is prudent to follow a phased and graduated approach for two reasons.

One, the defaulting vendor gets unambiguous message that the Government means business and the vendor should exercise due caution in further dealings. Secondly, should blacklisting become inescapable, the Government can time it to suit own requirements. In the case of HDW, hasty action to ban the company deprived India of catalogues and drawings. India could have easily waited for a few months.

India must also remember that banning a major foreign vendor may have little effect on his business and India may suffer more. Thus the whole exercise of punishing a foreign vendor for his alleged misdemeanor may become counter productive and end up boomeranging on India. In fact this is exactly what has happened in all cases. We have ended up shooting in our own foot. There cannot be another example of immature and reckless decision making. While trying to fix a vendor for his misconduct, we put our own defence modernisation plans in disarray, with consequent critical capability gaps and cost overruns.

The Government seems to have realised the foolhardiness of its policy. It has decided to tread cautiously. Blacklisting of Bofors has been revoked as the company is now owned by SWS Defence with considerable equity being held by a US based company. The Government should similarly allow HDW to do business with India. Nearly 20 years have lapsed and India has not been able to collate conclusive proof of wrong-doings. It is time to close the old chapter and start afresh. Although Denel has been proscribed recently, the Government should offer a way out by asking it to make good financial loss with stiff penal deduction. For generating maximum competition to obtain best deals, the Government has to show maturity, practicality and adroit handling. Outright blacklisting is the easiest and the most imprudent way of managing a delicate and highly critical issue.

A sustained and inspired media campaign was carried out by a small section of press to sabotage Scorpene submarine deal. It is to the credit of the Government that it resisted all demands to reopen the case. It is similarly hoped that the current reports against IAI would be looked into judiciously and an objective view taken. In case any misdemeanor is proved, appropriate and balanced action should be taken against both the vendor and the functionaries involved. Blacklisting, however, must remain the last resort. Cutting off your nose to spite your face can never be considered a prudent policy.

NEW POLICY ON DEFENSE CONTRACTS OFFSETS

India's policies on defense-related acquisitions from abroad and production within India are believed to have been directed not only at ensuring India's security interests but also at promoting self-reliance and indigenous capability in this vital sector often involving advanced technologies. Whatever one's opinions about intentions, questions have often been raised, including in these columns, as to whether these goals have actually been achieved. Again, while the point may be debated, clearly there are major problems going by the evidence in the past two decades. India has been buying ever larger quantities of increasingly sophisticated military hardware from foreign suppliers, while its defense forces have not been able to acquire necessary comparable equipment from Indian state-sector manufacturers due to inadequate performance, inordinate time delays and massive cost overruns.

Fighter aircraft such as the Light Combat Aircraft (LCA), jet trainers, helicopters, main battle tanks, submarines are all military equipment in which India has had active indigenous or collaborative R&D or manufacturing programs over several decades. But, as inventories have reached the end of their life cycles calling for replacements, India has repeatedly been forced to go in for costly foreign acquisitions while requisite indigenous capability has continued to languish even for the next generation of technology. This has not only increased India's dependence on imports, and vulnerability to technology denial regimes, in such a vital sector, it has also meant huge lost opportunities for enhancing science and technology capabilities, and downstream spread effects, in important sectors of national industry. Very belatedly, India had set in place over the past two years a policy of "offsets" in major defense contracts worth over Rs 300 crore in value.

Under this clause, a party securing such a contract was obligated to plough back to Indian parties at least 30 per cent of the contract value by way of buy-back of products and services, with a provision for a higher percentage in special cases. Of course, there still remained the danger that even such offsets may amount to little more than some sub-contracts or assembly-line operations, not resulting in any upgradation or absorption of know-how or capability, but it least it was a beginning. Unfortunately, under pressure from major manufacturers in the US and some other Western countries, there are moves to dilute even this offset clause in important ways to the detriment of the long-term Indian interests. As we go to press, Defense Ministry officials have confirmed that a modified DPP will be notified by April 2008.

OFFSET POLICY

The policy on offsets, first enunciated in 2005, was further elaborated along with rules and procedures in the Defense Purchase Policy (DPP) of 2006 under which a new Defense Offset Facilitation Agency (DOFA) was also set up to work with vendors on implementation and monitoring. Offsets could include buy-back of products or services, foreign direct investment (FDI) in Indian public or private companies for such products or services or co-development and infrastructure, or even FDI in Indian entities engaged in defense R&D. All these were envisaged to be "direct offsets" that is directly related to the contract, the procurement of items under it, and their cost. In the short period DPP-2006 had been in operation, two major contracts had been concluded with offset clauses.

Israeli firm ELTA System had been awarded a contract worth Rs 900 crore for supplying radars. Under the offset provision, ELTA signed contracts with two Indian firms for purchase of components, with Astra Microwave securing a contract worth Rs 100 crore. Similarly, in the $1 billion (Rs 4000 crore) contract awarded to the Russian manufacturers of the Mig-29 for upgrades of the IAF's fleet, the vendor has agreed to offsets of $300 million. Several other pending deals such as for refueling tankers also contain offset clauses.

Interestingly, even the controversially cancelled deal to purchase 196 military helicopters from the French-led European conglomerate Eurocopter (most probably cancelled under pressure from its US rivals Bell Helicopters as revealed in these columns a few months ahead of the cancellation) had contained offset provisions with Eurocopter having agreed to 30 per cent offsets as required. Two points must be noted here.

First, such offset clauses are not unique to India nor are they some archaic leftovers of an earlier "socialistic" self-reliance policy incommensurate with the contemporary realities of globalization. Many countries have, and continue to successfully enforce, such offset clauses in the interests of their economies and in order to boost their knowledge base and industrial capabilities. Israel, Malaysia, Thailand to name a few are among many other countries in Asia and South America having even more stringent offset conditionalities than India.

Take for instance Israel's $2.5 billion order for 50 F-16 fighter aircraft from the US giant Lockheed Martin which had lost out to its American rival Boeing (both now pushing aggressively for the Indian 126-aircraft deal).

Israel secured an offset package of $850 million or about 35 per cent of the contract value spread over 10 years. Within 3 years of signing the deal, Lockheed Martin had already invested over $250 million in 12 Israeli firms for sourcing various components, assembly and post-production services. Israel not only enhanced their capabilities in these sectors it also ensured that it acquired new knowledge in advanced areas. Lockheed Martin was made to invest and participate in co-development of flight simulators and helmet-mounted display systems, as well as other technologies relating to space applications and electronics. Israel also made full use of its option clause for acquisition of a further 50 F-16s to add pressure on the US vendor.

Offsets for What?

Second, as also brought out by the above example, offsets should not be seen merely as commercial propositions by which India could earn additional money thus reducing capital outflows in defense contracts. Merely obtaining orders for some components, or securing servicing and overhaul contracts, or even assembly and license-production is not sufficient to ensure absorption of know-how and building up the capacity to independently develop and manufacture equipment using the next generation technology. Indeed, India's own experience of serial license-production agreements clearly reveals the yawning gap between certain types of licensed manufacture and development of indigenous capability. India manufactured the French Alouette helicopter (Cheetah) and its engine at HAL, Bangalore, in the '70s and '80s but, not having absorbed the technology, was forced to go for imports of the next generation helicopters such as the Eurocopter.

HAL's bottom line was certainly boosted, its turnover substantially increased for several years, but this does not appear to have translated into capability to develop and make its own helicopters, forcing the government to go in for another sequence of imports and license arrangements. Similarly, India is now in the market reportedly for 200 howitzer artillery guns building up through licensed manufacture towards an inventory of 1500 guns worth an estimated $2.5 billion (Rs 10,000 crore), and even had to buy howitzers on an emergency basis during the Kargil conflict, despite having had full access to the Bofors technology since the '80s. Therefore, in working out offsets, quite apart from the commercial angle, it is very important to see that offset arrangements are properly planned and channelized to projects and institutions with a clear vision of what is required in the short and medium term in terms of developing independent indigenous capability and know-how.

NEW POLICY

Despite this past experience, and in spite of some success in pressurizing vendors into more meaningful collaboration through the policy of direct offsets under DPP-2005/6, the defense ministry is in the process of modifying the DPP particularly is respect of offsets. It is no coincidence that this process has been initiated at a time when major Western military hardware vendors are salivating at the $30 billion Indian acquisition budget, and especially the massive $10 billion deal for multi-role combat aircraft, in the tender for which India has specified a 50 per cent offset condition, much to the open displeasure of US aviation majors Lockheed Martin and Boeing.

It is also no surprise that defense ministry spokesmen confirmed the advent of a new offsets policy just prior to the opening of the large arms expo in Delhi on February 18. The revised policy proposes three major departures all leading to a framework of "indirect" offsets in contrast to the earlier system of direct offsets. The first allows for "banking" of offsets wherein offsets accumulated under one project can be shown against any subsequent project too. The second, although apparently an extension of the first, allows companies engaged in civilian contracts to "bank" such offsets and show them against offset requirements in military contracts.

Clearly, this is purely a commercial consideration and makes no allowance for the fact that the main purpose of offsets is, or ought to be, building capability and know-how in the defense technology sector albeit with spin-offs in the civilian sector. It is also a measure that will clearly favour Boeing which can show offsets and "bank" its sub-contracts to Indian parties making fuselage parts for the passenger jets being bought by Air India and Indian Airlines while tendering for the combat aircraft order. The third modification and perhaps the most dangerous is to allow vendors to charge for technology transfer, show these charges as part of the offsets and deduct these charges from the actual offset payments. This is a specious provision and opens the door to all sorts of underhand manipulations, will render the entire offsets mechanism useless and make its processes completely non-transparent.

Who is to define what constitutes transfer of technology and what price to attach to it? In any sub-contracting or license production, there is some technology transfer involved. Under the direct offset clause operational hitherto in India, and practiced elsewhere in the world, licensed production includes technology transfer for manufacture. Under the modified provision, it can be charged separately, and an arbitrarily determined technology fee can be subtracted from any buy-back arrangement! With a 50 per cent offset provision for the fighter deal, about Rs 20,000 crore worth of business was expected to come to Indian firms but, with the new technology transfer clause, this could easily be reduced to half or even less!

Vested Interests Vs National Interests

It is significant that pressure has been brought on India to change its offsets provisions particularly by US companies especially in the aviation sector. The US Defense Department has always opposed offset clauses, but has not stood in the way of contracts including such clauses when it serves US policy or when US companies push for them, as with the Israeli case cited above.

In the case of India, the US India Business Council (USIBC) constituted and empowered under the US-India Strategic Partnership has been pushing hard for precisely such modifications in offsets policy as are now being made in the soon-to-be-revised DPP. At the Bangalore air show in 2007 when US aviation companies made a big show of their various offerings, Nikhil Khanna, Director of Policy Advocacy at USIBC in Washington said: "We have encouraged the broadening of the definition of offsets to include indirect offsets, so other areas of India's economy may gain from the massive investments that are sure to flow from aerospace and defense contracts." and added that this would credit for technology transfer, limitation of liability, and the ability to "bank" the value of current projects as offsets for future defense contracts. At that time Khanna stated that new Delhi was "considering the suggestions". Defense minister A K Antony stated that "if there is scope for improvement, we will adjust and make minor changes to the policy." It now seems that he has! Only thing is, the changes are not minor!

Indian industry has reason to feel deeply aggrieved. The Confederation of Indian Industry (CII), through a Committee chairmanship of Rahul Bajaj had advocated an aggressive offsets policy as far back as 1999. CII had strongly recommended that "direct offsets be implemented as a matter of National Policy for Defense Procurement [so as to] get state-of-the-art technologies for both Public and Private Sectors [and] give major thrust to Self Reliance."

The proposed modified offsets policies, being instituted at the instigation of US companies backed by political pressure, will negate these aims. It is therefore imperative that pressure be brought upon the UPA government to abandon these changes, stay the course with direct offsets and ensure that the offsets are properly directed and monitored so as to reduce India's dependence on imports and consequent vulnerability to technology denial regimes while simultaneously leading to significant enhancement in science and technology capabilities, as well as a spread effect in important industrial and research sectors of the national economy.

8

India's Nuclear and the Non-Proliferation Treaty

The Bush Administration's initiative to sell civilian nuclear technology to India, a *de facto* nuclear-weapon state, is a landmark decision that will have a broad and lasting impact on the international nonproliferation regime. The challenge will be to develop cooperative nuclear energy relationships with friendly, democratic, *de facto* nuclear powers such as India while maintaining America's long-term nonproliferation goals.

Carving out exceptions for individual countries is an obvious but controversial solution to the dilemma. Regrettably, exceptions can become precedents for even more exceptions. For example, Russia or China could cite the U.S.-India deal as an excuse to carve out country-specific exceptions for client states, such as Iran and Pakistan. To meet the new challenges presented by the growing impact of *de facto* nuclear-weapon states on U.S. security, American policymakers should pursue a two-track policy for nuclear nonproliferation and develop criteria-based policies for emerging nuclear technology relationships with *de facto* nuclear-weapon states.

- The first track is the broad regime to prevent nuclear proliferation built around the 1968 Treaty on the Non-Proliferation of Nuclear Weapons (NPT), which does not account for the presence of *de facto* nuclear-weapon states. Indeed, the central purpose of the NPT is to prevent the emergence of such states.

- The second track should focus on addressing the regional security imbalances that motivate non-nuclear-weapon states to seek nuclear weapons. The purpose of the second track is not to abandon the first track, but to explore means for convincing *de facto* nuclear-weapon states to abandon their nuclear weapons and return to the first track.

THE INDISPENSABLE TREATY

The NPT is the world's most important diplomatic tool for controlling the spread of nuclear weapons and technology. In 1968, the United Nations endorsed the treaty, and 62 nations signed it. Today, 187 countries are signatories with the notable exceptions of Cuba, India, Pakistan, Israel, and North Korea, which withdrew in 2003.

The goal of the NPT was to stop proliferation by limiting the number of states with nuclear weapons. It designated countries that had detonated a nuclear device prior to January 1967 (i.e., the United States, the United Kingdom, France, China, and the Soviet Union) as "nuclear-weapon states." Countries that do not possess nuclear weapons and promise not to pursue them are designated as "non-nuclear-weapon states." In return, they are guaranteed access to peaceful nuclear technology as long as they continue to forswear nuclear weapons and do not pursue nuclear weapon programs.

Since its inception, the treaty has preempted the nuclear weapon programs of a number of states, including Germany, Italy, Japan, Sweden, and Switzerland. In pursuit of the NPT's goals, the United States and the international community have pressured countries that subsequently began nuclear weapon programs-including South Africa, South Korea, Taiwan, Brazil, and Argentina-to give up those programs. At the end of the Cold War, the international community pursued NPT goals in the former Soviet republics and persuaded all of the republics except Russia to give up the weapons that they had inherited from the Soviet Union. Today, a large and growing number of countries, including Canada and Australia, possess the technological capability to build the bomb but have not done so because they believe that the NPT effectively prevents the uncontrolled spread of nuclear weapons.

There are fears that by cooperating with India's civilian nuclear program, the United States could create the appearance of disregarding NPT strictures and thereby undermine its integrity. To maintain the authority and credibility of the NPT, the U.S. government should therefore develop a criteria-based policy, rather than an India-based policy, for addressing America's relationship with the *de facto* nuclear powers. A criteria-based policy will also reassure the other NPT member countries that the U.S.-India agreement will not undermine the international nonproliferation regime.

The Problem of *De Facto* Nuclear-Weapon States

During the Cold War, the five NPT-approved nuclear-weapon states were divided between East and West. On one side stood the NATO countries of the U.S., France, and the U.K., and on the other side was the Soviet Union. Although Communist China was a nuclear-weapon state under the NPT, Beijing played almost no role in the arms control debates of the period because of its limited capability. The Cold War antagonists possessed sufficient nuclear weapons to destroy one another, but from the perspective of a nonproliferation regime, negotiations were eased because there were so few parties with which to negotiate.

Today, there are at least four additional nuclear-weapon states-India, Pakistan, Israel, and North Korea-and Iran could soon join their ranks. The *de facto* nuclear-weapon states are developing nuclear capability for a variety of reasons other than the familiar motivations of the Cold War. For example, while Israel is presumed to have the weapons for traditional threat-based deterrence, North Korea appears to possess nuclear weapons for use as a bargaining tool as well as a deterrent.

In India's case, New Delhi considers the balance of power with China to be lopsided in China's favor, not only because of India's previous lack of a nuclear deterrent, but also because of China's place as a permanent member of the U.N. Security Council. Hence, New Delhi is not ashamed to admit that one of the reasons for testing its weapons was to gain the trappings of a great power that it believes are denied India by the United Nations and the international nonproliferation regime.

In addition, not all of the *de facto* nuclear-weapon states behave in the same way. Israel does not regularly threaten its neighbours with total destruction as North Korea has threatened South Korea. Neither does India proliferate nuclear technology as Pakistan has done to Iran, Libya, and North Korea.

INDIA AND THE INTERNATIONAL NONPROLIFERATION REGIME

India's nuclear technology is not homegrown; it was imported from the U.S. and its allies. Under the Eisenhower Administration's Atoms for Peace program, the United States assisted non-nuclear states in the development of peaceful nuclear capability. Beginning in 1955, the United States trained foreign nuclear scientists and engineers and declassified thousands of reports on plutonium processing and other nuclear-related information.

In 1955, members of the U.S. Joint Committee on Atomic Energy visited India to promote the peaceful uses of atomic energy, and Indian Prime Minister Jawaharlal Nehru succeeded in persuading the international community to make Homi Bhahba (father of India's nuclear establishment) president of the first U.N. Conference on the Peaceful Uses of Atomic Energy, held in Geneva in July and August. This conference facilitated the flow of U.S., Canadian, and British assistance to the Indian nuclear programs in the mid-1950s.

Also in 1955, Canada agreed to supply India with a powerful research reactor-the 40 megawatt Canada-India Reactor (CIR). Then, in February 1956, Washington supplied 21 tons of heavy water for this reactor, now dubbed the Canada-India Reactor, U.S. or CIRUS.

Acquisition of CIRUS was a turning point for India's nuclear weapons ambitions. The reactor's design was ideal for producing weapons-grade plutonium. CIRUS produced the plutonium used in India's first nuclear test in 1974, provided the design prototype for India's more powerful Dhruva plutonium production "research" reactor, and is directly responsible for producing nearly half of the weapons-grade plutonium currently believed to be in India's stockpile. Although U.S. cooperation on the CIRUS project was granted on the understanding that the reactor would be used only for peaceful purposes, there were no international safeguards available to regulate and verify the use of transferred technology.

After India's 1974 nuclear weapon test-which India described as a "peaceful" explosion-the United States and other countries that produced nuclear technology formed the Nuclear Supplier's Group (NSG). The goal of the NSG was to prevent exports of commercial and civilian nuclear and dual-use technologies from being diverted to the weapons programs of other countries. For 30 years, U.S.-India nuclear technology transfers stopped.

Nevertheless, New Delhi did not stop its nuclear weapons programs. At the end of the Cold War, India's patron, the Soviet Union, was gone, the Indian economy was a crumbling socialist relic, and China was the new emerging power. To reassert itself on the world stage, India embarked on an effort to reform its economy in 1991, began courting a closer relationship with the United States, and tested its nuclear weapons again in 1998 as a demonstration of strength. Although the test brought another storm of international condemnation, both the Bush and Clinton Administrations soon began to seek out ways to cooperate with India as a friendly, *de facto* nuclear power that shared American values and interests.

The United States and India agreed to the Next Step for a Strategic Partnership (NSSP) in July 2005 and to a follow-up agreement in March 2006 in which the United States and India agreed to civilian nuclear and space cooperation. These agreements, if implemented, run counter to the spirit of the NPT. The NPT encourages cooperation in the civilian nuclear power field only with non-nuclear-weapon states in exchange for their clear commitments not to seek nuclear weapons.

In the past, the U.S. has withheld nuclear cooperation from and has severely limited defense cooperation with countries openly seeking nuclear weapons, including India. The new willingness of the U.S. to engage in cooperative activities in the civilian nuclear power field with a state outside of the NPT raises questions about the future of U.S. nuclear nonproliferation policy.

Despite its snub of international proliferation controls, New Delhi has many policies that serve broader U.S. interests and demonstrate a respect for nonproliferation goals, including the following:

- Although not a signatory of the NPT, India has no record of proliferating nuclear technology to other countries, while China, a *de jure* nuclear-weapon state, is suspected of sharing nuclear weapons technology with both Pakistan and North Korea. Pakistan has admitted to sharing nuclear technology with North Korea, Libya, and Iran. Russia is also bargaining to sell nuclear technology to Iran, a country that is known to be violating its NPT safeguards agreement.
- India is a democracy. While the governments of other *de jure* and *de facto* nuclear-weapon states (e.g., China, Pakistan, and North Korea) are less than democratic, there is a high correlation between the quality of democracy and a country's proliferation record.
- India and the United States have a sophisticated and mutually beneficial defense relationship. India generally shares American and Western concerns about regional security issues.
- India has agreed to separate its civilian and military nuclear facilities and to place its civilian reactors under International Atomic Energy Agency (IAEA) safeguards-a move warmly approved by IAEA Director General Mohammed ElBaradei, who called India "an important partner in the nonproliferation regime." North Korea and Iran have withdrawn from or have violated their IAEA safeguard agreements.
- While India has not signed the Comprehensive Test Ban Treaty (CTBT), it has declared a unilateral moratorium on testing nuclear weapons.

India and Pakistan

Despite India's appearance as a model of moderation and stability, there are perceptions of India's nuclear weapons programs that, if not properly addressed, could ignite a regional arms race. Most important is the perception of India in Pakistan. The primary purpose of Pakistan's nuclear deterrent is India. Islamabad has largely accepted that New Delhi needs a minimum nuclear arsenal, but Islamabad asserts that India should not substantially exceed Pakistan's deterrent in size or capability. There are also three U.S. policies toward India that unfavorably affect Islamabad's security perceptions.

First, India and the United States are cooperating on regional missile defense, which could someday counter Pakistan's missile delivery capability.

Second, the proposed U.S.-India nuclear deal excludes eight of India's nuclear reactors, including its fast breeder reactor. Fast breeder reactors are known to be very efficient at creating weapons-grade fuel. Islamabad is afraid that without international controls, India will continue to produce nuclear weapons until it has an overwhelming advantage.

Finally, the United States is not including Pakistan in a civilian nuclear deal. Islamabad feels that it needs a conventional military deterrent against India to avoid escalation in the event of war or border confrontation. Pakistan is already insecure about India's much greater size, and Islamabad worries about an American alliance with its greatest enemy.

That said, there is little motivation in Washington to change policies. Specifically:

- Pakistan has an extensive nuclear proliferation network, and its belated efforts to stop proliferating nuclear weapons technology are incomplete and will not recall technology that is already spread to North Korea and Iran.
- Pakistan is not a democracy. President Pervez Musharraf's claim that only continued army control can keep Pakistan together is a self-serving sham.
- The United States and Pakistan have a long and mutually beneficial defense relationship, but Pakistan's past support of terrorist groups and current ineffectual attacks on the same groups are the reasons the United States does not want to extend civil nuclear cooperation to Pakistan.

Nevertheless, it is in America's interests to reassure Pakistan and the international community that a criteria-based second-track policy does not present open-ended exceptions to qualifying non-nuclear-weapon states. Indeed, reassuring Pakistan is a central goal of the second track of the two-track policy proposed in this chapter.

While properly crafted legislation and international agreements should establish criteria that permit only qualifying *de facto* nuclear-weapon states to benefit from civil nuclear cooperation, second-track negotiations should reassure Islamabad that Washington will not permit New Delhi to use its nuclear deal with the U.S. to dominate Pakistan or accelerate the arms race in Asia. In fact, the U.S. should press for the resolution of regional disputes in the second track with the ultimate goal of convincing both India and Pakistan that neither country needs nuclear weapons. Success in the second track, therefore, will serve the purpose of the NPT, which is to limit nuclear weapons to the five *de jure* nuclear-weapon states identified by the treaty.

What the U.S. Should Do

The United States should develop a criteria-based policy rather than an exception-based policy for engaging *de facto* nuclear states in civil nuclear cooperation and other forms of cooperation. Engagement with *de facto* nuclear states that meet American criteria could include military-to-military contacts, conventional arms sales, space cooperation, missile defense cooperation, and joint military exercises. In deference to the nuclear nonproliferation goals and treaty obligations of the United States, however, under no circumstances should cooperation extend to nuclear weapons and delivery systems designed for nuclear weapons. The criteria for nuclear power technology transfers should include:

- A stable democracy and rule of law. Democracy is not a shallow political ideology; it is a necessity for any effective nonproliferation regime. Of the current 10 *de jure* and *de facto* nuclear-weapon states, the ones with the best nonproliferation records are the democracies. The United States and its allies did assist India in developing its nuclear industry, indirectly assisting its weapons program; but when India tested a nuclear weapon in 1974, cooperation halted, and the democracies moved to block further technology transfers. Furthermore, India has no record of passing nuclear technology to other countries. On the other hand, all the non-democratic nuclear-weapon states are aggressive and indiscriminate proliferators.

- A record of not proliferating nuclear technology "to other states" and a demonstrated respect for the international nuclear nonproliferation regime's obligations for nuclear-weapon states.India has no record of transferring nuclear technology to any other country-consistent with the NPT. India has also declared a unilateral moratorium on testing nuclear weapons-consistent with the Comprehensive Test Ban Treaty (CTBT)-and has demonstrated an interest in participating in the Proliferation Security Initiative (PSI). It is American reluctance to accept a country that is not an NPT member that has delayed India's participation in PSI activities.
- Not being a state sponsor of terrorism. The nexus of state-sponsored terrorism and nuclear weapons is America's greatest nightmare.
- Firm separation between civilian and military nuclear programs. Commercial power reactors are an area in which the United States can accomplish multiple goals with *de facto* nuclear powers. For example, an energy trade deal with India should include provisions that prevent India from subsidizing civilian reactors and prevent the United States and other nuclear suppliers from providing nuclear technologies or facilities at prices below the cost of production. Without government assistance, a nuclear power plant would not be economically viable if it was diverting resources to expensive military projects, such as building bombs. At the same time, a trade agreement that eliminated government subsidies and allowed India's power plants to operate for profit would force substantial reform in India's energy sector and contribute to the country's economic development.
- Non-aggressive security policies. This criterion addresses

the fundamental security pretexts for developing nuclear weapons in ways that will encourage *de facto* nuclear states to abandon or reduce their nuclear weapons programs. For example, the threat posed by Pakistan is one of many reasons for India to possess nuclear weapons, but India is Pakistan's only reason for possessing nuclear weapons. This criterion would require India to engage in substantive negotiations to resolve disputes.

India, however, does meet this criterion. The ongoing armistice at the Line of Control and the Kashmir border talks between Pakistan and India are making remarkable progress. Although neither country is close to making a fundamental compromise on Kashmir, they have reached a range of agreements on other matters, particularly on controls for their nuclear weapons.

- A willingness to consider limits on the number of nuclear weapons. Arms control advocates assert that this agreement, when implemented, would free India's domestic capacity to produce the fissile material (highly enriched uranium and plutonium) needed to build nuclear weapons and would set a bad precedent for other *de facto* nuclear-weapon states. The Bush Administration's proposed legislation to implement the agreement with India addresses this issue by conditioning U.S. support for India's civil nuclear program on India's assistance to the U.S. in concluding a multilateral Fissile Material Cut-off Treaty.

Ultimately, the size of a state's nuclear arsenal depends on more than just the volume of fissile material that it can produce. Perceived threats and military doctrine regarding the use of nuclear weapons are at least as important. This issue is best addressed in the second track of the two-track nonproliferation policy, which focuses on regional security issues. The broader purpose of the second track is to address the underlying security concerns that prompted India to obtain nuclear weapons in such a way that India concludes that it no longer needs nuclear weapons. Clearly, the second-track agenda should address the threat and doctrinal issues in ways that, among other issues, lessen the threats that the state faces.

THEORETICAL BACKGROUND: NUCLEAR PROLIFERATION AND CIVIL-MILITARY RELATIONS

Ever since the advent of nuclear weapons in global politics in 1945, theorists and practitioners alike have focused on the causes and consequences of nuclear weapons proliferation. The first generation of nuclear strategists that included Bernard Brodie, Albert Wohlstetter, and Thomas Schelling, among others, tried to grapple with the central dilemma that confronted global politics with the advent of nuclear weapons. On the one hand, the presence of survivable and deliverable strategic weapons made it imperative for the nuclear powers to try to limit war. On the other hand, nuclear powers also viewed nuclear weapons as political instruments, whereby the threat of nuclear war could be used to attain political ends. This dilemma has continued to define the work of later scholars, including the "optimist-pessimist debate" on the proliferation of nuclear weapons.

Kenneth Waltz, the leading proponent of the optimist school, has long argued that the gradual spread of nuclear weapons is inevitable but not a cause for worry. Waltz has contended that "whatever the number of nuclear states, a nuclear world is tolerable if these states are able to send a convincing deterrent message: It is useless to attempt to conquer because you will be severely punished." In fact, he argues proliferation should be welcomed as nuclear weapons, being defence oriented, make wars less likely. According to him, proliferation of nuclear weapons will lead to neither domestic nor regional instability, because "uncertainty about the course that a nuclear war might follow, along with the certainty that destruction can be immense, strongly inhibits the first use of nuclear weapons."

While there were several dissenting voices against Waltz's provocative argument, the most powerful critique of this proliferation-optimism school came from Scott Sagan. Sagan argued that the civilian control of the military in the emerging nuclear states seems to be weak, or that in many cases these states have military-run governments. In such states, the biases and parochial interests of the military might determine state behaviour, thereby leading to deterrence failures as "professional military organizations, if left on their own, are unlikely to fulfill the operational requirements for rational nuclear deterrence." Sagan used his argument to bring the issue of civil-military relations in emerging nuclear states to the center of the debate on the implications of nuclear proliferation.

The study of civil-military relations has a long pedigree. In fact, it can be traced to Clausewitz, for whom war was the continuation of politics by other means. When he argued that war's grammar may be its own but not its logic, he was making it clear that the logic of war belonged to the domain of civilians. But ever since then, there has not been a consensus on how to define the boundaries of the domains claimed by the civilians and the military.

The central problem that animates much of the debate in the scholarly literature on civil-military relations has been termed as the civil-military problematic— how to ensure that the very institution created to protect the polity, that is, the military does not itself become a threat to the polity. While the military must be strong and efficient enough to prevail in a war against an outside enemy, it must function in a manner so as not to destroy the society it is supposed to guard.

Samuel Huntington, in his seminal work, *The Soldier and the State*, proposed to resolve this dilemma by examining how military effectiveness, and therefore national security, was a function of differing patterns of civil-military relations, arguing that civilian respect for military autonomy is necessary for military effectiveness. He proposed a policy of "objective civilian control," whereby civilians would set the policy objectives but the military would be free to determine what military operations were called needed to successfully attain those objectives.

Building on this work and using it in the study of nuclear proliferation, other scholars have demonstrated that different patterns of civil-military relations lead to different forms of nuclear command and control and therefore to different implications for the nuclear proliferation dynamic. In a way, the very structure of nuclear deterrence rests on effective command and control organizations and technologies. A failure of command and control systems would mean the failure of nuclear deterrence, which therefore makes it imperative to examine the question of civil-military relations in order to fully comprehend the consequences of nuclear proliferation.

The issue of civil-military relations and concomitant command and control issues in new nuclear nations is not of much concern for the proliferation optimists. For some optimists like Waltz, there are huge strategic incentives for new nuclear nations to have effective command and control systems to manage their nuclear weapons. In his words, "we do not have to wonder if they [the new nuclear states] will take good care of their weapons. They have every incentive to do so."

In fact, he goes on to say, "if the weakness or absence of civilian control of the military has not led America to use its plentiful nuclear weapons, we hardly have reason to think that new nuclear countries will misuse theirs because of an absence of civilian control." Other proliferation optimists like Mearsheimer and Van Evera are, however, more guarded in their optimism regarding the strategic consequences of nuclear proliferation. In this view, if "well-managed," nuclear proliferation does not pose much of a problem. But this literature does not deal with command and control issues in new nuclear states directly.

This optimistic appraisal of command and control in emerging nuclear states was countered by the pessimists who have argued that despite claims to the contrary, the command and control situation faced by the two superpowers during the cold war was not perfect and that command and control problems would be even difficult to tackle in the new nuclear states. And, therefore, nuclear proliferation should be dreaded, much less encouraged.

It has been further argued that while a nation's use of its nuclear weapons will not be determined by its command and control systems, the nature of command and control in emerging nuclear nations may suggest the likelihood of the use of nuclear weapons when the nation does not want them used. According to Peter Feaver, command and control in emerging nuclear nations will be a function of the nature of civil-military relations and the time urgency of the nuclear arsenal.

These factors can push states into developing command and control systems that do not necessarily enhance strategic stability. Not to be left behind, the optimists came back with another set of arguments in support of their position. Termed as "neooptimists," this position holds that the emerging nuclear states are much less likely to face critical command and control problem because of the small size of their nuclear arsenals, even as it concedes that large and complex nuclear arsenals like those of the two superpowers during the cold war are prone to command and control problems.

Because most of the new nuclear states are interested in developing small nuclear arsenals for the purpose of minimum deterrence and because of cost considerations, they will be able to achieve safe nuclear practices rather easily. As Jordan Seng argues, "the organizational features, strategic imperatives, and resource limitations of minor nuclear proliferators could make it very difficult for them to reproduce the command and control methods of advanced nuclear powers; but, at the same time, these enable minor proliferators to employ alternative methods of command and control that are equally or more effective."

This debate remains irreconcilable and unresolved because of the paucity of evidentiary support for either side from the emerging nuclear states. This is because not many countries have emerged as nuclear weapon states and even those that can be termed as "emerging" are either doing their best to conceal their activities, like Iran and North Korea, or are following the "opaque" route to nuclear weaponization.

The two obvious exceptions to this trend are India and Pakistan, which declared themselves as "nuclear weapon states" in 1998 in defiance of the international community and have since moved slowly, but steadily, towards nuclear weaponization that can be defined as the process of developing, testing, and integrating warhead components into a militarily usable weapons system. Though much still remains shrouded in mystery, India and Pakistan have been trying to be more open about their nuclear postures in order to be seen as responsible nuclear states. India's case is particularly interesting, because it is the first among the new or emerging nuclear states that has come out with an explicit nuclear doctrine and command structure. India's recent attempts to integrate the military into the realm of nuclear policy can only be examined by placing it in the broader historical context of civil-military relations in India.

CIVIL-MILITARY RELATIONS IN INDIA: A HISTORICAL OVERVIEW

Indian politicians after independence in 1947 viewed the Indian army with suspicion as including the last supporters of the British Raj and did their best to isolate the military from policy and influence. This attitude was further reinforced by the views of two giants of the Indian nationalist movement, Mahatma Gandhi and Jawaharlal Nehru. Gandhi's ardent belief in non-violence left little room for accepting the role of the use of force in an independent India.

It also shaped the views on military and defence of the first generation of postindependence political leaders in India. But more important has been the legacy of Nehru, India's first prime minister, who laid the institutional foundations for civil-military relations in India. His obsession with economic development was only matched by his disdain and distrust of the military, resulting in the sidelining of defence planning in India.

He also ensured that the experiences in neighboring Pakistan, where the military had become the dominant political force soon after independence, would not be repeated in India by institutionalizing civilian supremacy over the country's military apparatus. The civilian elite also did not want the emergence of a rival elite with direct access to political leadership. Two significant changes immediately after independence that reduced the influence of the military and strengthened civilian control were the abolition of the post of commander in chief that had hitherto been the main military adviser to the government, and the strengthening of the civilian-led Ministry of Defence.

Other organizational changes followed that further strengthened civilian hold over the armed forces. It has been argued that, as a consequence, India is among only a handful of nations where civilian administrations wield so much power over the military.

Along with Nehru, another civilian who left a lasting impact on the evolution of civil-military relations was V. K. Krishna Menon, India's minister of defence from 1957 to 1962. During his tenure, which has been described as the most controversial stewardship of the Indian Defence Ministry, he heralded a number of organizational changes that were not very popular with the armed forces.

The first major civil-military clash in independent India also took place under his watch, when B. K. Thimayya, the then well-respected chief of army, decided to bypass Menon in 1959 and went straight to the prime minister with his litany of complaints that included, among others, Menon's interference in the administration of the armed forces.

The situation was so precarious that Thimayya even submitted his resignation to Nehru, which he was persuaded to withdraw later. While this episode demonstrated that the strength of civil-military relations in India in so far as Thimayya used the due process to challenge his civilian superior, it also revealed the dangers of civilian intervention in matters the military feels belong to its domain. And the consequences of such civil-military friction would be grave for India in the 1962 war with China.

Despite any military experience, Nehru and Menon were actively involved in operational-level planning before the outbreak of the Sino-Indian war of 1962. They "directly supervised the placement of individual brigades, companies, and even platoons, as the Chinese and Indian forces engaged in mutual encirclement of isolated outposts." As a consequence, when China won the war decisively, the blame was laid on the doors of Nehru and Menon. Menon resigned, while Nehru's reputation suffered lasting damage. It also made it clear, both to the civilians and the military, that purely operational matters were best left to the military. Some have argued that since then a convention has been established whereby, while the operational directive is laid down by the political leadership, the actual planning of operation is left to the chiefs of staff.

Two significant consequences followed the Indian army's debacle in 1962 in so far as the topic under study is concerned. One, Indian pursuit of nuclear weapons became a serious concern of successive Indian governments, especially after China became a nuclear weapon state in 1964 and emerged as Pakistan's main arms supplier after 1965. Second, sections of the Indian armed forces became more creative in thinking about operational and strategic defence issues. When there was no movement on the nuclear front after India's "Peaceful Nuclear Explosion" of 1974, the chiefs of all three Indian armed services wrote to the then prime minister of India, Indira Gandhi, in 1983 that India should develop its own nuclear capability. This was the first time in India's history that armed forces had explicitly stated their views on India's nuclear policy. But it was General K. Sundarji who became one of the first Indian armed forces officials to systematically think about nuclear weapons and Indian military strategy.

He wrote his masters thesis on the viability of nuclear weapons and headed a secret interservices committee in 1985 that examined India's nuclear option. He was unabashedly for India acquiring nuclear weapons and argued that India need not go the mutual assured destruction (MAD)route taken by the two superpowers. He also estimated that India needed around ninety nuclear weapons to have a "credible minimum deterrent." His ambitions also led him to organize a massive military exercise, Operation Brasstacks, in 1986. Though the actual goals of this operation still remain shrouded in mystery, most analysts agree that this was India's attempt to undertake a preemptive strike on Pakistan's nuclear capability to destroy it before Pakistan emerged as a mature nuclear power. But the danger of the crisis getting out of hand led Indian's political leadership to pull back from the brink after the international uproar. This crisis also brought to light the consequences of the non-involvement of the Indian armed forces in the nation's nuclear programme, because even as the crisis raged on, the armed forces had no idea if they had a delivery vehicle for nuclear warheads if things came to such a pass. Sundarji's term as the chief of the Indian army was probably the most ambitious tenure in the Indian history. But even he could not dictate policy with regard to nuclear weapons, which remained firmly under the civilian control, and its pace was set by how much cost the civilian leadership in India was willing to bear. While the Indian army has traditionally feared that nuclear weapons would lead to a reduction in its own influence in the interservices hierarchy, it has been suggested that after Sundarji it had positioned itself such that once the government had taken a decision to acquire nuclear weapons, the Indian army would be the first to stake a claim. And thus the Indian nuclear weapons programme continued apace without any meaningful involvement of the Indian armed forces.

There is little evidence that the Indian government consulted the Indian armed forces when it decided to go openly nuclear in 1998. It was primarily a civilian decision, with the involvement of the Indian armed forces being only peripheral to the whole exercise.

FRAMING OF INDIA'S NUCLEAR DOCTRINE: 1998–2003

After declaring itself as a nuclear weapon state (NWS) in May 1998, India took its first major step of converting that rhetoric into reality in January 2003 when it made explicit its nuclear doctrine and the nature of its command and control over its nuclear arsenal. The Cabinet Committee on Security (CCS) of the Indian government, composed of the prime minister and the ministers of home affairs, defence, finance, and external affairs, decided to share with the Indian public and the world some major aspects of the Indian nuclear weapons doctrine and operational arrangements governing India's nuclear assets.

It is important to recognize that the salient aspects of the Indian nuclear doctrine had been enunciated immediately by the Indian government after it conducted its nuclear tests in May 1998. India decided to adopt a no-firstuse (NFU) policy and declared that it would never use nuclear weapons against a non-nuclear state. India also made clear its intention of working consistently towards the goal of universal nuclear disarmament. India was also engaged in high-level arms control negotiations with the United States that were trying to define the broad contours of Indo-U.S.

relationship post–Pokharan II. While India had voluntarily declared a moratorium on further nuclear testing, the United States was also pressing India to accept a moratorium on fissile material production and to participate in the Fissile Material Cut-off Treaty (FMCT) negotiations, strengthen its export control system, and engage in a security dialogue with Pakistan.

India's nuclear doctrine, as finally announced, largely conformed to the draft nuclear doctrine that was produced by the National Security Advisory Board (NSAB). The NSAB is part of the National Security Council (NSC) that was established in 1998 as part of the larger organizational shake-up in national security decision-making apparatus of India. There has been considerable debate in India on the need to establish a NSC since late 1980s, but nothing concrete emerged out of it for a long time. Some of the issues raised in this debate related to the authority of the National Security Adviser (NSA) and how a NSC should be restructured so that it reflected that requirements of a parliamentary democracy. In fact, a former prime minister, P. V. Narasimha Rao, made it clear that he found it pointless to have a NSC in India, because the concept of a NSC was more appropriate for a presidential form of government as opposed to the Indian parliamentary system, where the cabinet was the supreme decision-making body.

The Hindu nationalist Bhartiya Janata Party (BJP) promised in its election manifesto in 1998 that, if elected, it would establish a NSC to "undertake India's first ever Strategic Defence Review to study and analyze the security environment and make appropriate recommendations." The NSC was established in November 1998 after India had conducted its nuclear tests earlier that year. It has been suggested that the NSC was designed "to assuage global concerns that, despite conducting its nuclear tests, India had no institutional framework to evaluate security threats or evolve a nuclear doctrine."

The NSC that has emerged is headed by the prime minister and includes the ministers for home affairs, defence, external affairs, and finance as well as the deputy chairman of the Planning Commission. The NSC is supported by a three-tier structure involving a Strategic Policy Group, a NSAB, and a Secretariat, whose nucleus is provided by the Joint Intelligence Council. However, the armed forces have no direct access to the political leadership at the apex level and continue to be deprived of participation in the decisionmaking process of the NSC. It was the NSAB that played the central role in the crafting of the Indian nuclear doctrine. The twenty-two-member NSAB is composed of former civil and military officials, academics, scientists, and journalists "with expertise in Foreign Affairs, External Security, Defence, Strategic Analysis, Economics, Science and Technology, Internal Security, and Armed Forces."

The NSAB's first convenor, K. Subrahmanyam is the doyen of Indian strategic thinkers and has long been a proponent of nuclear weaponization for India. It has been argued that the draft nuclear doctrine reflected the personal inclinations of the members of the NSAB, because nineteen of the NSAB's twenty-two members were known to be in favour of nuclear weapons. Some have also argued that the government ensured that the NSAB members would advocate its nuclear policies by writing and speaking in its support. But this is strongly denied by the members of the NSAB themselves, who claim that the BJP government kept out of the NSAB deliberations completely. The draft doctrine that was produced by the NSAB was a consensus document incorporating, by and large, all of the disparate opinions expressed in the deliberations.

As one critic has noted, "The nuclear doctrine's only virtue is that nothing in it went very strongly against the sentiment of any member of the NSAB and conversely all members could identify themselves with some portions of it." A member of the NSAB has himself made it clear that the draft doctrine was a "document that the members of the NSAB drafting group discovered early on could accommodate differing views about what those concepts actually entailed in terms of structuring a nuclear deterrent force, deploying such a force, and the scenarios in which nuclear weapons can probably be used."

The draft nuclear doctrine was released 1999, but it was not formally accepted by the Indian government, because it generated a lot of debate and strong reactions on all sides. When the draft nuclear doctrine was released, it was seen by many as too close to the viewpoint of the BJP, which was then running a caretaker government, and was perceived as a blatant ploy by the BJP to secure votes in the coming elections. The draft recommended an open-ended nuclear force posture that many thought might lead to an arms race on the subcontinent.

Reflecting the terminology employed by the established nuclear weapon states, the draft doctrine called on India to develop an "integrated operational plan" for nuclear use and a "triad of aircraft, mobile land-based missiles, and sea-based assets." Not only did Pakistan and China react with alarm to the draft, but the United States also made its disappointment very clear to India. Even as the debate on India's draft nuclear doctrine continued in India and abroad, India started exploring the possibility of enunciating a limited war doctrine in early 2000. It was a result of the lessons learned from the Kargil conflict of May–June 1999. Kargil was the first crisis situation between India and Pakistan in an openly nuclearized regional environment.

Kargil confirmed the beliefs of Indian policymakers that Pakistan was an unreliable and adventurous state, especially as the crisis came soon after the then Indian prime minister, Atal Bihari Vajpayee, had taken a personal initiative in resurrecting the long-moribund Indo-Pak peace process and had traveled to Lahore to start talks with his Pakistani counterpart. The strategic surprise of Kargil once again highlighted endemic deficiencies in India's intelligence infrastructure and the need for India to develop a set of strategic rapidresponse capabilities to strengthen deterrence.

There were many indications that for the Pakistani military, the acquisition of nuclear weapons by India and Pakistan had virtually eliminated the possibility of an all-out conventional war between the two adversaries and had increased the salience of proxy wars. Still, Kargil came as a tactical and strategic surprise for the Indian political and military leaders. The newly formed NSC came in for a lot of flak, because it failed to play a leadership role either prior to or during the Kargil crisis. The NSC had been made dysfunctional with the appointment of a part-time NSA by the government, and it was not vested with full powers of intelligence oversight, coordination, arbitration, implementation, and performance review to ensure accountability. Intelligence agencies, more often than not, produce varied, incomplete, or even conflicting intelligence in security matters and therefore need arbitration by an intelligence coordinator.

The NSC was supposed to play this role for strategic assessment and was supposed to be the central body for the formulation of national security strategies, thereby providing the basis for the formulation of national military strategies by the military hierarchy. It failed to do this in 1999, renewing a debate on its utility and effectiveness.

While the U.S. role in restraining Pakistan during this crisis and thereby bringing it to an early end is now well accepted, several other operational factors have also been cited for tilting the conflict in India's favour. These include an effective use of air power on the Indian side of the Line of Control (LOC), creation of overwhelming superiority of land forces, and use of massive concentrations of artillery. This is despite the fact that many in Pakistan argue that while Kargil might have been a strategic failure for Pakistan, at the operational and tactical level, it was a success for the Pakistani army. Some in India also do not view India's victory in Kargil as unequivocal, arguing that the "structure and conditions of the withdrawal [rendered] what most likely would have been an unconditional military victory into a profoundly complex and problematic one."

As a consequence, in the aftermath of the Kargil conflict, a belief emerged in the higher echelons of the Indian government and armed forces that the changed strategic milieu in South Asia, because of the nuclearization of India and Pakistan, makes it imperative for India to be able to fight a limited conventional war, thereby disabusing Pakistan of the belief that India would be deterred in any war imposed on it and would not fight back. It was a fairly specific example of efforts to achieve escalation dominance, because it was argued that in a war with limited political and military objectives, "the escalatory ladder can be climbed in a carefully controlled ascent wherein politicodiplomatic factors would play an important role."

Despite skepticism in the West and in some sections of the Indian security establishment about the ability of India and Pakistan to limit their conflicts below the nuclear threshold, for India the Kargil crisis was a demonstration of its ability to fight and win a limited war and the possibility of more limited conventional wars in the future. This gave rise to a policy of compellence, with India deciding to adopt a proactive posture vis-à-vis Pakistan by retaining the ability to launch limited conventional war.

The real test for these changing doctrinal assumptions came during the crisis that erupted between India and Pakistan after India's parliament was attacked by terrorists in December 2001. It has been suggested by some that it was the failure of "Operation Parakram"—the 2002 army mobilization on the border—that forced the Indian political leadership to explicate the Nuclear Command Authority (NCA) and provide an outline of the nuclear doctrine. A major factor in this failure was that India lacked the capacity, conventional and nuclear, to bend Pakistan to its will. The top political leadership failed to give the Indian armed forces any clear directives as to what objectives India wanted to achieve through the mobilization of its army. The threat of the use of nuclear weapons by Pakistan deterred India from undertaking a military offensive, even a limited one. In fact, the Pakistan army claimed that the Indian army's "redeployment," or withdrawal, was their "victory."

Not everyone agrees that the Operation Parakram was a failure for India, with some claiming that it led to President Musharraf 's famous January 2002 speech in which he promised not to allow Pakistani territory to be used by terrorists operating in Kashmir and banned a number of terrorist groups that India had held responsible for the attack on the parliament building, and a debate still continues in Indian policy circles on its exact ramifications. But the constraints under which the Indian armed forces operated during Operation Parakram reinforced many of the lessons learned during the Kargil conflict, leading finally to the official unveiling of India's "Cold Start" war doctrine by the Indian army in 2004. This doctrine signifies a salient shift from defensive to offensive operations at the very outset of a conflict, relying on the element of surprise and not giving Pakistan any time to bring diplomatic leverage into play vis-à-vis India.

Musharraf 's speech to Pakistan air force officers in December 2002 brought South Asia under further international scrutiny. Musharraf asserted that it was Pakistan's threat to use "unconventional tactics" that prevented India from launching a full-scale war against Pakistan in 2002. India chose to interpret the general's words as an undisguised threat of the first use of nuclear weapons and reacted vigorously, warning Pakistan that a nuclear strike against India would be met with "massive retaliation." Musharraf 's speech seemed to India a signal to take stock and to respond to what many view as constant nuclear blackmail from across the border and might have accelerated the finalization of the nuclear doctrine that had been under discussion for the previous four and a half years.

Finally, in January 2003, the Indian government unveiled a final set of political principles and administrative arrangements to manage its arsenal of nuclear weapons.

The main elements of the Indian nuclear doctrine are:

- Building and maintaining a credible minimum deterrent;
- A posture of NFU;
- Retaliatory attacks only to be authorized by the civilian political leadership through the Nuclear Command Authority;
- Nonuse of nuclear weapons against non-nuclear weapons states;
- India to retain the option of retaliating with nuclear weapons in the event of a major attack against India or Indian forces anywhere, by biological or chemical weapons;
- A continuance of controls on export of nuclear and missile related materials and technologies, participation in the FMCT negotiations, observance of the moratorium on nuclear tests, and working towards the goal of universal nuclear disarmament.

Given that India had declared itself a nuclear weapon power in 1998 after its nuclear tests, the setting up of a formal command

and control structure was also long overdue. There was already a loosely knit structure in operation, but the need for formalizing it and making it public had become apparent to India. India has decided to put its nuclear arsenal under the control of a formal command chain.

A two-layered structure, the NCA, will have the overall control of nuclear weapons. The NCA is composed of the Political Council, headed by the prime minister, and the Executive Council, presided over by the national security adviser. Though the actual composition of the NCA at its political and executive levels has not been made explicit by the government, according to some reports in the Indian media, the Political Council includes the members of the CCS and the national security adviser, while the Executive Council is composed of the chairman of the Chiefs of Staff Committee (COSC) of the three services, heads of intelligence agencies, and members of the scientific community associated with the nuclear programme.

The prime minister will be the sole authority to issue orders to release the use of nuclear weapons in the event of a nuclear war. The national security adviser, who chairs the executive council of the NCA, will execute the directives of the political council. It is the job of the security adviser and the Executive Council to assist the Political Council, headed by the prime minister, in taking the decision on the use of nukes and then ensuring that the orders are carried out. A triservice command called the Strategic Forces Command (SFC) will be NCA's operational arm, having its own commander in chief reporting to the chairman of the Joint Chiefs of Staff, and will control all of India's nuclear warheads and delivery systems. Two operational missile groups of the Indian army with 150–250 kilometer short-range Prithvi and longer version 2,500-kilometer Agni-II missiles, both capable of carrying nuclear warheads have been transferred to form the nucleus of the new SFC. India has also started the production of Agni-I, 700-kilometer medium-range ballistic missile, is working on operationalization of the 3,500-kilometer Agni-III and plans to double its nuclear strike range to 6,000 kilometers with Agni-IV. The SFC will also locate assets like some squadrons of Mirage 2000 and Su-30 MKI and nuclear-capable naval warships and submarines to form the country's first ever nuclear arm.

The Indian government has also "approved the arrangement for alternate chains of command for retaliatory nuclear strikes in all eventualities." In its first-ever formal meeting in September 2003, the NCA reviewed the state of the Indian nuclear arsenal, especially the command and control structure and the alternate chains of command.

The establishment of the nuclear command post in concrete underground bunkers at "secure locations" was the highlight of the meeting. However, details regarding the chain of command and control if the prime minister is incapacitated or in the event of decapitating nuclear attacks are still not in the public domain.

There was a smooth transfer of control over nuclear assets when the BJPled government was defeated in the Indian parliamentary elections in May 2004. The Congress Party–led coalition government swiftly took control of the nuclear assets by naming a new NSA, thereby ensuring the continuity of the nation's NCA. The Congress Party, when in opposition, had argued that the previous government had only made cosmetic changes in the institutional arrangements and the NSC in particular had not been strengthened.

However, after almost four years in power, it's not clear if the United Progressive Alliance (UPA) government is serious about implementing its promise of establishing a fully functional and institutionally cohesive NSC. The formal declaration of its nuclear doctrine and creation of the NCA by India brought into effect a long-standing requirement, thereby formalizing what was essentially a set of unstructured arrangements among senior members of the politico-military-scientific establishment. It was India's attempt to set at rest some doubts over nuclear issues while reiterating the promises it made to the international community. The new framework accords the necessary doctrinal underpinning to India's evolving nuclear posture and the sanctity of government approval for the use of nuclear weapons.

Maximum restraint in the use of nuclear forces, absolute political control over decision making, and an attempt to evolve an effective interface between civilian and military leaders in the administration of its nuclear arsenal have emerged as the basic tenets of India's nuclear weapons policy. The declaration of its nuclear doctrine and the NCA by India marked a significant step in India's plan to develop an effective and robust command and control and indications-and-warning systems and infrastructure for its strategic nuclear forces commensurate with India's strategic requirements.

An effective command and control arrangement for the Indian nuclear force, however, continues to remain a challenge for India's ability to develop a credible minimum deterrent, especially as it involves an integration of the Indian military with the civilian authorities for the management of the nation's nuclear arsenal.

INDIA'S NATIONAL SECURITY AND DEFENCE

India has been subjected to wars in every decade of its Post – Independence existence and increased armed insurgencies, proxy wars and terrorism of the Islamic fundamentalist variety.

India has been so subjected to aggression because in the last fifty years, it exhibited the propensity to be pacifist or defensive in nature. It shied away from the use of power despite its size and resources. The resultant effect was that India's adversaries perceived India as a "Soft State" incapable of strong military responses even when its national security interests were threatened and trampled upon both externally and internally.

The Need for a Strategic Vision for the Twenty first Century

India sadly lacks a 'Strategic Vision'. Vision is defined as 'imaginative insight, statesman like foresight, political sagacity.' 'Strategic Vision' would imply the application of imaginative, statesmanlike foresight and political sagacity by India's political leadership to the nation's national security management and long-range strategic planning to counter both external and internal security threats.

Hence 'Strategic Vision' for India would imply the need for:

- Political statesmanship that can have a penetrative foresight of how India can be led to its aspirational goals of being a leading regional and global power.

- Political leadership that can translate India's 'Strategic Vision' into time-bound implementation plans. These implementation plans should incorporate short term, medium term and long term goals.
- Political leadership which is resolute, forceful and determined to direct an integrated national effort towards achieving strategic goals, cutting through bureaucratic red-tapism and lethargy. National security and strategic implementation should have an over-riding priority over all other national activities.
- Political leadership that is bold and audacious and which will ensure that in the pursuit of India's 'strategic vision', any attempts to thwart it by external or internal threats are met with prompt, decisive and crippling military responses. Power is meant to be used to nip any emerging threats to India's national security.

India's 'Strategic Vision' for the 21st century should incorporate the following goals and components and which should be reflected in appropriate declaratory policies binding across the entire Indian political spectrum:

- India is to be the predominant power in the Indian sub-continent. It already is in terms of size, natural resources and human resources. It has an unbridgeable lead in the sub-continent in terms of economy, industrial development and infrastructure and hi-technology wherewithal. India however is not the pre-dominant military power, as Pakistan has been built up as the 'regional spoiler' state by China in terms of a nuclear weapons and missile arsenal. China has been engaged for the last two decades specifically to arrest India's emergence as the predominant power in South Asia by its proxy efforts through Pakistan.
- India is one of the major powers of Asia, along with China and Japan. To this end India's strategic strengths should be built at an accelerated pace and strategic partnerships evolved to ensure that India becomes a determinant in any regional or global power considerations in political, economic and military terms.

To achieve this ' strategic vision' for the 21st century India needs to develop strategically and in military terms, the following capabilities:

- Military preponderance in both the nuclear and conventional military fields. In terms of levels, it should have an overwhelming military superiority in South Asia and relative parity with China.
- India needs to develop 'force projection' capabilities, especially naval and air. Sizeable air-mobile and naval task forces should be available for rapid deployment in India's area of interest and 'areas of influence'.
- India's naval power should be built to levels which would permit sea-denial if not sea-control in the entire Indian Ocean region.
- Nuclear deterrence strong enough to deter even major powers to attempt political or military coercion i.e., development of an ICBM and SLBM arsenal. India after fifty years of being a 'Soft State' needs to get into a resurgent mode befitting her size and resources. The time has come not only to have the will to build up her power attributes but also to learn and have the will to use power.

Political leadership of a very high order and calibre is required to lead India towards the achievement of the 'strategic vision' thus envisioned.

INDIA'S NEED FOR DECLARATORY STRATEGIC DOCTRINES

India having formalised its "strategic vision" should then spell out in declaratory terms the strategic doctrines the country would follow henceforth. In the last 50 years, India has shied away from declaratory strategic doctrines. Declaratory strategic doctrines are necessary for the following reasons:

- India's strategic intentions are made clear in declaratory form. Ambiguity is the weapon of the weak and the passive. India should move away from ambiguous policies.
- Strategic doctrines should define in unambiguous terms the "red lines" whose crossing or attempts to breach by

any country will not be tolerated. These "red lines" should flow from the enunciation of India's national security interests. The use of force and swift retaliation should be declared in these strategic doctrines.

- Strategic doctrines so declared will leave no doubt to potential aggressors or those tempted to stir and generate internal security threats in India as to what India's responses would be.
- Declaratory strategic doctrines are especially necessary for combating terrorism, hijacking and other disruptive activities resorted to by adversaries. Doctrines should spell out that even the roots of terrorism and insurgency from across Indian borders will not be immune from India's retaliatory responses.
- On the practical plane, declaratory strategic doctrines would provide the template on which planning for India's national security apparatus and force-planning and force structures can be configured.
- Declaratory strategic doctrines should therefore essentially reflect India's will to use power both in terms of pre-emptive military operations and launching of offensive operations.

In the realms of Indian military strategy, the absence of declaratory strategic doctrines has been most keenly felt. India's military responses to both external and internal threats, so far, perforce, have been defensive and re-active in nature. Our entire national ethos, political and military mind-sets and tactical thinking have been oriented in defensive terms

Such defensive and reactive policies have had a debilitating impact on India's military preparedness and also on India's intelligence machinery. As soon as the crisis blows over, in the absence of strategic doctrines, combat equipment acquisitions and build-up of strategic needs is shelved. It has also led to neglect of our build-up of force-projection capabilities and the development of our offshore island territories into strong military bases for force projection capabilities.

India's Political Governance: The Need For a Qualitative Change

Good political governance is an imperative requirement of the power attributes of any nation aspiring to be a big power. Power status, decisive political leadership, strategic vision, military preparedness, economic advancement and national cohesion cannot be achieved without good political governance.

The indicators of power potential which foreign countries look for pertaining to India all centre around and are focussed on political stability and good governance. In India's march towards her future goals of being a major power, the weakest link in that achievement is India's political governance and the quality of her polity. This is not an individual opinion but the general opinion of one and all, namely, contempt for the politicians and their ethical standards.

Qualitative change in the polity and political governance of India can only be brought about by a conscious and deliberate effort by political leaders of major political parties. It is they who have to set irreproachable high standards personally and also ensure that party tickets are given to intelligent, mature and dedicated men and women of substance. Leaders of major political parties need to discipline their unruly parliamentarians and legislators. India's polity should not take it for granted that they are not under scrutiny. Ironically this polity which claims to have a prerogative on national leadership stands paralysed qualitatively. This has a grave effect on India, strategically and militarily.

India's Strategic Culture: The Need for Re-Invention

India's geographical boundaries stood changed after 1947 and so also the nature and relief of terrain configurations on which present boundaries rest. Historically and culturally, India went through three widely separated stages–Hindu, Muslim and British, Each of these periods had a religious and cultural disconnect and therefore do not provide the consistency of the evolution of a strategic culture, like China for example. India today stands faced with the daunting task of re–inventing its strategic culture for two good reasons :

- India today faces strategic threats to its national security both external and internal, which are in marked variance to its earlier geographical, historical or cultural configurations.
- Secularism does not define or arise from any strategic culture. India's strategic culture needs to be reinvented by drawing on its most ancient and indigenous roots and blending it with India's contemporary strategic ambitions and the global strategic environment. It is India's political leadership and its elites who have failed to grasp this critical strategic requirement.

India's history of the last fifty years indicates that India was unable to re-invent a strategic culture, appropriate and commensurate enough to meet the threats to its security. India was passive, defensive, reactive and soft in her strategic cultures. India needs to re-invent its strategic culture in a more resurgent mode of proactive, directed and aggressive responses to threats to her national security.

National Security Issues Should Not be Politicised

India presents a regrettable phenomenon where political opposition parties, in the absence of any other political issue, tend to politicise national security issues. In this process and in their zeal to discomfit the ruling party at any cost, they fail to realise the impact it has on the Armed Forces of India – their morale, their will to fight and their entire confidence in the political structure of the Indian nation state is seriously jeopardised. The most recent examples of this politicisation of India's national security issues pertain to the then opposition parties reaction to India's nuclear weaponisation in 1998, their ill-informed criticisms during the Pakistan aggression in Kargil in 1999 and thereafter and their attitudinal problems to the Indian Army operations against the Pakistan sponsored proxy war in Jammu and Kashmir State.

National security issues have hardly been discussed by political parties during Defence budget debates in Parliament. The parliamentary attendance then presents a sorry spectacle. Yet when grave national crises occur every second politician becomes a master strategist or tactician minus the grasp of the essentials of strategy and the intricacies of military operations and oblivious to the fact that the parliamentarians own strategic incompetence brought about the military aggression in the first place.

India's political leaders need to get together and work out conventions where during a crisis they can discuss the issues away from the glare of publicity and arrive at a consensus on how the Indian nation state has to meet the security challenges that arise.

National Security and Indian Media

The Indian media both print and electronic has developed imperialistic attitudes towards the coverage, analysis and projection of national security issues. Nothing exemplifies this more than the 'Tehelka Tapes' episode. In a bid to make money, national security interests were given a go by this portal. A noble mantle was sought to be worn by depicting it as a crusade against corruption. The media elite including notable editors-in-chief ganged up to support Tehelka not on the grounds of objectivity but for sheer defence of one of their flock. Some Indian journals, indulged in politicising the issues of military commanders performances on the basis of leaked classified documents. They did not even bother to think that such irresponsible journalism not only affects the national security of the country but also the morale of the Indian Armed Forces. It also affects the confidence of the uniformed personnel in the Indian media, who should really strive to be a pillar of the state rather than a money-spinning enterprise of some industrial house, depending on sensationalism for its wider circulation.

India as a nation state is still in the formative stages and many challenges both external and internal threaten its existence and integrity. The Indian media should refrain from applying western templates of journalism as neither the political & strategic context nor the national cohesion as existent in the West is presently obtainable in India.

INDIA'S NUCLEAR PROGRAM: ILLUSORY GAINS AND UNAFFORDABLE RISKS

In May 1998, India conducted five nuclear tests. Even if one were to concede the tests were understandable, the question arises: What did India gain? The short answer, contrary to facile claims of strategic, military or political utility, and cost-effectiveness is: not much.

Unilateral nuclear disarmament is unlikely by any of the nuclear-armed states, including India, and is thus unrealistic as a policy goal. However, a denuclearized world that includes the destruction of India's nuclear stockpile would favorably affect the balance of India's security and other interests like development and social welfare, national and international interests, and material interests and value goals.

Although prospects for nuclear disarmament look dim, especially after the Ukraine crisis, the goal of an eventually denuclearized world is both necessary and feasible. For nuclear peace to hold, deterrence and fail-safe mechanisms must work every single time.

For nuclear Armageddon, deterrence or fail-safe mechanisms need to break down only once. This is not a comforting equation. As long as any one country has nuclear weapons, others will want them. As long as nuclear weapons exist, they will be used again someday by design, miscalculation, rogue launch, human error or system malfunction. And any nuclear war fought by any set of nuclear-armed states could be catastrophic for the whole world.

Nuclear weapons may be sought for (1) compellence, (2) defense, (3) deterrence and/or (4) status.

"Compellence" means the use of coercion to force an adversary to stop or reverse something already being done, or to do something he would not otherwise do. There is no demonstrable instance of a nonnuclear state having been cowed into changing its behavior by the threat of being bombed with nuclear weapons. Indian doctrine, backed by deployment patterns, explicitly eschews any intent to use nuclear weapons as tools of coercion.

It is hard to see any role for India's nuclear armaments as instruments of defense. India's no-first-use doctrine disavows use of nuclear weapons in response to conventional attacks. Nuclear weapons cannot be used for defense by nuclear-armed rivals whose mutual vulnerability to second-strike retaliatory capability guarantees that any escalation through the nuclear threshold would be mutual national suicide.

India's nuclear arsenal offers no defense against a major conventional attack by China, Russia or the U.S. — the only three countries with the capability to do so. As for intent, Russia is a diplomatic ally and friend of long standing. Relations with the U.S. have warmed to a remarkable degree, including a just concluded high-profile visit by Prime Minister Narendra Modi, which was remarkable for the fact that a person denied a U.S. visa from 2005 until May 2014 was hosted to a state dinner by President Barack Obama.

Deepening and broadening bilateral Sino-Indian relations, and cooperation on several major international issues based on converging interests in forums like the group of Brazil, Russia, India, China and South Africa (BRICS), provide considerable substance, texture and ballast to that relationship today. During his recent visit, Chinese President Xi Jinping signed agreements to invest $20 billion to upgrade India's woeful infrastructure.

With nuclear weapons being unusable for defense, their sole operational purpose and role is mutual deterrence. Deterrence stability depends on rational decision-makers being always in office on all sides: a shaky precondition. It depends equally critically on there being no rogue launch, human error or system malfunction: an impossibly high bar. Nuclear weapons have failed to stop wars between nuclear and nonnuclear rivals (Korea, Afghanistan, Falklands, Vietnam, 1991 Persian Gulf War).

To believe in deterrence is to argue that Iran should be encouraged, indeed facilitated in getting the bomb in order to contribute to the peace and stability of the Middle East where presently Israel is the only nuclear-armed state. Good luck and good night.

The subcontinent's history since 1998 gives the lie to the then-hopes and expectations, on both sides of the border, that nuclearization would prove to be a largely stabilizing factor.

Powerful domestic constituencies have grown in both countries to identify multiple threats that justify a matching expansion of a highly elastic nuclear posture. The low-cost, low-risk covert war in the shadow of the subcontinent's nuclearization had three attractions for Pakistan: It would weaken India by raising the human and economic costs of Kashmir's occupation; the fear of nuclear escalation would raise the threshold for cross-border Indian retaliatory raids; and it would help internationalize the Kashmir dispute by highlighting the risk of nuclear escalation.

Pakistan has invested in terrorist groups as part of its unconventional inventory against India. In responding to a terrorist attack, any deliberate escalation by India through the nuclear threshold would be extremely high-risk. The development of tactical missiles and battlefield nuclear weapons by the two sides, whose utility is contingent on proximity to battlefields, multiply the risks. India must also live with the nightmare possibility of jihadists getting their hands on Pakistan's nuclear weapons. While obviously more acute for Pakistan, the threat is grave for India also.

Just what is a "credible minimum deterrent" — India's official doctrine — that would dissuade nuclear blackmail and coercion and permit second-strike nuclear retaliation? China and Pakistan are incommensurate in their national power, strategic frames and military capabilities. The requirements of numbers, reach, deployment patterns and locations, and the distribution between land-based, air-launched and sea-borne platforms, are as mutually incompatible between them. That which is credible toward China cannot be the minimum toward Pakistan, and vice versa.

Few analysts would take issue with the claim that currently nonnuclear-armed Germany has a higher status, weight and clout in Europe and the world than nuclear-armed Britain and France. Nuclear brinkmanship earns North Korea neither prestige, power nor friends; nonnuclear-armed South Korea fares better on all three counts.

India does have a higher international profile today than in 1998. This is despite, not because of, nuclear weapons, and rests in its economic performance and information technology credentials. No serious Indian analyst is likely to claim that Pakistan's profile has risen alongside India's since 1998, despite

Islamabad's more focused efforts on expanding, deepening and broadening its nuclear weapons capability.

If India's economy stutters, its social pathologies intensify and multiply and its political system proves incapable of making and implementing hard decisions. The fact that India has nuclear weapons will add to international unease and worries rather than enhance its global stature and international prestige.

If India's economic future is mortgaged to bad governance rooted in populist politics pursued by corrupt politicians, other countries will return India to the basket of benign neglect while offering ritual but empty praise for its rich civilization and culture. Prime Minister Modi at least seems to get this.

A nuclear catastrophe was averted during the Cold War as much owing to good luck as wise management. The number of times that we have come frighteningly close to nuclear holocaust is simply staggering.

According to one study by a U.S. nuclear weapon laboratory in 1970, more than 1,200 nuclear weapons were involved in accidents from 1950 to 1968 because of security breaches, lost weapons, failed safety mechanisms or accidents resulting from weapons being dropped or crushed in lifts, etc.

In the 1962 Cuban missile crisis, U.S. strategy was based on intelligence that indicated there were no nuclear warheads in Cuba. In fact there were 162 warheads already stationed there and the local Soviet commander had taken them out of storage to deployed positions for use against an American invasion. Intelligence agencies are necessary even in democratic societies to protect us against quotidian threats, for example wannabe terrorists who will discuss targets and tactics on open international phone lines. But it's amazing how often they fail to forewarn us of the big picture like the erection and fall of the Berlin Wall, the end of the Cold War, 9/11, etc.

Recently declassified documents show there was another near-miss in November 1983, when strategic arsenals were far more lethal on both sides. In response to NATO war games exercise Able Archer, which Moscow mistook to be real, the Soviets came close to launching a full-scale nuclear attack against the West under the misapprehension that a NATO nuclear attack was imminent. And the West was blissfully unaware of this at the time.

On Jan. 21, 1961, a 4-megaton bomb (260 times more powerful than the Hiroshima blast) was one ordinary switch away from detonating over North Carolina; the effects would have covered Washington, Baltimore, Philadelphia and even New York. Days after President John F. Kennedy's inauguration, a B-52 bomber on a routine flight went into an uncontrolled spin. Two hydrogen bombs fell loose over Goldsboro, North Carolina. One, assuming it had been deliberately released over an enemy target, began the detonation process. Three of four fail-safe mechanisms failed and only the final, a simple dynamo-technology low-voltage switch, averted what would have been the greatest disaster in U.S. history with millions of lives at risk.

In addition to close calls based on miscalculations and misperceptions and accidental near misses, the nuclear age has left a trail of grave environmental damage. There is also a significant economic cost. Nuclear weapons have not permitted any of the states that have them to buy defense on the cheap.

In terms of opportunity costs, heavy military expenditure amounts to stealing from the poor. India's core expenditure on nuclear weapons are around $4 billion, and the full nuclear costs amount to $5 billion. Yet nuclear weapons do not help to combat India's real threats of Maoist insurgency, terrorism, pandemics, poverty, illiteracy, malnutrition and corruption.

As demonstrated in the 1999 Kargil war, the possession of nuclear weapons by both sides in a conflict does not rule out either an initial military incursion across a disputed border or a conventional military retaliation. But it did dampen a full-scale conventional attack by India in order to avoid escalating to the nuclear threshold. If India is to retain the option of being able to respond to provocations (border skirmishes, incursions and state-sponsored terrorist attacks) with calibrated use of conventional military power, it must invest still more heavily in conventional military capability than would have been required in the absence of a nuclear overhang in the subcontinent.

In a convergence of Indian military-nuclear thinking with international norms, India's military doctrine has begun to emphasize prompt offensive action with division-sized battle groups upon provocation. India's maritime strategy also increasingly emphasizes offensive action with power-projection capability both to the east and west across the Indian Ocean. Indian weapons scientists are working on a successor Agni-VI missile with a 10,000-km range (that is, covering all of China) with a projected test flight date of 2017.

In the absence of an official strategic defense or nuclear posture review, it is hard to discern how India will ensure that a capability meant to deter does not in fact provoke, including additional Chinese assistance to Pakistan's nuclear capabilities. There is the added risk of proliferation to extremist elements through leakage, theft, state collapse and state capture.

Domestically, meanwhile, a nuclear program encourages excessive centralization of political control and obsessive secrecy. Nuclear weapons can lead to the creation of a national security state with a premium on governmental secretiveness, reduced public accountability and increased distance between citizens and government.

Relying on secrecy and obfuscation, a nuclear program undermines democratic accountability and contributes instead to a culture of lies and evasions. Shielding the program from public scrutiny hides the inefficiency, malpractice, mismanagement and dangers — and nuclear technology is unforgiving when things go wrong with grave safety and environmental concerns. Just ask the former residents of Fukushima.

In other words, India is caught in an escalating cycle of increased nuclear and conventional military expenditures with no net gain in defense capability against the most likely threat contingencies. Internationally India has shifted from being a disarmament champion to a nuclear-armed state. While the former was informed by a strategic vision, the latter has been ad hoc and episodic.

As a disarmament crusader, India was the foremost critic of the Non-Proliferation Treaty-centered "nuclear apartheid" regime.

As a non-NPT nuclear-armed state, India has been gradually integrating with the global nuclear orders while hypocritically preaching nuclear abstinence to others like North Korea and Iran. Nuclear weapons confer neither power, prestige nor influence. South Asia's insecurity dilemma has intensified since May 1998.

India still lacks effective deterrent capability against China. History and geography make the India-Pakistan nuclear equation less stable than Cold War U.S.-Soviet deterrence. Nuclear weapons failed to deter Pakistani infiltration and Indian retaliation and escalation in the two-month Kargil war in 1999, and a year-long full military mobilization by both in 2002. Nuclear weapons are not going to help India combat internal insurgency, cross-border terrorism or parasitical corruption.

Nor can nuclear weapons help to solve any of the real problems of poverty, illiteracy and malnutrition. And they are irrelevant to India's security needs against any other country.

While not advocating unilateral nuclear disarmament, such a conclusion should at least encourage India to be a champion of phased, regulated and verifiable global nuclear disarmament governed by a nondiscriminatory nuclear weapons convention.

This would be in keeping with: the legacy of Indian initiatives on nuclear arms control and disarmament, including the Rajiv Gandhi Action Plan of 1988; the fact that India was the most reluctant nuclear weapons possessor of all the nine nuclear-armed states; and its official nuclear doctrine that lists global nuclear disarmament as a national security objective.

With more than 90 percent of the global nuclear weapons arsenal, the U.S. and Russia bear primary and heaviest responsibility for nuclear disarmament. That is no reason for the other nuclear powers to abdicate their responsibility commensurate with their status as nuclear weapons possessor states.

9

Pakistan and Weapons of Mass Destruction

Pakistan began focusing on nuclear weapons development in January 1972 under the leadership of Prime Minister Zulfiqar Ali Bhutto, who delegated the program to the Chairman of PAEC Munir Ahmad Khan. In 1976, Abdul Qadeer Khan also joined the nuclear weapons program, and, with Zahid Ali Akbar, headed the *Kahuta Project*, while the rest of the program being run in PAEC and comprising over twenty laboratories and projects was headed by nuclear engineer, Munir Ahmad Khan. This program would reach fruition under President General Muhammad Zia-ul-Haq, then-Chief of Army Staff.

Pakistan's nuclear weapons development was in response to neighboring India's development of its nuclear programme. Bhutto called a meeting of senior scientists and engineers on 20 January 1972, in Multan, which came to known as "*Multan meeting*". Bhutto was the main architect of this programme, and it was here that Bhutto orchestrated nuclear weapons programme and rallied Pakistan's academic scientists to build the atomic bomb for national survival.

At the Multan meeting, Bhutto also appointed Munir Ahmad Khan as chairman ofPakistan Atomic Energy Commission (PAEC), who, until then, had been working as Director at the nuclear power and Reactor Division of the International Atomic Energy Agency (IAEA), in Vienna, Austria. In December 1972, Abdus Salam led the establishment of Theoretical Physics Group (TPG) as he called scientists working at ICTP to report to Munir Ahmad Khan. This marked the beginning of Pakistan's pursuit of nuclear deterrence capability. Following India's surprise nuclear test, codenamed*Smiling Buddha* in 1974, the first confirmed nuclear test by a nation outside the permanent five members of the United Nations Security Council, the goal to develop nuclear weapons received considerable impetus.

Finally, on 28 May 1998, a few weeks after India's second nuclear test (*Operation Shakti*), Pakistan detonated five nuclear devices in the Ras Koh Hills in the Chagai district, Balochistan. This operation was named *Chagai-I* by Pakistan, the underground iron-steel tunnel having been long-constructed by provincial martial law administrator General Rahimuddin Khan during the 1980s. The last test of Pakistan was conducted at the sandy Kharan Desert under the codename *Chagai-II*, also in Balochistan, on 30 May 1998. Pakistan's fissile material production takes place at Nilore, Kahuta, and Khushab/Jauharabad, where weapons-grade plutonium is refined. Pakistan thus became the seventh country in the world to successfully develop and test nuclear weapons.

HISTORY OF PAKISTAN'S NUCLEAR WEAPONS PROGRAM

Nuclear Development and Non-weapon Policy

The uneasy relationships with India, Afghanistan, the former Soviet Union, and the energy shortage explains its motivation to become a nuclear power as part of its defence and energy strategies. On 8 December 1953, Pakistan media welcomed the U.S.Atoms for Peace initiatives, followed by the establishment of Pakistan Atomic Energy Commission in 1956. In 1953, Foreign minister Sir Zafarullah Khan publicly stated that "Pakistan does not have a policy towards the atom bombs". Following the announcement, on 11 August 1955, the United States and Pakistan reached an understanding concerning the peaceful and industrial use of nuclear energy which also includes a $350,000 worth pool-type reactor. Before 1971, Pakistan's nuclear development was peaceful but an effective deterrent against India, as Benazir Bhutto maintained in 1995. Pakistan followed a strict non-nuclear weapon policy from 1956 until 1971, and major proposals were made in the 1960s by several officials and senior scientists, but PAEC under its chairman Ishrat Hussain Usmani made no efforts to acquire nuclear fuel cycle for the purposes of active nuclear weapons programme.

After the 1965 Indo-Pakistan war, Foreign minister (later Prime minister) Zulfikar Ali Bhutto aggressively began the advocating the option of "nuclear weapons programmes" but such attempts were dismissed by Finance minister Muhammad Shoaib and chairman I.H. Usmani. Pakistani scientists and engineers' working at IAEA became aware of advancing Indian nuclear program towards making the bombs.

Therefore, In October 1965, Munir Khan, director at the Nuclear Power and Reactor Division of the International Atomic Energy Agency (IAEA), met with Bhutto on emergency basis in Vienna, revealing the facts about the Indian nuclear programme and a weapon production facility in Trombay. At this meeting Munir Khan concluded: "a (nuclear) India would further undermine and threaten Pakistan's security, and for her survival, Pakistan needed a nuclear deterrent...".

Understanding the sensitivity of the issue, Bhutto arranged a meeting with President Ayub Khan 11 December 1965 at Dorchester Hotel in London. Munir Khan pointed out to the President that Pakistan must acquire the necessary facilities that would give the country a nuclear weapon capability, which were available free of safeguards and at an affordable cost, and there were no restrictions on nuclear technology, that it was freely available, and that India was moving forward in deploying it, as Munir Khan maintained. When asked about the economics of such programme, Munir Ahmad Khan estimated the cost of nuclear technology at that time. Because things were less expensive, the then costs were not more than US$150 million. After hearing the proposal President Ayub Khan swiftly denied the proposal, saying that Pakistan was too poor to spend that much money and that, if Pakistan ever needed the atomic bomb, it could somehow acquire it off the shelf.

Although Pakistan began the development of nuclear weapons in 1972, Pakistan responded to India's 1974 nuclear test with a number of proposals toprevent a nuclear competition in South Asia. On many different occasions, India rejected the offer.

Nuclear Energy Development

Pakistan's nuclear energy programme was established and started in 1956 following the establishment of PAEC. Pakistan became a participant in U.S. President Eisenhower's "Atoms for Peace Program." PAEC's first chairman was Dr. Nazir Ahmad. In 1961, the PAEC set up a Mineral Center at Lahore and a similar multidisciplinary Center was set up in Dhaka, in the then East Pakistan. With these two centres, the basic research work started.

The first thing that was to be undertaken was the search for uranium. This continued for about three years from 1960 to 1963. Uranium deposits were discovered in the Dera Ghazi Khan district, and the first-ever national award was given to the PAEC. Mining of uranium began in the same year. Dr. Abdus Salam and Dr. Ishrat Hussain Usmani also sent a large number of scientists to pursue doctorate degrees in the field of nuclear technology and nuclear reactor technology. In December 1965, then-foreign minister Zulfikar Ali Bhutto visited Vienna where he met IAEA nuclear engineer, Munir Ahmad Khan. At a Vienna meeting on December, Khan informed Bhutto about the status of Indian nuclear program.

The next landmark under Dr. Abdus Salam was the establishment of PINSTECH – Pakistan Institute of Nuclear Science and Technology, at Nilore near Islamabad. The principal facility there was a 5MW research reactor, commissioned in 1965 and consisting of the PARR-I, which was upgraded to 10 MWe by Nuclear Engineering Division under Munir Ahmad Khan in 1990. A second Atomic Research Reactor, known as PARR-II, was a Pool-type, light-water, 27–30 kWe, training reactor that went critical in 1989 under Munir Ahmad Khan.

The PARR-II reactor was built and provided by PAEC under the IAEA safeguards as IAEA had funded this mega project. The PARR-I reactor was, under the agreement signed by PAEC and ANL, provided by the U.S. Government in 1965, and scientists from PAEC and ANL had led the construction. Canada build

Pakistan's first civil-purpose nuclear power plant. The Ayub Khan Military Government made then-science advisors to the Government Abdus Salam as the head of the IAEA delegation. Abdus Salam began lobbying for commercial nuclear power plants, and tirelessly advocated for nuclear power in Pakistan. In 1965, Salam's efforts finally paid off, and a Canadian firm signed a deal to provide 137MWe CANDU reactor in Paradise Point, Karachi. The construction began in 1966 as PAEC its general contractor as GE Canada provided nuclear materials and financial assistance. Its project director was Parvez Butt, a nuclear engineer, and its construction completed in 1972. Known as*KANUPP-I*, it was inaugurated by Zulfikar Ali Bhutto as President, and began its operations in November 1972. Currently, Pakistan Government is planning to build another 400MWe commercial nuclear power plant. Having known as *KANUPP-II*, the PAEC completed its feasibility studies in 2009. However, the work is put on hold since 2009.

The PAEC in 1970 began work on a pilot-scale plant at Dera Ghazi Khan for the concentration of uranium ores. The plant had a capacity of 10,000 pounds a day. In 1989, Munir Ahmad Khan signed a nuclear cooperation deal and, since 2000, Pakistan has been developing two more nuclear power plants with an agreement signed with China. Both these plants are of 300 MW capacity and are being built at Chashma city of Punjab province. The first of these, *CHASNUPP-I*, began producing electricity in 2000, and 'CHASNUPP-II', began its operation in fall of 2011. In 2011, the board of governors of International Atomic Energy Agency gave approval of Sino-Pak Nuclear Deal, allowing Pakistan legally to build the 300-MW 'CHASNUPP-III' and 'CHASNUPP-VI' reactors.

Development of Nuclear Weapons

The Indo-Pakistani War of 1971 was a crushing defeat for Pakistan, which led to Pakistan losing roughly 56,000 square miles (150,000 km^2) of territory as well as losing millions of its citizens to the newly created state of Bangladesh. It was a psychological setback for Pakistanis; Pakistan had lost its geopolitical, strategic, and economic influence in South Asia. Furthermore, Pakistan had failed to gather any significant material support or assistance from its key allies, the United States and the People's Republic of China. Isolated internationally, Pakistan seemed to be in great mortal danger and felt that it could rely on no one but itself. At United Nations Security Council meeting, Prime Minister Zulfiqar Ali Bhutto drew comparisons with the Treaty of Versailles, which Germany was forced to sign in 1919. There, Bhutto vowed never to allow a repeat. Bhutto was "obsessed" with India's nuclear program, and that is why Bhutto immediately came up with the idea of obtaining nuclear weapons to prevent Pakistan from signing another 'Treaty of Versailles' as it did in 1971.

In 1969, after a long negotiation, the United Kingdom Atomic Energy Authority (UKAEA) signed a formal agreement to supply Pakistan with a nuclear fuel reprocessing plant capable of extracting 360 g of weapons-grade plutonium annually. The PAEC selected a team five senior scientists, including geophysicist Dr. Ahsan Mubarak, were sent to Sellafield to receive technical training. Later, the team under Ahsan Mubarak advised the government not to acquire the whole reprocessing plant but key parts important to building the weapons, while the plant would be built indigenously.

At the Multan meeting on 20 January 1972, Bhutto stated, "What Raziuddin Siddiqui, a Pakistani, contributed for the United States during the Manhattan Project, could also be done by scientists in Pakistan, for their own people." Raziuddin Siddiqui was a Pakistani theoretical physicist who, in the early 1940s, worked on both the British nuclear program and the U.S. nuclear program. Although a few Pakistanis who worked on the Manhattan Project were also willing to return and do the same for their native Pakistan, Prime Minister Bhutto still needed to recruit and bring in other Pakistani nuclear scientists and engineers who never worked in the United States. This is where Dr. Abdul Qadeer Khan, a German-educated metallurgical engineer, came into the picture. Some of the initial funding came from oil-rich Arab states, particularly Saudi Arabia.

In later years, some funding for the continuation of the nuclear development programme came from the large British

Pakistani population. In December 1972, the science advisor to the President, Dr. Abdus Salam, had called theoretical physicists from the ICTP to report of Munir Ahmad Khan, Chairman of Pakistan Atomic Energy Commission. This marked the beginning of the "Theoretical Physics Group" (TPG). Later, Pakistani theoretical physicists at Institute of Theoretical Physics of Quaid-e-Azam University also joined the TPG headed by Salam. The TPG, which directly reported to Abdus Salam in PAEC, was assigned to do research in the development of nuclear weapon devices, and conduct mathematical calculations on complex hydrodynamical phenomenons and the fast neutron calculations. Professor Salam also had done the groundbreaking work of the "Theoretical Physics Group", which was initially headed by Salam until in 1974 when he left the country in protest. The TPG division at PAEC closely collaborated and completed its physics and mathematical calculations on fast-neutron calculations with the Mathematics Group led by Raziuddin Siddiqui and others, a division which contained the pure mathematicians. On other side, Munir Ahmad Khan began to work on indigenous development of nuclear fuel cycle and the weapons programme. Munir Ahmad Khan, with his lifelong friend Abdus Salam, had done a groundbreaking work in the nuclear development, and after Salam's departure from Pakistan, scientists and engineers who were researching under Salam, began to report to directly to Munir Ahmad Khan. In 1974, Munir Ahmad Khan, days after *Operation Smiling Buddha*, launched the extensive plutonium reprocessing and uranium enrichment programme, and the research facilities were expanded throughout the country.

In 1965, amidst skirmishes that led up to the Indo-Pakistan War of 1965, Zulfikar Ali Bhutto announced:

"If India builds the bomb, we will eat grass and leaves for a thousand years, even go hungry, but we will get one of our own. The Christians have the bomb, the Jews have the bomb and now the Hindus have the bomb. Why not the Muslims too have the bomb? "

In 1983, Khan was convicted in absentia by the Court of Amsterdam for stealing the blueprints, though the conviction was overturned on a legal technicality. A. Q. Khan then established a proliferation network through Dubai to smuggle URENCO nuclear technology to Khan Research Laboratories. He then established Pakistan's gas-centrifuge program based on the URENCO's Zippe-type centrifuge.

Through the late 1970s, Pakistan's program acquired sensitive uranium enrichment technology and expertise. The 1975 arrival of Dr. Abdul Qadeer Khan considerably advanced these efforts. Dr. Khan was a German-trained metallurgist who brought with him knowledge of gas centrifuge technologies that he had acquired through his position at the classified URENCO uranium enrichment plant in the Netherlands. He was put in charge of building, equipping and operating Pakistan's Kahuta facility, which was established in 1976. Under Khan's direction, Pakistan employed an extensive clandestine network to obtain the necessary materials and technology for its developing uranium enrichment capabilities.

"It took only two weeks and three days for Pakistan to master the field... and (detonate) the nuclear devices of our own..." — Benazir Bhutto, on first nuclear tests on May 1998,

A new directorate, known as Directorate of Technical Development (DTD) under Dr. Zaman Sheikh and Hafeez Qureshi, was established in March 1974 by Munir Ahmad Khan. The DTD was tasked to manufacture chemicalexplosive lenses, trigger mechanism, and tampers used in atomic weapon. The DTD was later charged with testing Pakistan's first implosion design in 1978, which was later improved and tested on 11 March 1983 when PAEC carried out Pakistan's first successful cold test of a nuclear device, codename *Kirana-I*. Between 1983 and 1990, PAEC carried out 24 more cold tests of various nuclear weapon designs. DTD had also manufactured a miniaturised weapon design by 1987 that could be delivered by all Pakistan Air Force fighter aircraft.

Dr Ishrat Hussain Usmani's contribution to the nuclear energy programme is also fundamental to the development of atomic energy for civilian purposes as he, with efforts led by Salam, established PINSTECH, that subsequently developed into Pakistan's premier nuclear research institution. In addition to sending hundreds of young Pakistanis abroad for training, he laid the foundations of the Muslim world's first nuclear power reactor KANUPP, which was inaugurated by Munir Ahmad Khan in 1972. Thus, Usmani laid solid groundwork for the civilian nuclear programme. Scientists and engineers under Munir Ahmad Khan developed the nuclear capability for Pakistan within the early 1980s, and under his leadership the PAEC had carried a cold test of nuclear device at Kirana Hills, evidently made from non-weaponized plutonium. The former chairman of the PAEC, Munir Ahmad Khan, was credited as one of the pioneers of Pakistan's atomic bomb by a study from the International Institute for Strategic Studies (IISS), London's dossier on Pakistan's nuclear weapons program.

Policy

Pakistan acceded to the Geneva Protocol on 15 April 1960. As for its Biological warfare capability, Pakistan is not widely suspected of either producing biological weapons or having an offensive biological programme. However, the country is reported to have well developed bio-technological facilities and laboratories, devoted entirely to the medical research and applied healthcare science. In 1972, Pakistan signed and ratified the Biological and Toxin Weapons Convention (BTWC) in 1974. Since then Pakistan has been a vocal and staunch supporter for the success of the BTWC. During the various BTWC Review Conferences, Pakistan's representatives have urged more robust participation from state signatories, invited new states to join the treaty, and, as part of the non-aligned group of countries, have made the case for guarantees for states' rights to engage in peaceful exchanges of biological and toxin materials for purposes of scientific research.

Pakistan is not known to have an offensive chemical weapons programme, and in 1993 Pakistan signed and ratified the Chemical Weapons Convention (CWC), and has committed itself to refrain from developing, manufacturing, stockpiling, or using chemical weapons.

Pakistan is not a party to the Non-Proliferation Treaty (NPT) and is not bound by any of its provisions. In 1999, Prime

Ministers Nawaz Sharif of Pakistan and Atal Bihari Vajpayee of India signed the *Lahore Declaration,* agreeing to a bilateral moratorium on further nuclear testing. This initiative was taken a year after both countries had publicly tested nuclear weapons.

Since the early 1980s, Pakistan's nuclear proliferation activities have not been without controversy. However, since the arrest of Abdul Qadeer Khan, the government has taken concrete steps to ensure that Nuclear proliferation is not repeated and have assured the IAEA about the transparency of Pakistan's upcoming Chashma Nuclear Power Complexseries of Nuclear Power Plants. In November 2006, The International Atomic Energy Agency Board of Governors approved an agreement with the Pakistan Atomic Energy Commission to apply safeguards to new nuclear power plants to be built in the country with Chinese assistance.

Protections

U.S. Secretary of State Hillary Rodham Clinton informed that Pakistan has dispersed its nuclear weapons throughout the country, increasing the security so that they could not fall into terrorist hands. Her comments came as new satellite images released by the ISI suggested Pakistan is increasing its capacity to produce plutonium, a fuel for atomic bombs. The institute has also claimed that Pakistan has built two more nuclear reactors at Khoshab increasing the number of plutonium producing reactors to three.

In May 2009, during the anniversary of Pakistan's first nuclear weapons test, former Prime Minister of Pakistan Nawaz Sharif claimed that Pakistan's nuclear security is the strongest in the world. According to Dr. Abdul Qadeer Khan, Pakistan's nuclear safety program and nuclear security program is the strongest program in the world and there is no such capability in any other country for radical elements to steal or possess nuclear weapons.

Modernisation and Expansion

Pakistan is increasing its capacity to produce plutonium at its Khushab nuclear facility, a Washington-based science think tank has reported. The sixth nuclear test (codename: Chagai-II) on 30 May 1998, at Kharan was a quiet successful test of a sophisticated, compact, but "powerful plutonium bomb" designed to be carried by aircraft, vessels, and missiles. The Pakistanis are believed to be spiking their plutonium based nuclear weapons with tritium. Only a few grams of tritium can result in an increase of the explosive yield by 300% to 400%." Citing new satellite images of the facility, the Institute for Science and International Security (ISIS) said the imagery suggests construction of the second Khushab reactor is "likely finished and that the roof beams are being placed on top of the third Khushab reactor hall". A third and a fourth reactor and ancillary buildings are observed to be under construction at the Khushab site.

In an opinion published in *The Hindu*, former Indian Foreign Secretary Shyam Saran wrote that Pakistan's expanding nuclear capability is "no longer driven solely by its oft-cited fears of India" but by the "paranoia about U.S. attacks on its strategic assets. Noting recent changes in Pakistan's nuclear doctrine, Saran said "the Pakistan Military andcivilian elite is convinced that the United States has also become a dangerous adversary, which seeks to disable, disarm or take forcible possession of Pakistan's nuclear arsenals and its status as nuclear power."

As of 2014, Pakistan has been reportedly developing smaller, more tactical nuclear weapons for potential use on the battlefield exclusively.

This is consistent with earlier statements from a meeting of the National Command Authority (which directs nuclear policy and development) saying Pakistan is developing "a full-spectrum deterrence capability to deter all forms of aggression."

Bilateral Arms Control Proposals and Confidence Building Measures

Pakistan has over the years proposed a number of bilateral or regional non-proliferation steps to India, including:

- A joint Indo-Pakistan declaration renouncing the acquisition or manufacture of nuclear weapons, in 1978.
- South Asian Nuclear Weapons Free Zone, in 1978.
- Mutual inspections by India and Pakistan of each other's nuclear facilities, in 1979.

- Simultaneous adherence to the NPT by India and Pakistan, in 1979.
- A bilateral or regional nuclear test-ban treaty, in 1987.
- A South Asia Zero-Missile Zone, in 1994.

India rejected all six proposals.

However, India and Pakistan reached three bilateral agreements on nuclear issues. In 1989, they agreed not to attack each other's nuclear facilities. Since then they have been regularly exchanging lists of nuclear facilities on 1 January of each year. Another bilateral agreement was signed in March 2005 where both nations would alert the other on ballistic missile tests. In June 2004, the two countries signed an agreement to set up and maintain a hotline to warn each other of any accident that could be mistaken for a nuclear attack. These were deemed essential risk reduction measures in view of the seemingly unending state of misgiving and tension between the two countries, and the extremely short response time available to them to any perceived attack. None of these agreements limits the nuclear weapons programs of either country in any way.

Disarmament Policy

Pakistan has blocked negotiation of a Fissile Material Cutoff Treaty as it continues to produce fissile material for weapons. In a recent statement at the Conference on Disarmament, Pakistan laid out its nuclear disarmament policy and what it sees as the proper goals and requirements for meaningful negotiations:

- A commitment by all states to complete verifiable nuclear disarmament;
- Eliminate the discrimination in the current non-proliferation regime;
- Normalize the relationship of the three ex-NPT nuclear weapon states with those who are NPT signatories;
- Address new issues like access to weapons of mass destruction by non-state actors;
- Non-discriminatory rules ensuring every state's right to peaceful uses of nuclear energy;

- Universal, non-discriminatory and legally binding negative security assurances to non-nuclear weapon states;
- A need to address the issue of missiles, including development and deployment of Anti-ballistic missile systems;
- Strengthen existing international instruments to prevent the militarisation of outer space, including development of ASATs;
- Tackle the growth in armed forces and the accumulation and sophistication of conventional tactical weapons.
- Revitalise the UN disarmament machinery to address international security, disarmament and proliferation challenges.

Pakistan has repeatedly stressed at international forums like the Conference on Disarmament that it will give up its nuclear weapons only when other nuclear armed states do so, and when disarmament is universal and verifiable. It rejects any unilateral disarmament on its part.

INFRASTRUCTURE

Uranium Infrastructure

Pakistan's uranium infrastructure is based on the use of gas centrifuges to produce Highly-Enriched Uranium (HEU) at the Khan Research Laboratories (KRL) at Kahuta. Responding to India's nuclear test In 1974, Munir Khan launched the uranium program, codename *Project-706* under the aegis of the PAEC. Physical chemist, dr. Khalil Qureshi, did the most of the calculation as the member of the uranium division at PAEC, which undertook research on several methods of enrichment, including gaseous diffusion, jet nozzle and laser enrichment techniques, as well as centrifuges. Abdul Qadeer Khan officially joined this program in 1976, bringing with him centrifuge designs he mastered inURENCO, the Dutch firm where he had worked as a senior scientist. Later, the government separated the program from PAEC and moved the program to Engineering Research Laboratories (ERL), with A.Q. Khan as its senior scientist. To acquire the necessary equipment and material for this program, Khan developed an illicit procurement network, which was later used to provide enrichment technology to Libya, North Korea, and Iran. The uranium program proved to be a difficult, challenging and most enduring approach.

Commenting on the difficulty, one mathematician who worked with A.Q. Khan quoted in the book *"Eating grass"* that "hydrodynamical problem in centrifuge was simply stated, but extremely difficult to evaluate, not only in order of magnitude but in detailing also." Many of Khan's fellow theorists were unsure about the feasibility of the enriched uranium on time despite A.Q. Khan's strong advocacy. One scientist recalled his memories in *Eating Grass*: "No one in the world has used the [gas] centrifuge method to produce military-grade uranium.... This was not going to work. He [A.Q. Khan] was simply wasting time." Despite A.Q. Khan had difficulty getting his peers listening to him, Khan aggressively continued his research and the program was made feasible by Pakistan in shortest time possible. His efforts won him the praise from country's elite politicians and the military science circles, and he was now debuted as the "father of the uranium" bomb. On 28 May 1998, it was the KRL's HEU that ultimately created the nuclear chain reaction which led the successful detonated of boosted fission devices in a scientific experiment codenamed as: Chagai-I.

Plutonium Infrastructure

As opposed to uranium, the parallel plutonium programme is indigenous, locally developed and culminated under the scientific directorship of PAEC chairman Munir Ahmad Khan. Since 1972, earlier efforts were directed towards plutonium and necessary infrastructure was built by Bhutto as early as the 1970s. Contrary to popular perception, Pakistan did not forego or abandon the plutonium program and pursued it along with the uranium route. Despite many setbacks and international embargo, PAEC continued its research on plutonium and created a separated electromagnetic isotope separation program alongside the enrichment program, under Dr. G D Allam, a theoretical physicist.

Towards the end of the 1970s, the PAEC began to pursue Plutonium production capabilities. Consequently Pakistan built the 40–50 MW (megawatt, thermal) Khushab Reactor Complex at Joharabad, and in April 1998, Pakistan announced that the nuclear reactor was operational.

The Khushab reactor project was initiated in 1986 by Munir Khan, who informed the world that the reactor was totally indigenous, i.e. that it was designed and built by Pakistani scientists and engineers.

Various Pakistani industries contributed in 82% of the reactor's construction. The Project-Director for this project was Sultan Bashiruddin Mahmood. According to public statements made by the U.S. Government officials, this heavy-water reactor can produce up to 8 to 10 kg of plutonium per year with increase in the production by the development of newer facilities, sufficient for at least one nuclear weapon. The reactor could also produce H^3 if it were loaded with Li^6, although this is unnecessary for the purposes of nuclear weapons, because modern nuclear weapon designs use ^6Li directly. According to J. Cirincione of Carnegie Endowment for International Peace, Khushab's Plutonium production capacity has allowed Pakistan to develop lighter nuclear warheads that would be easier to deliver to any place in the range of the ballistic missiles.

The Plutonium electromagnetic separation takes place at the *New Laboratories*, a reprocessing plant, which was completed by 1981 by PAEC and is next to the Pakistan Institute of Nuclear Science and Technology (PINSTECH) near Islamabad, which is not subject to IAEA inspections and safeguards.

In late 2006, the Institute for Science and International Security released intelligence reports and imagery showing the construction of a new plutonium reactor at the Khushab nuclear site. The reactor is deemed to be large enough to produce enough plutonium to facilitate the creation of as many as "40 to 50 nuclear weapons a year." The*New York Times* carried the story with the insight that this would be Pakistan's third plutonium reactor, signalling a shift to dual-stream development, with Plutonium-based devices supplementing the nation's existing HEU stream to atomic warheads. On 30 May 1998, Pakistan proved its plutonium capability in a scientific experiment and sixth nuclear test: codename Chagai-II.

Stockpile

Estimates of Pakistan's stockpile of nuclear warheads vary. The most recent analysis, published in the Bulletin of the Atomic Scientists in 2010, estimates that Pakistan has 70–90 nuclear warheads. In 2001, the U.S.-based Natural Resources Defense Council (NRDC) estimated that Pakistan had built 24–48 HEU-based nuclear warheads with HEU reserves for 30–52 additional warheads. In 2003, the U.S. Navy Center for Contemporary Conflict estimated that Pakistan possessed between 35 and 95 nuclear warheads, with a median of 60. In 2003, the Carnegie Endowment for International Peace estimated a stockpile of approximately 50 weapons. By contrast, in 2000, U.S. military and intelligence sources estimated that Pakistan's nuclear arsenal may be as large as 100 warheads.

The actual size of Pakistan's nuclear stockpile is hard for experts to gauge owing to the extreme secrecy which surrounds the program in Pakistan. However, in 2007, retired Pakistan Army's Brigadier-General Feroz Khan, previously second in command at the Strategic Arms Division of Pakistans' Military told a Pakistani newspaper that Pakistan had "about 80 to 120 genuine warheads."

Pakistan tested plutonium capability in the sixth nuclear test, codename Chagai-II, on 30 May 1998 at Kharan Desert. The critical mass of a bare mass sphere of 90% enriched uranium-235 is 52 kg. Correspondingly, the critical mass of a bare mass sphere of plutonium-239 is 8–10 kg. The bomb that destroyed Hiroshima used 60 kg of U-235 while the Nagasaki Pu bomb used only 6 kg of Pu-239. Since all Pakistani bomb designs are implosion-type weapons, they will typically use between 15–25 kg of U-235 for their cores. Reducing the amount of U-235 in cores from 60 kg in gun-type devices to 25 kg in implosion devices is only possible by using good neutron reflector/tamper material such as beryllium metal, which increases the weight of the bomb. And the uranium, like plutonium, is only usable in the core of a bomb in metallic form.

However, only 2–4 kg of plutonium is needed for the same device that would need 20–25 kg of U-235. Additionally, a few grams of tritium (a by-product of plutonium production reactors and thermonuclear fuel) can increase the overall yield of the bombs by a factor of three to four. "The sixth Pakistan nuclear test, codename Chagai-II, (30 May 1998) at Kharan Desert was a successful test of a sophisticated, compact, but powerful bomb designed to be carried by missiles. A whole range and variety of weapons using Pu-239 can be easily built, both for aircraft delivery and especially for missiles (in which U-235 cannot be used). So if Pakistan wants to be a nuclear power with an operational weapon capability, both first and second strike, based on assured strike platforms like ballistic and cruise missiles (unlike aircraft), the only solution is with plutonium, which has been the first choice of every country that built a nuclear arsenal.

As for Pakistan's plutonium capability, it has always been there, from the early 1970s onwards. However, there were only two logistic problems faced by PAEC. One was that Pakistan did not want to be an irresponsible state and the PAEC did not divert spent fuel from the safeguarded KANUPP for reprocessing at the New Labs. This was enough to build a whole arsenal of nuclear weapons straight away. The PAEC built its own plutonium and tritium production reactor at Khushab, known as Khushab-I reactor, beginning in 1985. The second one was allocation of resources.

Ultra-centrifugation for obtaining U-235 cannot be done simply by putting natural uranium through the centrifuges. It requires the complete mastery over the front end of the nuclear fuel cycle, beginning at uranium mining and refining, production of uranium ore or yellow cake, conversion of ore into uranium dioxide (UO2) (which is used to make nuclear fuel for natural uranium reactors like Khushab and KANUPP), conversion of UO_2 into uranium tetrafluoride (UF4) and then into the feedstock for enrichment (UF6).

The complete mastery of fluorine chemistry and production of highly toxic and corrosive hydrofluoric acid and other fluorine compounds is required. The UF_6 is pumped into the centrifuges for enrichment. The process is then repeated in reverse until UF_4 is produced, leading to the production of uranium metal, the form in which U-235 is used in a bomb.

It is estimated that there are approximately 10,000–20,000 centrifuges in Kahuta. This means that with P2 machines, they would be producing between 75–100 kg of HEU since 1986, when full production of weapons-grade HEU began. Also the production of HEU was voluntarily capped by Pakistan between 1991 and 1997, and the five nuclear tests of 28 May 1998 also consumed HEU. So it is safe to assume that between 1986 and 2005 (prior to the 2005 earthquake), KRL produced 1500 kg of HEU. Accounting for losses in the production of weapons, it can be assumed that each weapon would need 20 kg of HEU; sufficient for 75 bombs as in 2005.

Pakistan's first nuclear tests were made in May 1998, when six warheads were tested under codename Chagai-I and Chagai-II. It is reported that the yields from these tests were 12 kt, 30 to 36 kt and four low-yield (below 1 kt) tests. From these tests Pakistan can be estimated to have developed operational warheads of 20 to 25 kt and 150 kt in the shape of low weight compact designs and may have 300–500 kt large-size warheads. The low-yield weapons are probably in nuclear bombs carried on fighter-bombers such as the Dassault Mirage III and fitted to Pakistan's short-range ballistic missiles, while the higher-yield warheads are probably fitted to the Shaheen series and Ghauri series ballistic missiles.

Second Strike Capability

According to a U.S. congressional report, Pakistan has addressed issues of survivability in a possible nuclear conflict through second strike capability. Pakistan has been dealing with efforts to develop new weapons and at the same time, have a strategy for surviving a nuclear war. Pakistan has built hard and deeply buried storage and launch facilities to retain a second strike capability in a nuclear war. In January 2000, two years past after the atomic tests, U.S. intelligence officials stated that previous intelligence estimates "overstated the capabilities of India's homegrown arsenal and understate those of Pakistan". The United States Central Command commander, General Anthony Zinni, a friend of Musharraf, told the NBC that longtime assumptions, that "India had an edge in the South Asian strategic balance of power, were questionable at best. Don't assume that the Pakistan's nuclear capability is inferior to the Indians", General Zinni quoted to NBC.

It was confirmed that Pakistan has built Soviet-style road-mobile missiles, state-of-the-art air defences around strategic sites, and other concealment measures. In 1998, Pakistan had 'at least six secret locations' and since then it is believed Pakistan may have many more such secret sites. In 2008, the United States admitted that it did not know where all of Pakistan's nuclear sites are located.

MIRV Capability

Pakistani engineers are also said to be in the advance stages of developing MIRV technology for its missiles. This would allow the military to fit several warheads on the same ballistic missile and then launch them at separate targets.

Personnel

In 2010, Russian foreign ministry official Yuriy Korolev stated that there are somewhere between 120,000 to 130,000 people directly involved in Pakistan's nuclear and missile programs, a figure considered extremely large for a developing country.

Allegations of Foreign Assistance

Historically, the People's Republic of China (PRC) has been repeatedly charged with allegedly transferring missile and related materials to Pakistan. Despite China strongly dismissing the charges and accusations, the United States alleged China to have played a major role in the establishment of Pakistan's atomic bomb development infrastructure. There are also unofficial reports in Western media that the nuclear weapon technology and the weapon-grade enriched uranium was transferred to Pakistan by China. China has consistently maintained that it has not sold any weapon parts or components to Pakistan or anyone else. On August 2001, it was reported that U.S. officials confronted China numerous times over this issue and pointed out "rather bluntly" to Chinese officials that the evidences from intelligence sources was "powerful." But they had been rebuffed by the Chinese, who have retorted by referring to the U.S. support for Taiwan's military build-up which Beijing says is directed against it.

The former U.S. officials have also disclosed that China had allegedly transferred technology to Pakistan and conducting putative test for it in 1980. However, senior scientists and officials strongly dismissed the U.S. disclosure, and in 1998 interview given to Kamran Khan, Abdul Qadeer Khan maintained to the fact that, "due to its sensitivity, no country allows another country to use their tests site to explode the devices," although the UK conducted such tests in Australia and the United States.

His statement was also traced by Samar Mubarakmand who acknowledged that cold tests were carried out, under codename *Kirana-I*, in a test site which was built by the Corps of Engineers under the guidance of the PAEC. According to a 2001 Department of Defense report, China has supplied Pakistan with nuclear materials and has provided critical technical assistance in the construction of Pakistan's nuclear weapons development facilities, in violation of the Nuclear Non-Proliferation Treaty, of which China is a signatory. In 2001 visit toIndia, the Chairman of the Standing Committee of the National People's Congress Li Peng rejected all the accusations against China to Indian media and strongly maintained on the ground that "his country was not giving any nuclear arms to Pakistan nor transferring related-technology to it." Talking to a media correspondents and Indian parliamentarians, Li Peng frankly quoted: "We do not help Pakistan in its atomic bomb projects. Pakistan is a friendly country with whom we have good economic and political relations."

In 1986, it was reported that both countries have signed a mutual treaty of peaceful use of civil nuclear technology agreement in which China would supply Pakistan a civil-purpose nuclear power plant. A grand ceremony was held in Beijing where Pakistan's then-Foreign Minister Yakub Khan signed on behalf of Pakistan in the presence of Munir Khan and Chinese Prime Minister. Therefore, in 1989, Pakistan reached agreement with China for the supply of the 300-MW commercial *CHASHNUPP-1* nuclear power plant.

In February 1990, President François Mitterrand of France visited Pakistan and announced that France had agreed to supply a 900 MWe commercial nuclear power plant to Pakistan. However, after the Prime Minister Benazir Bhutto was dismissed in August 1990, the French nuclear power plant deal went into cold storage and the agreement could not be implemented due to financial constraints and the Pakistani government's apathy. Also in February 1990, Soviet Ambassador to Pakistan, V.P. Yakunin, said that the USSR was considering a request from Pakistan for the supply of a nuclear power plant. The Soviet and French civilian nuclear power plant was on its way during the 1990s. However, Bob Oakley, the U.S. Ambassador to Pakistan, expressed U.S. displeasure at the recent agreement made between France and Pakistan for the sale of a nuclear power plant. After the U.S. concerns the civilian-nuclear technology agreements were cancelled by France and Soviet Union.

Declassified documents from 1982, released in 2012 under the U.S. Freedom of Information Act, said that U.S. intelligence detected that Pakistan was seeking suspicious procurements from Belgium, Finland, Japan, Sweden and Turkey.

According to more recent reports, it has been alleged that North Korea had been secretly supplying Pakistan with ballistic missile technology in exchange for nuclear weapons technology.

Doctrine

Pakistan refuses to adopt a "no-first-use" doctrine, indicating that it would strike India with nuclear weapons even if India did not use such weapons first. Pakistan's asymmetric nuclear posture has significant influence on India's decision ability to retaliate, as shown in 2001 and 2008 crises, when non-state actors carried out deadly attacks on Indian soil, only to be met with a relatively subdued response from India. A military spokersperson stated that "Pakistan's threat of nuclear first-use deterred India from seriously considering conventional military strikes." India is Pakistan's primary geographic neighbour and primary strategic competitor, helping drive Pakistan's conventional warfare capability and nuclear weapons development: The two countries share an

1800 mile border and have suffered a violent history—four wars in less than seven decades. The past three decades have seen India's economy eclipse that of Pakistan's, allowing the former to outpace the latter in defence expenditure at a decreasing share of GDP. In comparison to population, India is more powerful than Pakistan by almost every metric of military, economic, and political power—and the gap continues to grow," a Belfer Center for Science and International Affairs report claims.

THEORY OF DETERRENCE

The theory of "N-deterrence" has been frequently being interpreted by the various government-in-time of effect of Pakistan. Although the nuclear deterrence theory was officially adopted in 1998 as part of Pakistan's defence theory, on the other hand, the theory has had been interpreted by the government since in 1972. The relative weakness in defence warfare is highlighted in Pakistan's nuclear posture, which Pakistan considers its primary deterrent from Indian conventional offensives or nuclear attack. Nuclear theorist Brigadier-General Feroz Hassan Khan adds: "The Pakistani situation is akin to NATO's position in the Cold War. There are geographic gaps and corridors similar to those that existed in Europe... that are vulnerable to exploitation by mechanized Indian forces ... With its relatively smaller conventional force, and lacking adequate technical means, especially in early warning and surveillance, Pakistan relies on a more proactive nuclear defensive policy."

Indian political scientist Vipin Narang, however, argues that Pakistan's asymmetric escalation posture, or the rapid first use of nuclear weapons against conventional attacks to deter their outbreak, increases instability in South Asia. Narang supports his arguments by noting to the fact that since India's assured retaliation nuclear posture has not deterred these provocations, Pakistan's passive nuclear posture has neutralised India's conventional options for now; limited retaliation would be militarily futile, and more significant conventional retaliation is simply off the table."

The strategists in Pakistan Armed Forces has ceded nuclear assets and a degree of nuclear launch code authority to lower-level officers to ensure weapon usability in a "fog of war" scenario, making credible its deterrence doctrine. On further military perspective, the Pakistan Air Force (PAF), has retrospectively contended that "theory of defense is not view to enter into a "nuclear race", but to follow a policy of "peaceful co-existence" in the region, it cannot remain oblivious to the developments in South Asia." ThePakistan Government officials and strategists have consistently emphasised that nuclear deterrence is intended by maintaining a balance to safeguard its sovereignty and ensure peace in the region.

Pakistan's motive for pursuing a nuclear weapons development program is never to allow another invasion of Pakistan. President Muhammad Zia-ul-Haq allegedly told the Indian Prime Minister Rajiv Gandhi in 1987 that, "If your forces cross our borders by an inch, we are going to annihilate your cities."

Pakistan has not signed the Non-Proliferation Treaty (NPT) or the Comprehensive Test Ban Treaty (CTBT). According to the United States Department of Defense report cited above, "Pakistan remains steadfast in its refusal to sign the NPT, stating that it would do so only after India joined the Treaty. Pakistan has responded to the report by stating that the United States itself has not ratified the CTBT. Consequently, not all of Pakistan's nuclear facilities are under IAEA safeguards. Pakistani officials have stated that signature of the CTBT is in Pakistan's best interest, but that Pakistan will do so only after developing a domestic consensus on the issue, and have disavowed any connection with India's decision."

The Congressional Research Service, in a report published on 23 July 2012, said that in addition to expanding its nuclear arsenal, Pakistan could broaden the circumstances under which it would be willing to use nuclear weapons.

Nuclear Command and Control

The government institutional organisation authorised to make critical decisions about Pakistan's nuclear posturing is the NCA. The NCA has its genesis since the 1970s and has been constitutionally established in February 2000. The NCA is composed of two civic-military committees that advises and console both Prime minister and thePresident of Pakistan, on the development and deployment of nuclear weapons; it is also responsible for war-time command and control. In 2001, Pakistan further consolidated its nuclear weapons infrastructure by placing the Khan Research Laboratories and the Pakistan Atomic Energy Commission under the control of one Nuclear Defense Complex. In November 2009, Pakistan President Asif Ali Zardari announced that he will be replaced by Prime Minister Yusuf Raza Gilani as the chairman of NCA.

The NCA consists of the Employment Control Committee (ECC) and the Development Control Committee (DCC), both now chaired by the Prime Minister. The Foreign minister and Economic Minister serves as a deputy chairmen of the ECC, the body which defines nuclear strategy, including the deployment and employment of strategic forces, and would advise the prime minister on nuclear use.

The committee includes key senior cabinet ministers as well as the respective military chiefs of staff. The ECC reviews presentations on strategic threat perceptions, monitors the progress of weapons development, and decides on responses to emerging threats. It also establishes guidelines for effective command-and-control practices to safeguard against the accidental or unauthorised use of nuclear weapons.

The chairman of the Joint Chiefs of Staff Committee is the deputy chairman of the Development Control Committee (DCC), the body responsible for weapons development and oversight which includes the nation's military and scientific, but not its political, leadership. Through DCC, the senior civilian scientists maintains a tight control of scientific and ethical research; the DCC exercises technical, financial and administrative control over all strategic organisations, including national laboratories and scientific research and development organisations associated with the development and modernisation of nuclear weapons and their delivery systems. Functioning through the SPD, the DCC oversees the systematic progress of weapon systems to fulfil the force goals set by the committee.

Under the Nuclear Command Authority, its secretariat, Strategic Plans Division (SPD), is responsible for the physical protection and to ensure security of all aspects of country's nuclear arsenals. The SPD functions under the Joint Chiefs of Staff Committee at the Joint Headquarters (JS HQ) and reports directly to the Prime Minister. The comprehensive nuclear force planning is integrated with conventional war planning at the National Security Council (NSC). According to the officials of Pakistan's military science circles, it is the high-profile civic-military committee consisting the Cabinet ministers, President, Prime minister and the four services chiefs, all of whom who reserves the right to order the deployment and the operational use of the nuclear weapons. The final and executive political decisions on nuclear arsenals deployments, operational use, and nuclear weapons politics are made during the sessions of the Defence Committee of the Cabinet, which is chaired by the Prime minister. It is this DCC Council where the final political guideles, discussions and the nuclear arsenals operational deployments are approved by the Prime minister. The DCC reaffirmed its policies on development of nuclear energy and arsenals through the country's media.

U.S. security assistance

From the end of 2001 the United States has provided material assistance to aid Pakistan in guarding its nuclear material, warheads and laboratories. The cost of the program has been almost $100 million. Specifically the USA has provided helicopters, night-vision goggles and nuclear detection equipment.

During this period Pakistan also began to develop a modern export control regulatory regime with U.S. assistance. It supplements the U.S. National Nuclear Security Administration Megaports program at Port Qasim, Karachi, which deployed radiation monitors and imaging equipment monitored by a Pakistani central alarm station.

Pakistan turned down the offer of Permissive Action Link (PAL) technology, a sophisticated "weapon release" program which initiates use via specific checks and balances, possibly because it feared the secret implanting of "dead switches". But Pakistan is since believed to have developed and implemented its own version of PAL and U.S. military officials have stated they believe Pakistan's nuclear arsenals to be well secured.

Security concerns of the United States

Since 2004 the U.S. government has reportedly been concerned about the safety of Pakistani nuclear facilities and weapons. Press reports have suggested that the United States has contingency plans to send in special forces to help "secure the Pakistani nuclear arsenal". Lisa Curtis of The Heritage Foundation giving testimony before theUnited States House Foreign Affairs Subcommittee on Terrorism, Nonproliferation, and Trade concluded that "preventing Pakistan's nuclear weapons and technology from falling into the hands of terrorists should be a top priority for the U.S." However Pakistan's government has ridiculed claims that the weapons are not secure.

Diplomatic reports published in the United States diplomatic cables leak revealed American and British worries over a potential threat posed by Islamists. In February 2009 cable from Islamabad, former US Ambassador to Pakistan Anne W. Patterson said "Our major concern is not having an Islamic militant steal an entire weapon but rather the chance someone working in [Pakistani government] facilities could gradually smuggle enough material out to eventually make a weapon."

A report published by *The Times* in early 2010 states that the United States is training an elite unit to recover Pakistani nuclear weapons or materials should they be seized by militants, possibly from within the Pakistani nuclear security organisation. This was done in the context of growing Anti-Americanism in the Pakistani Armed Forces, multiple attacks on sensitive installations over the previous 2 years and rising tensions. According to former U.S. intelligence official Rolf Mowatt-Larssen, U.S. concerns are justified because militants have struck at several Pakistani military facilities and bases since 2007. According to this report, the United States does not know the locations of all Pakistani nuclear sites and has been denied access to most of them. However, during a visit to

Pakistan in January 2010, the U.S. Secretary of Defense Robert M. Gates denied that the United States had plans to take over Pakistan's nuclear weapons.

A study by Belfer Center for Science and International Affairs at Harvard University titled 'Securing the Bomb 2010', found that Pakistan's stockpile "faces a greater threat from Islamic extremists seeking nuclear weapons than any other nuclear stockpile on earth".

According to Rolf Mowatt-Larssen, a former investigator with the CIA and the U.S. Department of Energy there is "a greater possibility of a nuclear meltdown in Pakistan than anywhere else in the world. The region has more violent extremists than any other, the country is unstable, and its arsenal of nuclear weapons is expanding."

Nuclear weapons expert David Albright author of 'Peddling Peril' has also expressed concerns that Pakistan's stockpile may not be secure despite assurances by both Pakistan and U.S. government. He stated Pakistan "has had many leaks from its program of classified information and sensitive nuclear equipment, and so you have to worry that it could be acquired in Pakistan,"

A 2010 study by the Congressional Research Service titled 'Pakistan's Nuclear Weapons: Proliferation and Security Issues' noted that even though Pakistan had taken several steps to enhance Nuclear security in recent years 'Instability in Pakistan has called the extent and durability of these reforms into question.'

In April 2011, IAEA's deputy director general Denis Flory declared Pakistan's nuclear programme safe and secure. According to the IAEA, Pakistan is currently contributing more than $1.16 million in IAEA's Nuclear Security Fund, making Pakistan as 10th largest contributor.

The Pakistani Government announced that it would train an additional 8,000 people to protect the country's nuclear arsenal. At the same time, the Pakistani Government also denounced the chapter. Training will be completed no later than 2013.

Pakistan consistently maintains that it has tightened the security over the several years. In 2010, the Chairman Joint Chiefs General

Tariq Majid exhorted to the world delegation at the National Defence University that, "World must accept Pakistan as nuclear power." While dismissing all the concerns on the safety of country's nuclear arsenal, General Majid maintains to the fact: "We are shouldering our responsibility with utmost vigilance and confidence. We have put in place a very robust regime that includes "multilayered mechanisms" and processes to secure our strategic assets, and have provided maximum transparency on our practices. We have reassured theinternational community on this issue over and over again and our track record since the time our atomic bomb programme was made overt has been unblemished".

On 7 September 2013, the U.S. State Department said "Pakistan has a professional and dedicated security force that fully understands the importance of nuclear security." Pakistan had earlier rejected claims in U.S. media that the Obama Administration was worried about the safety of Pakistani nuclear weapons, saying the country has a professional and robust system to monitor it nukes.

National Security Council

- Economic Coordination Committee (ECC)
- Development Control Committee (DCC)
- Employment Control Committee (ECC)
- Financial Monitoring Unit (FMU)

Strategic combat commands

- Air Force Strategic Command (AFSC)
- Army Strategic Forces Command (ASFC)
- Naval Strategic Forces Command (NSFC)

Weapons development agencies

National Engineering & Scientific Commission (NESCOM)

- National Development Complex (NDC), Islamabad
- Project Management Organization (PMO), Khanpur
- Air Weapon Complex (AWC), Hasanabdal
- Maritime Technologies Complex (MTC), Karachi

Ministry of Defense Production

- Pakistan Ordnance Factories (POF), Wah
- Pakistan Aeronautical Complex (PAC), Kamra
- Defense Science and Technology Organization (DESTO), Chattar

Pakistan Atomic Energy Commission (PAEC)

- Directorate of Technical Development
- Directorate of Technical Equipment
- Directorate of Technical Procurement
- Directorate of Science & Engineering Services
- Institute of Nuclear Power, Islamabad
- Pakistan Institute of Nuclear Science & Technology (PINSTECH)
- New Laboratories, Rawalpindi
- Pilot Reprocessing Plant
- PARR-1 and PARR-2 Nuclear Research Reactors
- Center for Nuclear Studies (CNS), Islamabad
- Computer Training Center (CTC), Islamabad
- Nuclear Track Detection Center (Solid State Nuclear Track Detection Center)
- Khushab Reactor, Khushab
- Atomic Energy Minerals Centre, Lahore
- Hard Rock Division, Peshawar
- Mineral Sands Program, Karachi
- Baghalchur Uranium Mine, Baghalchur
- Dera Ghazi Khan Uranium Mine, Dera Ghazi Khan
- Issa Khel/Kubul Kel Uranium Mines and Mills, Mianwali
- Multan Heavy Water Production Facility, Multan, Punjab
- Uranium Conversion Facility, Islamabad
- Golra Ultracentrifuge Plant, Golra
- Sihala Ultracentrifuge Plant, Sihala
- Directorate of Quality Assurance,Islamabad
- New Labs Nilore,Islamabad

Space and Upper Atmospheric Research Commission (SUPARCO)

- Aerospace Institute, Islamabad.
- Computer Center, Karachi.
- Control System Laboratories.
- Sonmian Satellite Launch Center, Sonmiani Beach.
- Instrumentation Laboratories, Karachi.
- Material Research Division.
- Quality Control and Assurance Unit.
- Rocket Bodies Manufacturing Unit.
- Solid Composite Propellant Unit.
- Liquid Composite Propellant Unit
- Space and Atmospheric Research Center (space Center), Karachi
- Static Test Unit, Karachi
- Tilla Satellite Launch Center, Tilla, Punjab

Ministry of Industries & Production

- State Engineering Corporation (SEC)
- Heavy Mechanical Complex Ltd. (HMC)
- Pakistan Steel Mills Limited, Karachi.

DELIVERY SYSTEMS

Land systems

As of 2011, Pakistan possesses a wide variety of nuclear capable medium range ballistic missiles with ranges up to 2500 km. Pakistan also possesses nuclear tipped Babur cruise missiles with ranges up to 700 km. In April 2012, Pakistan launched a Hatf-4 Shaheen-1A, said to be capable of carrying a nuclear warhead designed to evade missile-defense systems. The Babur cruise missile range can also be extended to 1000 km or more. These land-based missiles are controlled by Army Strategic Forces Commandof Pakistan Army.

Pakistan is also believed to be developing tactical nuclear weapons for use on the battlefield with ranges up to 60 km such as the Nasr missile. According to Jeffrey Lewis, director of the East Asia Non-proliferation Program at the Monterey Institute of International Studies, Pakistan is developing its own equivalent to the Davy Crockett launcher with miniaturised warhead that may be similar to the W54.

Aerial systems

The Pakistan Air Force (PAF) is believed to have practised "toss-bombing" in the 1980s and 1990s, a method of launching weapons from fighter-bombers which can also be used to deliver nuclear warheads. The PAF has two dedicated units (No. 16 *Black Panthers* and No. 26 *Black Spiders*) operating 18 aircraft in each squadron (36 aircraft total) of the JF-17 Thunder, believed to be the preferred vehicle for delivery of nuclear weapons. These units are major part of the Air Force Strategic Command, a command responsible for nuclear response. The PAF also operates a fleet of F-16 fighters, of which 18 were delivered in 2012 and confirmed by General Ashfaq Parvez Kayani, are capable of carrying nuclear weapons. With a third squadron being raised, this would bring the total number of dedicated nuclear capable aircraft to a total of 54. The PAF also possesses the Ra'ad air-launched cruise missile which has a range of 350 km and can carry a nuclear warhead with a yield of between 10kt to 35kt.

It has also been reported that an air-launched cruise missile (ALCM) with a range of 350 km has been developed by Pakistan, designated Hatf 8 and named Ra'ad ALCM, which may theoretically be armed with a nuclear warhead. It was reported to have been test-fired by a Mirage III fighter and, according to one Western official, is believed to be capable of penetrating some air defence/missile defence systems.

Naval systems

The Pakistan Navy was first publicly reported to be considering deployment of nuclear weapons on submarines in February 2001. Later in 2003 it was stated by Admiral Shahid Karimullah, then Chief of Naval Staff, that there were no plans for deploying nuclear weapons on submarines but if "*forced to*" they would be. In 2004, Pakistan Navy established the Naval Strategic

Forces Command and made it responsible for countering and battling naval-based weapons of mass destruction. It is believed by most experts that Pakistan is developing a sea-based variant of the Hatf VII Babur, which is a nuclear-capable ground-launched cruise missile. With a stockpile of plutonium, Pakistan would be able to produce a variety of miniature nuclear warheads which would allow it to nuclear-tip the C-802 and C-803 anti-ship missiles as well as being able to develop nuclear torpedoes,nuclear depth bombs and nuclear naval mines.

FUTURE DELIVERY SYSTEMS

Nuclear submarine

In response to INS *Arihant,* India's first nuclear submarine, the Pakistan Navy pushed forward a proposal to build its own nuclear submarine as a direct response to the Indian nuclear submarine program. Many military experts believe that Pakistan has the capability of building a nuclear submarine and is ready to build such a fleet. Finally in February 2012, the Navy announced it would start work on the construction of a nuclear submarine to better meet the Indian Navy's nuclear threat. According to the Navy, the nuclear submarine is an ambitious project, and will be designed and built indigenously. However, the Navy stressed that "the project completion and trials would take anywhere from between 5 to 8 years to build the nuclear submarine after which Pakistan would join the list of countries that has a nuclear submarine."

10

Nuclear Weapons in the Twenty-First Century

Nuclear weapons played a pivotal role in international security during the latter half of the twentieth century. Despite rapid increases in communications, transportation, and weapons technology, there has been no large-scale strategic conflict since the Second World War. Nuclear weapons, as the most destructive instruments ever invented, had a stabilizing effect on superpower relations by making any conflict unacceptably costly. However, geopolitical change and the evolution of military technology suggest that the composition of our nuclear forces and our strategy for their employment may be different in the twenty-first century. The time is right for a fundamental rethinking of our expectations and requirements for these unique weapons.

Nuclear weapons are one component of an integrated defense strategy that includes diplomacy and conventional forces. The principal role of nuclear weapons was and continues to be that of deterring any potential adversaries from an attack on America or our vital interests. This role is expected to continue for as long as nuclear weapons hold the appellation of supreme" instruments of military force. However, this does not mean that their role in military planning will not change at all. Changes in the geopolitical environment and the inexorable advance of military technology here and abroad suggest that the position of nuclear weapons in national security policy will evolve with time. Given the unique destructive power of nuclear weapons, it is essential that this evolution be planned, to the extent possible, with due consideration of the integration of strategic nuclear forces into a consistent and comprehensive policy for national security.

Even with the dramatic changes that have occurred in the world during the past decade, nuclear warplanning today is similar in many respects to what it was during the Cold War. The Single Integrated Operational Plan (SIOP) is focused on a massive counterattack strategy that aims to eliminate the ability of an adversary to inflict further damage to American interests. Nuclear weapons provide an assured retaliatory capability to convince any adversary that aggression or coercion would be met with a response that would be certain, overwhelming, and devastating. It is often, but not universally, thought that nuclear weapons would be used only in extremis, when the nation is in the gravest danger. While there has been some discussion of single weapon" strikes against isolated targets, such as sites of weapons of mass destruction, most of the attention in nuclear strategy has been and is directed toward large-scale engagements. This may not be true in the future.

The advance of conventional weapons technology may result in the ability of conventional weapons to perform some of the missions currently assigned to nuclear weapons. For example, take the case of a road mobile ballistic missile. If one knows the location of such a target and if one can place a conventional weapon on that target with meter-scale accuracy, then it can be destroyed without a nuclear weapon. On the other hand, if one does not know the location of the target to within many kilometers then even a nuclear weapon may not destroy it. The key parameters required for target destruction are intelligence and precision delivery, not the explosive force of the weapon. However, even if a weapon is precisely delivered to the correct target point, countermeasures as simple as steel netting, boulder fields, or decoys complicate reliance on conventional weapons with limited radii of destruction.

The role of nuclear weaponry as the ultimate deterrent to aggression and the ultimate destructive force in combat will likely lead to the retention of at least some nuclear forces for decades to come. However, the composition of our nuclear arsenal may undergo significant modification to respond to changing conditions, changing military needs, and changes in our confidence in our ability to maintain credible nuclear forces without nuclear testing or large-scale weapons production. Options for precision delivery of nuclear weapons may reduce the requirement for high yield. Lower yield weapons could be produced as modifications of existing weapons designs, or they could employ more rugged and simpler designs that might be developed and maintained with high confidence without nuclear testing and with a smaller nuclear weapons complex than we envision is required to maintain our current nuclear forces.

This chapter attempts to look forward to the role that nuclear weapons might play in the twenty-first century, starting about 2020. A twenty-year horizon was chosen because over this time scale it is possible to make reasonable projections of technology and some assumptions about the probable threat situation. It takes about twenty years for substantially new weapons technologies to be developed and fielded into dependable military systems. Since this is true for other countries as well as the United States, one can project the development of potential adversarial capabilities to some degree. Of course, changes in governments could occur quickly compared to this time scale, but the technology that would be employed against the United States would proceed more slowly. This chapter focuses on state-to-state defense and does not explicitly consider terrorism or the rapid evolution of entirely new state threats. It is unlikely that an emergent power would be able to develop the technology necessary to confront the United States on a time scale faster than two decades without some obvious indicators that would enable our technological or diplomatic response.

Why is this an important issue now? Current plans call for the deployment of the next generation" of strategic forces in about 2020, including replacements for intercontinental ballistic missiles (ICBMs), the Ohio-class ballistic missile submarine, and perhaps even the venerable B52 bomber. This strategic modernization will be expensive, and it is not too soon to begin the debate over what kinds of strategic forces are needed to meet future needs.

It takes at least a decade to deploy a new technology, and if research and development are required, additional time may be needed. For such a key component of national defense, it is not sufficient to merely demonstrate that new systems work. There must be sufficient time to shake out the inevitable problems associated with new systems so as to make them dependable beyond reasonable doubt of our own government and the governments of potential adversaries. Time must also be allowed for the negotiation of treaties or other international agreements that support the new force structure and that preclude the marginalization of our forces by either a massive breakout or any other action that would reduce the effectiveness of our forces. Finally, the twentieth century repeatedly demonstrated that sweeping geopolitical changes occur on a short time scale compared to our ability to respond with new technologies or doctrines. It is imperative to consider the widest range of potential options before a crisis develops and to maintain a sufficiently robust research and development base to enable a response at that time.

The development of naval air power during the 1930s is a prime example of the need to evaluate the role of new technologies well before any anticipated engagement. The development of radar and ballistic missiles during the 1940s is an example of technologies developed during a conflict using preexisting foundations of research and technology. Some investment in thinking about future strategic forces now could reap significant dividends in the future.

Planning for future strategic defense is a highly complex affair that requires the consideration of many possible contingencies. This chapter is not intended to be a complete analysis of such a complex topic. Rather, its purpose is to stimulate thinking about changes in the international environment and technology that might be expected to influence the makeup of our strategic warfighting capability.

In order to set the stage, I first present a brief overview of the geopolitical situation that might reasonably be expected to influence defense strategy in 2020. This is followed by a discussion of what weapons technology might be available to the United States and other countries. Next, a discussion is given of some force structures, including weapons and supporting infrastructure, that might satisfy future defense needs. The chapter concludes with a summary and suggestions for further work.

THE INTERNATIONAL SITUATION IN THE TWENTY-FIRST CENTURY

Before one can rationally discuss future defense needs, it is necessary to know what one is defending against. The past decade has demonstrated the difficulty and danger of predicting the geopolitical future, but there are some forecasts that can be made with reasonable confidence and which can be used to guide further discussion.

Strategic Threats to U.S. National Security in the Twenty-First Century

Future national security threats to the United States might be divided into three major categories: major power conflicts, especially those involving Russia and China; regional conflicts, including potential nuclear states such as Iran, Iraq, or North Korea; and conflicts involving terrorist groups and other nonstate organizations. Only the first two major categories will be considered here, since it is arguable whether there is any role for strategic nuclear forces in dealing with terrorism and substate threats. However, strategic conflicts can be sparked by terrorist acts, as was the case in the First World War and other conflicts.

Russia

During the past 200 years European Russia has sustained a series of catastrophes including the invasion of Napoleon, the Crimean War, the First World War, the Revolution, the Second World War, and now the transition from a communist state to something else. In each case the country recovered within a generation. Even after the Second World War, when the country was essentially in ruins, it came back to launch Sputnik within twelve years. While one cannot predict what will happen in a country so volatile as Russia, it is not unreasonable to assume that it will endeavor to return to a conventional military power while continuing to rely on a significant nuclear capability. It is clear from Russia's investment in conventional military technology that it wishes to reassert its status in this area and to continue a lucrative business in the international arms trade.

China

China's international aims are in development, but their long stated intention to reunify" Taiwan into the mainland and their territorial moves in the South China Sea indicate that they plan to play a broader role on the international stage. China has a small nuclear arsenal but one capable of inflicting unacceptable damage on American territory and interests. It is unclear at present what, if any, impact alleged Chinese nuclear espionage will have on the modernization of its nuclear arsenal. However, it is worth noting that China has several nuclear weapons systems in the advanced development stage including a new cruise missile, which presumably can carry a nuclear warhead, and new land-launched and sea-launched ballistic missiles. Road mobile nuclear capable missiles add a degree of survivability to China's limited nuclear arsenal. The desire to develop an operational ballistic missile submarine is another suggestion that China is concerned about the survivability of its nuclear forces and perhaps is a comment on its future goals of power projection outside of the immediate Pacific area.

Other Countries

The nuclear tests of India and Pakistan again demonstrate that countries will act in their own perceived national interests, sometimes in direct opposition to the wishes of the United States or to previous treaty commitments or arrangements. Continued tensions in South Asia, including Sino-Indian tensions, bear close monitoring, but they may not directly involve the United States. The Middle East will continue to be a problem area due to the misalignment of ethnic, cultural, and national borders. The prospects for Arab or Islamic unification do not appear imminent at present, but historically this unification has relied on a charismatic leader, whose advent is difficult to predict. Continued problems in the Balkans and elsewhere in the world may tax American and allied conventional capabilities, but such conflicts are not expected to assume a nuclear dimension in the foreseeable future. North Korea is presumed to have at least some nuclear capability and has demonstrated remarkable progress in ballistic missile technology, despite its perilous economic condition. Japan and South Korea look upon North Korea's nuclear ambitions with concern and could pursue their own nuclear programs if they felt uncertainty in the American nuclear umbrella. Similar concerns could apply to Taiwan in light of recent statements made by the People's Republic of China.

Nuclear engagement scenarios are not necessarily binary. Third countries may feel compelled to intervene in disputes between nuclear states or in conflicts involving weapons of mass destruction that could spill over into their territory or interests. For example, China may feel a need to act in a nuclear exchange between India and Pakistan.

Similarly, Israel may feel a need to act in a major conflict of its neighbors that involved weapons of mass destruction.

FOREIGN WEAPONS TECHNOLOGY IN THE TWENTY-FIRST CENTURY

Trends evident today suggest that by 2020 many countries in the world will have access to several important technologies.

- Weapons of mass destruction: India and Pakistan graphically demonstrated the ability of midlevel technology states to construct or obtain nuclear weapons. Chemical and biological weapons are assumed to be within the reach of many countries today.
- Long-range ballistic missile technology: It is apparent that countries like North Korea, Iran, India, Pakistan, and other countries have or will soon have the capability to project force at intercontinental distances. The developing international marketplace in these technologies may make long-range missiles available to almost any country that has the money and the basic technical capability to acquire and use them. Although such missiles may lack the precision of current U.S. weapons, they might be entirely adequate for the delivery of weapons of mass destruction.

- Space imaging: Commercial services already provide high-resolution images from space. The technical capability to provide these images in real time to customers around the world should be expected to develop. Whether international agreements will be enacted to prevent collection against sensitive sites remains to be seen. At some point, Third World countries will have the capability to launch their own intelligence satellites or will pay others to launch them, thus bypassing the need for commercial services.
- Russian weapons technology: Despite its economic troubles, Russia is committing significant resources to the research and development of advanced conventional weapons. Part of the reason for this is certainly to provide a credible defense of Russia and its vital interests. However, Russia also sees a lucrative international arms market that appreciates the low cost and operational simplicity of its weapons. One might expect more countries to have access to last generation" but quite capable Russian military technology including missiles, air defenses, submarines, tanks, and other systems.
- Advanced communications and computer technology: The spread of communications and computer technology will serve as a force multiplier for a growing number of countries. The ability to effectively employ a small number of electronic weapons against a technologically and/or numerically superior enemy is a cost-effective force-leveling tactic.

The United States will enjoy superiority in conventional and nuclear weapons as long as adequate investments are made in research and development and in the deployment of the resulting weapons systems. However, we should expect other countries to employ many of our ideas in their own defense strategy including the simple copying of our technology and doctrines, or the use of our technology to develop weapons systems of their own. They may also attempt to exploit weaknesses in our advanced technology through means such as electromagnetic weapons, chemical and/or biological weapons, and other "asymmetric means."

U.S. DEFENSE TECHNOLOGIES IN THE TWENTY-FIRST CENTURY

Conventional Military Technology

Advances in military technology have been much discussed in the literature and are said to be leading toward a revolution in military affairs. Relevant to the present discussion, there are several advances in conventional weapons technology that deserve mention.

- Advanced precision munitions: It is already possible for cruise missiles to deliver payloads to targets hundreds of miles from their launch point with few meter accuracy. High precision for intercontinental missiles, either land- or sea-launched, is also possible. Given that ballistic missile reentry vehicles arrive on target with velocities of thousands of meters per second, it is not necessary to have explosive payloads to destroy some classes of targets.
- Advanced real-time imagery and data fusion: Data collection from satellites and from unmanned forward platforms will enable real-time remote battle management, including the direction of precision munitions to distant, even mobile, targets.
- Antiballistic missile technology will mature if the appropriate investment is made, enabling some defense against limited missile attacks. Analogous defenses could be developed against cruise missiles and aircraft, although these threats are in many ways a tougher problem due to the greater number of potential entry points and the availability of stealth technology.
- Information warfare may develop in such a fashion to enable the United States to interdict enemy command, control, and communications.

There has been much discussion of other advanced conventional technologies including unmanned aircraft, sensor technology, beam weapons, and so on. In this chapter we will focus on those technologies that could have a strategic impact and that are related to the changing role of nuclear weapons. The importance of considering future defense against ballistic missiles, cruise missiles, and aircraft cannot be overestimated. The inexorable advance of technology will eventually make such defenses feasible and will put them within the grasp of any country that wishes to have them. Such is the case now with reasonably sophisticated air defenses. Long range strategic planners must at least consider the return of a traditional "armor/antiarmor" competition even for strategic forces. Stealth technologies, advanced countermeasures, and new technologies will affect these trades but will not change the fundamental ability of defense technologies to influence strategic thinking.

Nuclear Weapons-Related Technology

Nuclear weapons pack incredible destructive force into a small, deliverable package. In addition to their psychological deterrent value, they are the only current means of holding at risk several classes of targets.

- Mobile targets, such as road mobile and rail mobile missiles
- Fixed moderately hard targets, such as missile silos
- Distributed targets, such as airfields or naval bases
- Hard targets, such as deeply buried command structures
- Superhard targets, such as facilities located beneath mountains

Conventional weapons might be able to address some of the missions currently assigned to nuclear weapons, but not all of them. Some targets, like missile silos and command and control structures, are sufficiently hard that no conventional weapon will have the energy to defeat them. Other targets, such as airfields and naval bases, are sufficiently dispersed that a massive amount of conventional explosives would be required for their destruction. Even though conventional weapons could damage or destroy such targets, they could do so today only over an extended time frame and with the use of limited resources that may be required in other theaters of operation. Future conventional weapons designs may change this, but there are still limits on the amount of damage that can be caused with a given quantity of high explosive. For these and other reasons, nuclear weapons are expected to continue to play a role in strategic doctrine, independent of their role as a psychological deterrent to aggression.

The United States employs a counterforce strategy that targets military assets that could inflict damage to our national interests. We do not threaten cities or populations as in a countervalue policy, although there is an implicit threat of doing so that is a potent element of the deterrent calculus. American nuclear weapons systems are designed to hold specific classes of targets at risk, using the minimum explosive forces necessary to accomplish the mission. However, a sizable factor governing the explosive force required to defeat a target of given hardness is the precision with which weapons can be delivered. The evolution of accurate delivery systems could change engagement strategies for nuclear weapons, in some cases reducing the required yield or even eliminating the need for an explosion at all. Once again, the use of conventional weapons presumes a level of detailed information on the location and characteristics of the target that has so far eluded military planners. A reliance on precision conventional munitions for some strategic missions presumes a major investment in intelligence collection and analysis tools, including accurate means of assessing target damage following an attack. This is particularly important for strategic targets such as mobile missiles or weapons of mass destruction that could, if they survive, inflict significant damage.

Advances in military technology may change the makeup and use of our strategic forces in several ways.

- Some important classes of targets, such as mobile missiles, might be effectively dealt with by long-range precision conventional weapons. One can envision submarine-launched ballistic missiles (SLBMs) and intercontinental ballistic missiles (ICBMs), loaded with such precision weapons, which could be directed by real-time intelligence to targets anywhere on the planet within 30 minutes. Maneuvering reentry vehicles could enable these weapons to follow and destroy moving targets.
- A 5-kiloton (kt) nuclear explosive detonated on a 30-foot-thick missile silo door will vaporize that door, destroying the missile inside. With precision delivery many hard

targets might be able to be defeated with nuclear explosives having lower yield than we might currently employ. Such lower-yield weapons could use simpler and/or more robust designs than we have in our current arsenal. Simpler, more robust designs, in turn, might allow the nuclear arsenal to be maintained with a smaller maintenance and production complex than is required to support the sophisticated, highly optimized weapons in our stockpile. As in the case of advanced conventional weapons, the use of lower-yield nuclear weapons against hardened targets could be made problematic through the use of relatively simple countermeasures. In the example of a silo door, shielding could be used to separate the blast from the door area, reducing the effectiveness of the weapon.

- Widely dispersed targets require energy (yield) for assured destruction. Several dispersed lower-yield weapons will produce the same effect as a single higher-yield weapon. Using multiple weapons on a single target assumes that fratricide effects can be dealt with in planning multiple nuclear bursts in a single target area. Such an approach also requires a larger number of weapons, a factor that would be more challenging if deep cuts in weapons numbers are negotiated. A benefit of lower-yield weapons is that the collateral damage sustained by the near-target area may be reduced, an important factor in attacks near urban areas.
- Some very hard targets require high yield to destroy them. No application of conventional explosives or even lower-yield nuclear explosives will destroy such targets, which might include hardened structures buried beneath hundreds of feet of earth or rock. For such purposes it might be desirable to retain a small number of higher-yield nuclear weapons in the arsenal as deterrents against enemy confidence in the survival of such targets.
- Superhard targets, such as those found under certain Russian mountains, may not be able to be defeated reliably by even high-yield nuclear weapons. In this case, one might

> use a different strategy such as ýÿfunctional defeat" in which power, communications, or other vital functions are eliminated or denied without the physical destruction of the main target. Alternately, one might use negotiations to eliminate a target, bargaining away a limited set of special targets for concessions on our part.

These proposals are a departure from conventional thinking on nuclear issues. For example, our ability to negotiate away superhard targets would be very difficult at best. Others, such as the ability of precision advanced conventional munitions to hold at risk mobile and other soft-point targets, are more realistic and require only projections of current technology. In the latter case, a challenge may come from arms control concerns of other countries that see their own nuclear forces made marginal. Also, potential adversaries may use 'asymmetric means" to counter our advanced technology.

An important consideration in thinking about lower-yield nuclear forces for most of our strategic nuclear requirements is that such weapons could be much simpler than our current highly optimized nuclear designs. Given sufficient throw-weight on our missiles, we could use gun-assembled or other simple, rugged designs that might be maintained with high confidence without nuclear testing. Such designs would require a significantly smaller industrial plant for their maintenance than our current forces. If based on uranium weapons designs, a much smaller plutonium infrastructure would be required. Other technologies specific to high-yield nuclear weapons could be placed in a standby mode rather than a production mode. Finally, simpler weapons might be maintained with higher confidence for longer periods by a weapons staff that has little or no direct experience with nuclear testing. However, should the country elect to follow such a path it will still be necessary to retain expertise in more sophisticated nuclear designs as a hedge against changing conditions in the future.

There is an additional, nontechnical, consideration that will influence future nuclear policy. Given current and projected scientific capabilities, it is difficult or impossible to confidently field a new, highly optimized, nuclear warhead design without nuclear testing. For this and other reasons, the United States intends to maintain its existing nuclear designs into the indefinite future. This is a fundamental change in how we maintain our arsenal. Recent concerns about espionage in the weapons program raise questions about our ability to keep weapons designs secret over many decades.

Some in the intelligence community contend that a fixed target, such as our nuclear designs, will be compromised by a determined adversary given sufficient time. Information about our designs could provide important guidance to countries that wish to improve their own nuclear arsenals. Such information would also be advantageous to countries attempting to optimize some future ballistic missile defense system of their own for use against our systems. Finally, it could assist potential adversaries in deploying their strategic forces in a manner designed to make it difficult for us to assure their destruction.

Planners need to consider what we will do when, and not if, the details of our nuclear forces become known by a potential adversary. There are several paths that could be employed here, including disinformation, counterintelligence, etc. One path that has been proven to work has been to change our forces on a regular basis in response to evolving military requirements and technology options. The certification of substantially new nuclear weapons designs is difficult or impossible to do with high confidence without underground nuclear testing. However, the United States has a large archive of previously tested designs that might be fielded with reasonable confidence to meet evolving military needs. In addition, the current stockpile has significant flexibility for modification for new requirements. Such flexibility was most recently evidenced by the modification of the B61 bomb to provide earth-penetrating capability. A move toward a mixed force of long-range conventional and lower-yield nuclear weapons with improved accuracy would be another means of meeting this need. Such decisions need not be exclusive. It may be wisest to employ multiple technologies, both nuclear and nonnuclear, to create a robust future strategic posture.

STRATEGIC FORCES TO MEET FUTURE DEFENSE NEEDS

Planning strategic forces is a highly complicated affair that must include technical, geopolitical, and military considerations. A full analysis is not attempted here. The purpose of this section is to suggest some broad options that can be used as starting points for more detailed treatment. Although this section concentrates on strategic forces, it is worth noting that several countries possess potent nonstrategic" nuclear forces that are designed for tactical engagements. Nonstrategic forces include nuclear artillery shells, atomic demolition munitions, short-range missiles, and air-delivered bombs. While such weapons are typically lower in yield than most strategic bombs and warheads, they are still nuclear explosives with destructive power vastly greater than conventional weapons. One might expect the division between ýÿtactical" and strategic" weapons to blur in the future, especially if significant reductions in strategic arsenals occur.

Scenario 1: Status Quo

Nuclear weapons represent the ultimate defense of the nation, a deterrent against any and all potential adversaries. Combined with diplomacy and conventional military capabilities, nuclear weapons have helped to avoid a large-scale conflict between leading world powers for over fifty years. This is an astonishing achievement given the acceleration in communications and transportation that took place during this time. When the Cold War ended, the U.S. nuclear stockpile consisted of a set of highly optimized warheads and bombs on highly reliable missiles and aircraft. These weapons systems were designed primarily to counter the massive Soviet threat. They were and are the most advanced of their kind in the world. Current plans call for them to be retained essentially indefinitely. There are several good reasons for this.

- These weapons are safe, reliable, and meet performance requirements.
- We have nuclear test data that support our understanding of their operation.

- New warheads of comparable capability are difficult or impossible to field without nuclear testing.
- They can be modified in many ways to respond to changing military requirements, as was done when the B61 bomb was modified to give it an earth-penetrating capability.

This scenario maintains a triad of ICBMs, SLBMs, and bombers. More than one type of weapon is maintained in each leg of the triad to provide backup capability should one weapon type encounter a problem. This strategy served us well during the Cold War. Given the rapidity with which the geopolitical situation can change, there is merit in following a prudent and conservative path for future nuclear forces.

There are several potential disadvantages to maintaining the existing stockpile indefinitely. Over time such highly optimized systems may be less well suited to military requirements. Refurbishment and other changes will be made to aging warheads and bombs, changes that might be difficult to certify without nuclear testing. Also, the cost of maintaining these weapons is high for both DoD and DOE. In the case of DOE, an extensive infrastructure of laboratories and plants is required for the Stockpile Stewardship program, including a new manufacturing capability for plutonium pits. Finally, the current stockpile may not be credible against some set of potential adversaries. For example, if a national emergency were to develop that involved the imminent use of weapons of mass destruction against American interests, would an adversary consider our threat of a multiwarhead attack by the Peacekeeper ICBM or a Trident SLBM as overkill and hence not a realistic threat? Such a reliance on high-yield strategic weapons could lead to 'self-deterrence," a limitation on strategic options, and consequently a lessening of the stabilizing effect of nuclear weapons.

Scenario 2: Reduced Stockpile of Existing Designs

This scenario assumes that arms control initiatives have make it advantageous to the United States to greatly reduce our stockpile of existing nuclear weapons. It is similar to Scenario 1 with lower force levels. One can debate the merit of eliminating one arm of the strategic triad or the nonstrategic (i.e. tactical) nuclear forces under such circumstances, depending on the depth of the reductions. Cost savings associated with reduced numbers are not directly proportional to the number of weapons since a significant infrastructure is required to support any type of modern nuclear design. The cost advantage would be in the size of the required production plant and not in the diversity of technical capabilities that are required.

At very low stockpile numbers it may be useful to explicitly consider a ýÿflexible stockpile" strategy that takes advantage of the flexibility inherent in current nuclear weapon designs. The United States could have a mixed force of weapons based upon current types suitably modified to meet evolving military needs. Special consideration might be given to maneuvering reentry vehicles that can deal effectively with enemy defenses. One could consider tailored output weapons for special applications such as those that produce an enhanced electromagnetic pulse for the disabling of electronics or those that produce enhanced radiation for the destruction of chemical or biological weapons with minimum collateral damage. (There is serious doubt in the nuclear weapons community as to whether such systems could be introduced into the stockpile without additional nuclear testing.) Careful consideration must be given to single-point failure in a reduced stockpile. For example, the use of a common missile or a common warhead for ICBMs and SLBMs would save money but would introduce a potential single-point failure in the majority of strategic forces.

In selecting weapons that would be maintained in a smaller force structure, consideration might be given to those that are the most rugged, the easiest and cheapest to maintain, and the most flexible. Highly optimized weapons may be more efficient, but efficiency can come at the cost of complexity of maintenance. Without nuclear testing, small changes caused by natural aging or required component replacements will introduce some uncertainty into the stockpile, uncertainty that must be figured into military strategy. Understanding such uncertainty is especially important if the number of weapons types is reduced, admitting the possibility of single-point failure of a large part of the force. It may be advisable to view ruggedness and ease of maintenance as principal criteria for the selection of the types and distribution of weapons within a reduced stockpile. Given the uncertainty of future military needs, the ability of a weapon to be maintained, modified, and/or certified without nuclear testing may also be an important element in the decision process.

Scenario 3: Mixed Conventional and Nuclear Strategic Forces

Reasonable assumptions about the development of advanced conventional munitions leads to a scenario where the strategic workload is carried by a combination of nuclear and nonnuclear forces. It is possible to envision nonnuclear components to each of the arms of the strategic triad. Using conventional ICBMs and SLBMs, or their projected replacements, one could design reentry warheads to achieve high accuracy. These warheads would contain 'smart" guidance systems that would receive intelligence handoffs from satellites or other sources before and/or during flight. Such systems would know that a target exists in a general area, be aware of its potential movement and signatures, and be able to home in on it. Given the kinetic energy of a reentering warhead, it might not be necessary for the system to contain high explosives. Hitting the target might be sufficient to destroy it. Similar warheads could be developed for cruise missiles that could be launched from bombers, submarines, or surface warships. In the case of cruise missiles, the lower velocity of delivery would require a high-explosive warhead.

A nonnuclear long-range weapon would be especially useful against limited numbers of time-urgent weapons of mass destruction targets such as biological weapons warheads that were in preparation for use against U.S. forces. Long-range nonnuclear weapons would enable such targets to be destroyed without causing the United States to be the first to employ nuclear weapons in a conflict. The use of nonnuclear strategic weapons against Russia, China, or other nuclear states would require care, since the appearance of such a weapon on long-range sensors might be indistinguishable from a nuclear attack by the United States.

A word of caution is needed on the use of precision munitions for high-value strategic targeting: The Kosovo conflict demonstrated very clearly that just the ability to place a weapon on the designated aim point is not enough to ensure mission success. Inaccurate target coordinates provided to pilots sometimes resulted in weapons being delivered very precisely to the wrong spot. Effective utilization of precision munitions demand that a premium be placed on the collection and the analysis of target information. This includes postattack damage assessments that determine the need for follow-on attacks and the ability of the adversary to use its weapons for offense or defense.

The nuclear component in this scenario could take one of several forms. First, one could employ a small number of existing weapons designs to retain a traditional counterforce deterrent strategy. Second, one could modify existing designs to reduce their yield, relying on precision delivery to help achieve military objectives. In this case one could use existing reentry warheads or develop new ones with the precision guidance necessary to destroy moderately-hard-point targets with low yield.

Third, one could design and deploy a new set of nuclear weapons that do not require nuclear testing to be certified. Such weapons might be, but do not need to be, based on simple gun-assembled uranium designs that do not require a plutonium infrastructure and that do not require the same sophistication in nuclear weapons science and engineering as our current stockpile. However, nothing comes for free, and one must recognize that such simple weapons have important, perhaps fatal, tactical limitations that would preclude their use in some engagement scenarios.

Also, such simple devices would be based on a very limited nuclear test database and would require extensive and expensive flight testing to assure that they could be delivered with the required precision. Fourth, one could consider a combination of new or modified low-yield warheads and some existing higher-yield designs to be retained against the possibility of unexpected developments in adversaries defenses or of the need to hold very hard targets at risk. In this case one would need to retain much of the infrastructure of the current stockpile to ensure the continued performance of these highly optimized weapons. Savings could be achieved in the size of the plant complex required to remanufacture components and complete weapons.

Scenario 4: Prospects for Wholly Nonnuclear Strategic Forces

It is almost impossible to conceive of technological and political developments that would enable the United States to meet its defense needs in 2020 without nuclear weapons. There are several reasons for this. First, nuclear weapons continue to play a vital role in deterring other countries from launching significant military strikes against America, our allies, or our vital interests. The real threat of not just military defeat but national annihilation is a potent deterrent now and should be expected to remain so for at least the next few decades. Second, it does not appear possible with current or projected technology to assure ourselves that there are no-and never will be any nuclear weapons in the hands of potential adversaries. Given the unique destructive power of nuclear weapons, an asymmetry of this kind should be unacceptable to American military planners. Third, the development of antiballistic missile defense is encouraging, but the assumption that a leak-proof shield can be fielded by 2020 is debatable. Fourth, some targets will not be able to be held at risk by any type of conventional weapon because of their extreme hardness. Fifth, the ability of an adversary to deliver a nuclear weapon by aircraft, cruise missile, naval vessel, or by clandestine insertion into this country are additional concerns beyond the long-range ballistic missile threat. Lacking the ability to deter such threats and to respond in kind would open up the country to blackmail.

It is critical in any discussion of strategic forces to consider the overall stability provided by technology and policy. Such calculations have become considerably more complex in the multipolar world that is expected to persist at least over the time scale addressed in this chapter.

The future is unpredictable, but we can count on it to be dynamic. Strategic thinking must be flexible and must consider the evolution of several possible futures, each of which has branches that are contingent on the geopolitical situation and technological capabilities here and abroad. Countries will respond to technology and policy developments in the United States and elsewhere. We must be careful that any changes to our strategic position make the overall situation better and not worse.

Russia has already promised that it will use 'asymmetric means" to counter advanced U.S. technology. Official Chinese publications indicate that China will likely follow a similar strategy. The capabilities of their own research and development complex should not be underestimated. While Russia cannot yet match the United States in the most sophisticated technology, it has shown a remarkable ability to achieve military objectives through cleverness and sometimes through brute force. Finally, the development of advanced conventional strategic weapons could push the Russians to an even greater reliance on high-yield nuclear weapons. Rather than an evolution toward some fixed strategy, strategic thinking should be done along a flexible time line that recognizes changes in the world and in military technology. What may work at one time may not work at another time when the situation has substantially changed.

One 'asymmetric" counter to advanced technology is cyber-warfare, including non-explosive weapons that could disable or render ineffective advanced conventional or even nuclear munitions. Precision kill requires sophisticated electronics, and electronics can be affected by various means such as radio frequency or microwave weapons. Russia's electromagnetic weapons program is perhaps the most advanced in the world, and at least some of this technology has been shared with China. Given the uncertainty in future advanced weapons technology, the United States may wish to retain some higher-yield nuclear weapons as hedges against the development of potent point or area defenses. The development of antisatellite weapons would create a similar complication to the United States if we were to rely on advanced conventional weapons that require precise targeting information to be effective.

Arms control initiatives will play an important role in the planning of future strategic forces. Proposed deep reductions in nuclear stockpiles may be a motivation for using conventional weapons as part of the strategic weapons mix. Such a decision will strongly depend on whether warheads or launchers are the counted quantity. If nuclear warheads and not delivery vehicles are the counted quantity, then existing or new launchers can be equipped with advanced conventional warheads. If missiles and aircraft are the counted quantity, we will need to be careful about treaties that allow only one warhead, nuclear or conventional, on a missile. Maintaining an effective deterrent requires a minimum number of nuclear weapons, and the dilution of our forces with conventional weapons could drive us from a counterforce strategy (military targets) to a countervalue strategy (cities) with attendant ethical and perhaps legal problems.

Arms control agreements can assist in strategic planning by restricting certain classes of weapons or targets. If, in some scenario, our weapons are particularly susceptible to nuclear interceptors, then we may wish to negotiate the elimination of nuclear interceptors in return for some other concession. If we are unable to destroy one or more targets by any weapon in our arsenal, we may want to attempt to negotiate away the target in return for assurances that we will not construct similarly hard targets in the United States. Such negotiations are by nature complex because they involve giving up different commodities on each side. However, the advantages of reduced reliance on nuclear weapons, with their large radii of destruction, might be an incentive. Also, the development of new conventional strategic weapons, the use of which might be incorporated into nonnuclear war planning and that will not necessarily lead to national destruction, should be considered with care.

One of the features of nuclear weapons is that they are so destructive that their use is reserved for only the most extreme cases. Making strategic weapons more 'usable" could start the United States on a path of escalation that could exacerbate and not reduce the potential for war. Conversely, lowering the threshold for using nuclear weapons in response to a strategic situation could raise the level of care with which countries interact. This points to the need for a detailed stability analysis to be performed as a prelude to any arms control negotiations. Such an analysis must explicitly include the balance of nuclear forces, the state and projected future of ballistic missile defenses, and the ability of advanced conventional weapons to perform missions formerly assigned to nuclear weapons. The weapons research and development programs of potential adversaries will provide input to this analysis by providing pointers to future defense capabilities. And, of course, any analysis of future strategic weapons needs must necessarily consider the possible geopolitical situation that will be present at the time of their deployment. Finally, the distinction between tactical and strategic nuclear weapons will fade for small stockpiles. Both types of weapons must be included in negotiations for overall stability to be maintained.

Another important consideration in planning future strategic forces is cost. Nuclear weapons systems are sometimes considered expensive to maintain due to their complexity, their unique characteristics, and the lack of private industry support of some components of their infrastructure. In fact, nuclear weapons are cheaper to develop and to maintain than very large conventional force structures. This was the reason why NATO chose to rely on nuclear weapons as a principal part of its defense against the massive Soviet conventional threat in Europe. Nuclear weapons are considered expensive today because they are primarily strategic in nature and we are in the midst of a 'strategic pause" that has lessened the perceived need for strategic weapons.

For the DoD, costs include operations, maintenance, and the development of next generation capabilities that will replace current systems upon their obsolescence. For the DOE, costs include the operation of the weapons laboratories and production plants and the material costs associated with weapons refurbishment. To first order, the cost of maintaining the DOE nuclear weapons complex is independent of the number of weapons in the stockpile. Some capability in uranium, plutonium, and other special materials is required. Scientific capabilities must be maintained, especially in those classified areas unique to nuclear weapons, to enable informed decisions to be made on weapons aging, component replacements, and future modifications. Tritium has some variable cost, as it must be produced to support some fixed number of weapons. Plutonium pit production can be maintained at a small rate at Los Alamos, but any stockpile above about one thousand weapons will require the construction of a new large production plant to replace the Rocky Flats facility, which ceased production in 1989. Should the country go to a precision low-yield nuclear force that is based on uranium rather than plutonium, the cost of the large pit-production facility could be avoided, and the remaining high-yield weapons that did employ plutonium pits could be supported by a modified Los Alamos plutonium facility.

11

Avoiding Pakistan: India Naval Conflict

For much of its modern history, the Indian Ocean has been remarkably free of naval nuclear friction. Even during the second half of the Cold War, when both the United States and the Soviet Union expanded their military presence throughout the region, the bulk of their naval nuclear interactions occurred elsewhere, in the heavily patrolled Gulf of Finland or in the frigid waters of the Sea of Okhotsk.

South Asian military competition, for its part, has traditionally been primarily a terrestrial, rather than a maritime phenomenon. For over a decade following India's and Pakistan's decisions to burst out of the nuclear closet in 1998 and reveal their previously recessed capabilities to the world, the evolution of both nations' respective arsenals appeared to reflect these continental proclivities. Although it was common knowledge that India had initiated a nuclear submarine program some time in the 1970s, foreign analysts' attention remained squarely focused on the air-and land-based components of the subcontinental nuclear equation.

In July 2009, India launched its first ballistic missile submarine (SSBN), the Advanced Technology Vessel (ATV), or S-2. Subsequently named the INS *Arihant*, the submarine's nuclear reactor went critical in August 2013, and in 2014 it was announced that a second SSBN would be launched some time soon.

Meanwhile, Pakistan formally inaugurated a Naval Strategic Force Command headquarters in 2012 and has declared its intent to develop its own sea-based deterrent. Unlike their Indian counterparts, Pakistani security managers appear to have opted for a more unconventional naval nuclear force structure, strongly emphasizing dual-use platforms and strategic ambiguity.

Barring a few notable exceptions, commentary on these developments has been sparse and sporadic. This continued intellectual neglect is puzzling, considering the fact that the maritime space constitutes the only medium in which South Asian nuclear platforms are likely to find themselves in frequent interaction.

This study seeks, therefore, to raise awareness on an issue that is destined to become of great importance, not only to those who closely follow security issues in South Asia, but also to all those with an interest in the fascinating—and often troubling—intersections of naval and nuclear strategy. In particular, it seeks to explore how naval nuclear interactions might lead to friction, misperception, and escalation—and what can be done to prevent or forestall such developments.

The report is divided into three main sections. The first section engages in a granular analysis of South Asia's current naval nuclear developments, describing the motivations and aspirations of both actors, as well as the current limitations to these same ambitions. The report then draws on the history of naval nuclear operations during the Cold War before detailing how some of the debates and discussions held during that rich and variegated period in history could potentially apply to contemporary South Asia. Notwithstanding the reflexive skepticism of many in New Delhi and Islamabad, the intellectual contortions of previous generations of nuclear strategists hold an immense value in terms of thinking more deeply about issues as complex as conventional operations under a nuclear shadow, naval nuclear signaling, and escalation control.

The third and final section of the report explores the clouded future of naval nuclear dynamics in the Indian Ocean. Beijing might come to play a more important role, both as an enabler for Pakistani naval nuclearization and as a naval nuclear actor in its own right. Finally, ongoing technological developments in anti-submarine warfare (ASW) might have a sizable impact on sea-based deterrence and naval crisis stability in the region.

As India and Pakistan develop their naval nuclear deterrents, they will enter increasingly murky waters. By further institutionalizing relations between both navies and by insisting on stronger transparency with regard to naval nuclear developments, both countries may succeed in adding a greater degree of stability to what otherwise promises to be a dangerously volatile maritime environment.

SOUTH ASIA'S HETEROGENEOUS NAVAL NUCLEAR DEVELOPMENTS

India's and Pakistan's quests for sea-based nuclear capabilities have been motivated by different strategic premises, with an assortment of distinct objectives in mind.

Since the beginning of the atomic age, the quest for a nuclear deterrent has frequently been viewed as an imperative for middle powers facing prospective adversaries armed with vast nuclear or conventional superiority. In India's and Pakistan's cases, a feeling of conventional asymmetry combined with a strong threat perception act as the main drivers of their decisions to acquire a nuclear capability. In both nations, watershed moments helped give birth to a strong consensus among national decisionmakers around the strategic utility of nuclear weapons. New Delhi's primary concern was China, which had inflicted a humiliating defeat on India's ill-equipped and poorly prepared troops along the rugged Sino-Indian border in 1962. For Islamabad, the existential threat was India, particularly after the Indo-Pakistani war of 1971, which led to the amputation of Pakistan's eastern wing and the creation of the independent state of Bangladesh.

While New Delhi's and Islamabad's quests for a nuclear triad can be understood through the lens of traditional nuclear deterrence, there are also other, more complex factors to take into account. India's pursuit of a sea-based strike capability is the next logical step in the formulation of its nuclear triad, but Pakistan's motivations are more complex and should not be perceived solely as reactive.

INDIA'S FITFUL QUEST FOR A NUCLEAR TRIAD

Sea-Based Nuclear Strike and Assured Retaliation

Shortly after India's Pokhran-II series of nuclear tests in 1998, the Indian government announced that its future minimum nuclear deterrent would be structured around a triad composed of mobile land-based missiles, aircraft, and naval assets.

Having officially adopted a posture of no first use and assured retaliation, India considered it essential to acquire a capacity for continuous at-sea nuclear deterrence (CASD) to ensure the survivability of its nuclear second-strike capability. The importance attached to sea-based deterrence in India's nuclear posture has been repeatedly emphasized over the past decade, whether via the Standing Committee on Defense of the Lok Sabha (the Indian Parliament's lower chamber), or in the Indian Navy's maritime strategy and successive iterations of its Maritime Doctrine in 2004 and 2009.

One can clearly detect a bureaucratic rationale behind the Indian Navy's continued emphasis of the indispensability of its nuclear role, alongside that of the historically privileged army and air force, as well as a quest for prestige. This is made evident in the 2004 Maritime Doctrine, which states that, among no-first-use nuclear powers, "India stands out alone as being devoid of a credible nuclear triad." In August 2013, shortly after the S-2's nuclear reactor went critical, then prime minister Manmohan Singh relayed a strong and widely held sense of national pride at such an accomplishment, declaring that

today's development represents a giant stride in the progress of our indigenous technological capabilities. It is testimony to the ability of our scientists, technologists and defense personnel to work together for mastering complex technologies in the service of our nation's security.

Beyond the totemic significance of the *Arihant*, however, are powerful practical arguments in favor of India's deployment of nuclear-armed submarines. Placing nuclear assets at sea puts them at a safer distance from a so-called "splendid" first strike, and their mobility and discretion (in the case of a nuclear submarine) provide a greater measure of survivability.

Unlike the United States and the Soviet Union during the Cold War, whose strategic centers were separated by great distances, India is caught in between two prospective nuclear adversaries. The flight time of an incoming short-range ballistic missile launched from Pakistan toward an Indian metropolis, such as New Delhi or Mumbai, is estimated to be a couple of minutes, at the most. This deprives India of a crucial element in the event of a nuclear crisis—time to avert a crippling first strike. Furthermore, the increased militarization of the Chinese-controlled Tibet Autonomous Region and the proliferation of ballistic missile silos at strategically placed high-altitude vantage points along the long Sino-Indian border pose potential threats to the survivability of India's land-and air-based deterrent, which could be substantially weakened under a protracted missile saturation campaign.

Indian strategists frequently draw attention to China's recent advances in space-based surveillance, depicting them as a growing threat to the survivability of India's land-based arsenal. For example, Verghese Koithara, a retired Indian vice admiral, notes that

in China, India has an adversary that has considerable and fast improving space capabilities. Over the next two decades, its ability to zero in on India's siloes, and track and target its mobile forces could become considerable.

This reasoning is shared by Arun Prakash, a former chief of naval staff and one of India's most respected thinkers on maritime issues:

Given the kind of transparency provided by satellites and other technical means, no air base or missile site—fixed or mobile—can remain hidden for long and will eventually figure on an enemy target list. The best way for India to provide invulnerability to its deterrent is to remove it from the enemy's scrutiny and send it underwater, on an SSBN. Once the submarine dives into the deep waters of the open ocean it becomes virtually impossible to locate or attack.

Some Indian Navy officers have also opined that developing the sea-based leg could, in fact, prove more cost-effective in the long run, as deterrence would become less dependent on the size of the Indian arsenal and more on its invisibility from detection.

Indian decisionmakers have long understood the rationale behind an undersea deterrent, and initiated the ATV program some time in the 1970s. In 2012, a report on Indian grand strategy penned by a group of esteemed Indian strategists argued that

> *the pursuit and maintenance of nuclear capability has been integral to India's quest for strategic autonomy since independence.... In the absence of a credible nuclear deterrent, India would have few options when confronted with adversaries possessing nuclear weapons.... Our main effort must be devoted to the maritime leg of our nuclear capability and the accompanying command and control systems.*

A Long and Painful Gestation

Bureaucratic languor, technical challenges, and chronic difficulties in nuclear reactor miniaturization ensured that progress would be painstakingly slow. For some skeptically minded observers, it became uncertain whether the $2.9 billion project would ever come to fruition.

From 1988 to 1991, Indian mariners gained a measure of experience in the operation of a nuclear vessel when New Delhi leased a Charlie-class conventional attack submarine (SSN) from the Soviet Union. It has also been reported that the ATV project heavily benefited from Russian expertise during the design phase.

With the benefit of this technological know-how, and a renewed impetus after the overt nuclearization of the subcontinent in 1998, the *Arihant* was finally launched, with much publicity, in 2009. The *Arihant* is destined to be the first vessel in a flotilla of up to five indigenously produced SSBNs, and the Indian press reported in 2014 that a sister vessel at the classified Ship Building Center in Visakhapatnam was nearing completion. The second SSBN, INS *Aridhaman*, should be launched in 2015 or 2016, by which time India may have also acquired a second Akula-II-class SSN from Russia.

According to Raja Menon, a retired rear admiral in the Indian Navy, there has been a certain amount of intra-service discord surrounding the ATV project from its inception, and some naval officers had initially hoped that India would focus on indigenously developing a hunter-killer SSN rather than an SSBN. Revealingly, when the Indian press announced the beginning of construction on the INS *Aridhaman*, navy sources were quoted as saying that "the focus must also shift to surface vessels."

Such intra-service disputes are nothing new and are hardly specific to the Indian Navy. After all, when the U.S. Navy initiated the Polaris submarine-launched ballistic missile (SLBM) program in the mid-1950s, many in the navy hierarchy were hostile to what they viewed as a potential diversion of funds away from the surface fleet. Similar problems were encountered within the British Navy. Referring explicitly to the British Polaris program as a cautionary tale, one of India's former chiefs of naval staff stressed the importance of strictly disaggregating the funding of the nuclear and conventional components of India's fleet:

The funding of such a massive strategic project (for a continuous at-sea strike capability) must remain outside the Indian Navy's budget. We all know what happened to the Royal Navy after the British government opted for the Polaris-Trident program in the sixties. These strategic assets are created by the nation for a specific strategic purpose (only as a nuclear deterrent), but need to be assigned to the armed forces for operational management. For this reason, the sea-based deterrent project will be operationally managed by the IN [Indian Navy], but funded separately, and just cannot be part of the normally allocated budget of the IN. While a nuclear deterrent is a good bargaining chip, what really matters is conventional deterrence at sea.

The precise manner in which the financing of India's sea-based deterrent and its extensive supporting infrastructure will be split up between the Indian Navy and external government allocations remains, however, somewhat nebulous.

It is also unclear whether India's projected flotilla of SSNs will be tasked with SSBN protection, which would prevent it from fulfilling other potential roles, such as forward-deployed sea denial. According to Ravi Ganesh, a retired vice admiral who commanded India's first Charlie-class SSN and led India's ATV program from 2000 to 2004,

the SSNs' primary role will continue to be forward-deployed sea denial and surveillance missions. Carrier defense is possible, although that requires a level of sophistication in sonar and underwater communication technology that we are currently very far from. I do not visualize SSNs being deployed for defense of SSBNs. There are problems of mutual interference and we are unlikely to be able to devote assets to such a restricted role.

Nevertheless, as time goes by and India's SSBN fleet gradually grows in size and importance, a debate will no doubt unfold within the Indian Navy as to how many resources and platforms should be devoted to its protection. Difficult decisions will need to be made, particularly if India's underwater environment becomes more contested. Ensuring SSBN defense might bring about certain operational opportunity costs. Operational safety is also likely to become an increasingly important issue. Concerns have already been raised after a series of tragic accidents hobbled India's conventional submarine fleet last year, and a hatch on the future INS *Aridhaman* blew off during hydropressure testing, killing an engineer. Following such a string of unfortunate mishaps, the Indian Ministry of Defense finally cleared a long-standing request from the Indian Navy to procure two deep submergence rescue vehicles. In short, while the launch of India's first indigenous SSBN is, without doubt, a great achievement, it only constitutes the first step in what promises to be a long and onerous process.

Current Limitations to Deterrent Patrols

Another lingering question is when the submarines will truly be able to embark on deterrent patrols. The INS*Arihant* had first been described as a "technology demonstrator" rather than a combat vessel. In 2010, however, high-ranking naval officials appeared to indicate that the INS *Arihant* would eventually be deployed on deterrent patrols.

As of early 2015, the *Arihant* has commenced sea trials before its expected commissioning in the same year, and it is slated to be fitted with up to twelve Sagarika K-15 SLBMs. The Sagarika, however, reportedly only has a range of 750 to 800 kilometers (about 466 to 497 miles), which many Indian commentators have described as grossly inadequate. Indeed, with such a short strike radius, the *Arihant* could not effectively target Lahore or Islamabad, let alone China's strategic centers.

If the Indian Navy wished to enact credible deterrence vis-à-vis China, its SSBNs would need to be forward-deployed in congested Northeast Asian waters. While transiting through shallow and heavily trafficked waterways such as the Malacca Strait, they would be vulnerable to detection and interdiction. Within the closed maritime spaces abutting China's shores, the submarines could fall prey to the People's Liberation Army Navy's strategic ASW efforts. Moreover, the sheer distance involved in such journeys would pose some severe logistical challenges. The *Arihant*'s 83-megawatt pressurized water reactor is reportedly based on first-or second-generation Soviet-era technology and has a short refueling cycle. These technical limitations will inevitably reduce the length and frequency of the *Arihant*'s deterrent patrols. Due to all of these factors, it appears unlikely that the*Arihant* will be sent on deterrent patrols until it, or one of its successors, is fitted with longer-range SLBMs.

India's Defense Research & Development Organization (DRDO) is currently working on two longer-range SLBMs: the 3,500-kilometer-range K-4 (about 2,174 miles), which recently underwent a successful test launch from a submerged pontoon off the coast of Visakhapatnam, and the 5,000-kilometer-range K-5 (approximately 3,106 miles), which appears to still be in the design phase. According to a number of publicly available reports, the*Arihant* is fitted with four universal tube launchers that can each carry either three K-15 missiles or one K-4 missile. Doubts have been raised, however, about the compatibility of the K-4's height with the SSBN's 10.4-meter-diameter hull. If the length of the K-4 cannot be reduced to under 10 meters, the *Arihant* may need to be retrofitted with a hydrodynamic outer envelopment, or bump. Even if engineers from the Defense Research & Development Organization succeed somehow in squeezing the K-4 aboard the *Arihant*, the missile's range remains suboptimal, as it would require the submarine to operate on the northeastern fringes of the Bay of Bengal, skirting Burmese and Bangladeshi littoral waters, in order to target China's major political and economic hubs. The K-5, with a 5,000-kilometer range that would enable Indian SSBNs to target Beijing from India's eastern seaboard, is projected to be at least 12 meters in length, thus most likely ruling out its deployment aboard the *Arihant*.

In short, in order to enjoy an effective sea-based deterrent vis-à-vis China, New Delhi will need to develop larger SSBNs, with greater missile carriage capacity and more powerful nuclear reactors. Whereas the *Arihant*'s two successors will reportedly share its infelicitous specifications, the fourth planned submarine in the series—the S-5—will be larger and more advanced. It may take at least a decade, however, for the S-5 to be completed.

Supporting Infrastructure

Meanwhile, the Indian Navy announced in 2014 that it was planning to construct a major deepwater base in Rambilli on the Bay of Bengal, 50 kilometers (about 31 miles) southwest of Visakhapatnam. Because of its deep water and closer proximity to China, the bay is considered a better staging point for India's nascent undersea deterrent than the shallow, congested waters of the Arabian Sea. Nuclear submarines are typically most vulnerable during ingress and egress activities, and the depth of the water surrounding Rambilli will allow India's SSBNs to slip in and out without being detected by aircraft or satellites. The new facility, codenamed Project Varsha, will reportedly house India's proposed fleet of five to six SSBNs, along with its first indigenously built aircraft carrier, the INS *Vikrant*. The project represents a massive undertaking and will only be completed, at the very earliest, in 2022.

Maintaining the ability to communicate with deep-cruising nuclear submarines constitutes one of the most challenging prerequisites for effective CASD. When SSBNs are on deterrent patrol, they must avoid rising too close to the surface for fear of detection. Instead, communications must be sent via very low frequency (VLF) or extremely low frequency (ELF) messages. VLF can penetrate ocean waters up to about 20 meters, whereas ELF can reach far greater depths, but at a lower data rate—which means that the messages take significantly longer to transmit. Typically, SSBNs are instructed via ELF to rise to VLF depth in order to receive longer messages.

Until 2014, India only possessed one VLF station, INS Kattabomman, which was commissioned in 1990 at South Vijayanarayanam in Tamil Nadu State. In 2010, the Indian Navy authorized the construction of two new transmitter towers at INS Kattabomman, which has significantly improved the facility's data transmission speed. More recently, India built its first ELF station, which appears to be located on the same site. India's Eastern Naval Command has also reportedly acquired 2,900 acres of land in the state of Telangana for another transmission center, although at this stage it remains unclear whether the planned facility will be for ELF or VLF communications.

In the event of conflict, however, these large and highly visible targets would be acutely vulnerable to air and missile strikes. In order to strengthen the security of their subsurface communications, most nuclear powers during the Cold War began to deploy long-trailing ELF and VLF antennas aboard aircraft. In the United States' case, this airborne system of survivable communication links was designated by the acronym TACAMO (for Take Charge and Move Out).

If India aims to knit together a resilient, multilayered strategic communications network, it may need to funnel additional investments into a squadron of TACAMO-style aircraft. Indeed, according to Arun Prakash,

> *the modification of a multi-engined aircraft, with a trailing-wire VLF-ELF antenna, is entirely feasible and will probably be adopted for C2 [command and control] once SSBNs commence deterrent patrols.*

The Surface-Based Component

A somewhat puzzling development lies in India's decision to conduct a series of test firings, starting in 2000, of Dhanush-class short-range ballistic missiles (SRBMs) from offshore patrol vessels. The Dhanush has a reported range of 350 kilometers (about 217 miles). As of early 2015, it remains unclear whether the tests were intended to display a formal recognition of India's willingness to station nuclear-tipped ballistic missiles aboard conventional vessels or whether the Dhanush program has served primarily as a technology demonstrator.

For the Indian Navy, the program appears to be merely a temporary substitute for the SSBN fleet. However, it may take India at least another decade before it can credibly claim to have attained CASD. Uncertainties abound as to what role the Dhanush program will play during this potentially protracted interim period.

THE COMMAND AND CONTROL CHALLENGE

Last but not least, the submarine-based leg of the triad will have a major impact on India's nuclear command-and-control arrangements. As Vipin Narang, a professor at the Massachusetts Institute of Technology, notes:

Although India's force disposition and stewardship procedures have evolved over the decades, the key permanent feature of India's assured retaliation posture is that civilians not only maintain control over India's nuclear forces, but they maintain custody of it.... Thus, in peacetime and even in relatively intense crises, India's nuclear arsenal is kept under firm civilian control, which minimizes the risk of unintentional use.

With the advent of canisterized nuclear missiles aboard SSBNs, the issue of warhead mating, which involves Defense Research & Development Organization and Department of Atomic Energy personnel, will "no longer be germane," according to Arun Prakash. Civilian decisionmakers will be compelled to replace institutional or negative controls with procedural or positive controls. In discussions with this author, Indian naval officers frequently reiterated that civilians would not be permitted on an SSBN during deterrent patrols, and that as a result, negative controls would need to be replaced by fail-safe electronic permissive action links.

For the surface-based component of the naval deterrent, the issue is less pressing, as institutional separation and control could be maintained through the presence of civilian representatives on board.

PAKISTAN'S NAVAL NUCLEAR "FORCE IN BEING"

An Adjustable Nuclear Posture

Pakistan's nuclear posture over the years has been both catalytic and asymmetric. It has performed a catalytic diplomatic function by providing a medium of external signaling, which can be used to draw external powers into Indo-Pakistani disputes, most notably over the contested territory of Kashmir, and it has served an asymmetric military purpose by offsetting the growing conventional superiority of its overbearing neighbor.

Refusing to adhere to a no-first-use policy, Islamabad views its nuclear posture and arsenal as variables that can be adjusted in order to blunt India's conventional military advantage, which, notes retired Pakistani Commander Muhammad Azam Khan, is "most pronounced in the maritime field." In 2002, Lieutenant General Khalid Kidwai, then director of Pakistan's Strategic Plans Division, the entity responsible for safeguarding Pakistan's nuclear arsenal, laid out the conditions under which Pakistan would envisage nuclear use:

Nuclear weapons are aimed solely at India. In case that deterrence fails, they will be used if a) India attacks Pakistan and conquers a large part of its territory, b) India destroys a large part of either its land or air forces, c) India proceeds to the economic strangling of Pakistan, or d) India pushes Pakistan into political destabilization or creates a large-scale internal subversion in Pakistan.

The fact that economic strangulation was mentioned only three years after the Kargil War between India and Pakistan, during which the Indian Navy threatened a blockade by establishing a cordon sanitaire around the port of Karachi, is no coincidence. Clearly Islamabad is in the habit of adding a measure of elasticity to its redlines, depending on changes in strategic circumstances.

Developing a Sea-Based Deterrent

Some Pakistani officials and commentators have claimed that India's launching of the *Arihant* was the event that prompted Islamabad's development of a sea-based nuclear capability. Abdul Basit, then foreign office spokesman, described the "induction of new lethal weapon systems as detrimental to regional peace and stability," and journalists lamented the fact that India had behaved irresponsibly by choosing to take the Indo-Pakistani nuclear race to sea. Khan observed that it constituted the first step in "the military nuclearization of the Indian Ocean," adding that it "noticeably dents the strategic balance; it has the potential to trigger a nuclear arms race." In reality, however, Pakistan had begun seriously considering the acquisition of a sea-based deterrent long before the *Arihant* was launched. Eight years earlier, in February 2001, the Pakistan Navy publicly acknowledged that it was considering deploying nuclear weapons aboard its conventional submarines. This was reiterated in 2003 by Admiral Shahid Karimullah, then chief of naval staff, who announced that while no such immediate plans existed, Pakistan would not hesitate to take such steps if it felt so compelled.

In May 2012, Pakistan formally inaugurated the headquarters of the Naval Strategic Force Command. A press release from the country's Inter Services Public Relations stated the future naval strategic force "will strengthen Pakistan's policy of Credible Minimum Deterrence and ensure regional stability," and, perhaps most intriguingly, called it the "custodian of the nation's 2nd strike capability."

Although there have been some (unsubstantiated) reports of a secret project led by the Pakistan Atomic Energy Commission to design a miniaturized nuclear power plant for a submarine, it seems far more likely that Pakistan will attempt to mate nuclear-tipped cruise missiles with conventional diesel-electric submarines. When interviewed, Pakistani commanders mentioned the precedent set by Israel's alleged decision to place nuclear-tipped cruise missiles aboard conventional submarines and suggested that their country should follow suit.

In recent years, Pakistan has shifted from an earlier generation of enriched uranium nuclear weapons to a newer generation of plutonium weapons. This has allowed it to both significantly expand its nuclear arsenal and to make progress in the miniaturization of its nuclear warheads for cruise missiles and battlefield use. Mansoor Ahmed, a lecturer at Pakistan's Quaid-i-Azam University, has thus averred that

in Pakistan's case, availability of plutonium and possibly tritium from the Khushab Nuclear Complex in the last fourteen years and the expansion in the production capacity at this site will allow Pakistan to develop boosted-fission warheads for its SLCMs [submarine-launched cruise missiles], such as the naval version of Babar [Babur]. Such warheads can also be deployed on conventional attack submarines (SSKs) such as the Pakistani Air Independent Propulsion (AIP) equipped Agosta 90-Bs in the future.

Other Pakistani commentators have ventured that the Pakistan Navy may attempt to station tactical nuclear weapons aboard surface ships, or they have suggested that the service's P-3C Orion maritime patrol craft be given a tactical nuclear role.

Islamabad is currently developing a sea-based variant of its nuclear-capable, indigenously produced Babur missile, a subsonic, low-level, terrain-mapping land attack cruise missile with a reported range of 700 kilometers (about 435 miles). According to Feroz Khan, a former Pakistan Army brigadier, the project has been placed under the tutelage of Pakistan's Maritime Technologies Complex and is nearing completion. In December 2012, the Pakistan Navy conducted a series of cruise missile tests from naval platforms in the Arabian Sea. The official statement did not give the precise specifications of the missile in question, simply declaring that the test included "firings of a variety of modern missiles" and that it reaffirmed "credibility of deterrence at sea."

The Logic Behind Naval Nuclear Coercion

Pakistan's naval nuclear ambitions are fueled primarily by the sense of a growing conventional rather than strategic imbalance. Through the nuclearization of its own fleet, Islamabad hopes to prevent the Indian Navy from translating its conventional superiority into effective coercive power. Since the Indo-Pakistani war of 1971, when India's Osa-class missile boats conducted a daring nighttime raid against Karachi, Pakistani naval planners have sought, first and foremost, to prevent the Indian Navy from acquiring the ability to put debilitating pressure on Pakistan's maritime flank.

The Pakistan Navy's concerns were compounded by their Indian counterpart's actions during Operation Talwar, in the midst of the 1999 Kargil War, and during Operation Parakram in 2001–2002. In both cases, the Indian Navy surged elements from its Eastern and Western Fleets in order to engage in coercive maneuvering in the North Arabian Sea.

India's maritime strategy includes the following assessment of the 1999 deployment:

The Indian Navy short-listed three goals, namely to ensure safety and security of our maritime interests against a surprise attack, to deter Pakistan from escalating the conflict into a full-scale war and to win the war convincingly at sea. The lesson that emerges for the Indian Navy is on two counts. Firstly, there will be space and scope to conduct conventional maritime operations below the nuclear threshold. Secondly, a window of opportunity would exist to influence the land battle.

From the Indian Navy's point of view, such actions provided a means of projecting what some scholars have referred to as triadic deterrence—that is, using "threats and/or punishments against another state to coerce it to prevent non-state actors from conducting attacks from its territory"—all while maintaining the conflict below the nuclear threshold.

For Pakistani naval planners, however, both incidents were sobering reminders of their coastal nation's glaring vulnerability to blockade and strategies of commodity denial. Moeed Yusuf provides the following summary of how India's naval actions were perceived in Pakistan:

It would seem that the Kargil episode would have signaled to the Pakistani armed forces, army included, that if the advent of nuclear weapons had made the prospects of limited war more likely by allowing Pakistan to use the space below India's nuclear threshold with impunity, it also meant that India would counter Pakistan's advantage at the lowest rung of the escalation ladder by exploiting its naval superiority early on in the crisis. In essence, India was using the sea to neutralize Pakistan's low-end strategic space under the nuclear umbrella.

Islamabad appears particularly concerned over New Delhi's ability to interfere with its crude oil imports, which accounted for 31 percent of Pakistan's total energy supply in 2012. Energy shortages have frequently led to riots in Pakistan's major cities, and for many Pakistani security managers, any protracted disruption of sea-borne energy would automatically result in dangerous levels of unrest.

Unable to sustain any remotely symmetrical form of naval competition, the Pakistan Navy sees nuclearization as the most effective means of countering Indian maritime power projection. Writing in 2004, five years before India unveiled the *Arihant,* Pakistani Lieutenant Commander Raja Rab Nawaz posited that

limited conventional war at sea between India and Pakistan is more[,] not less likely in a future conflict. Overwhelming conventional superiority of the Indian Navy poses serious challenges in case of such an eventuality.... Pakistan must acquire a sea-based second-strike capability to maintain strategic balance in the region.

Security managers in New Delhi are probably unaware of the extent to which their nation's growing maritime strength is perceived as a threat in Pakistan.

An illustration of this perceptual mismatch was provided in the course of a crisis simulation exercise organized by the U.S. Naval Postgraduate School in 2013.

Held in Sri Lanka, the exercise included both Indian and Pakistani participants, ranging from retired military officials to civilian academics.

The simulation began with a mass terrorist attack in an Indian cricket stadium, which appeared to have originated in Pakistan. The Indian team immediately responded by initiating a number of moves that they considered "limited" and "punitive" in nature, including the implementation of a maritime exclusion zone (MEZ) along Pakistan's Makran coast.

Whereas the Indian participants deemed this action "restrained, justified, and short of war," the "enforcement of the MEZ off the Makran coast were deemed by the Pakistan team as acts of war." As the exercise continued to unfold, Pakistan began to heighten its nuclear readiness level and threatened first use.

This form of coercive nuclear signaling is entirely in line with weaker states' thinking with regard to the strategic utility of nuclear weapons.

By threatening either directly or indirectly to employ low-yield nuclear weapons at sea or against an advancing Indian aircraft carrier strike force, Islamabad can hope to acquire escalation dominance and considerably dilute its larger neighbor's coercive naval power.

PAKISTAN'S FEAR OF A PREEMPTIVE SEIZURE OR STRIKE ON ITS LAND-BASED NUCLEAR ASSETS

Stationing a portion of the nation's nuclear arsenal on or under the sea also guarantees an extra measure of reassurance for jittery officers in Pakistan's Strategic Plans Division.

The Pakistani military has long fretted over the possibility of foreign seizure or preemptive destruction of its land-based nuclear assets. The progressive fraying of Islamabad's ties with Washington and the way a U.S. Navy SEAL team was able to penetrate deep inside Pakistani territory and assassinate Osama bin Laden have only reinforced Pakistan's fears over the security of its nuclear arsenal. Meanwhile, as Washington and New Delhi's relations have continued on their upward trajectory, Pakistan has grown increasingly concerned that both democracies might share intelligence regarding the location of its nuclear stockpiles.

A Response to Cold Start

Frustrated by its inability to both deter and rapidly respond to violent acts of terrorism originating from Pakistan, the Indian military has been working to devise operational concepts that would enable it to safely wage a limited conventional war under a nuclear overhang. One such concept formulated by the army, termed Cold Start, envisions a type of blitzkrieg warfare, relying on fast integrated battle groups and closely synchronized army and air force operations in order to conduct lightning retaliatory strikes and potentially gain temporary control of shallow tracts of Pakistani territory. Cold Start has never been formally validated by India's official leadership, let alone the other services, and it is still very much viewed as something of a strategic hypothesis.

Unfortunately, however, the idea has gained traction in Pakistan, where commentators frequently depict it as proof of India's belligerence and alleged desire to further dismember its smaller neighbor.

Pakistan's doctrinal response has been to reemphasize its readiness to use nuclear weapons to destroy Indian mechanized forces, arguing that "the wider the conventional asymmetry, the lower the nuclear threshold." Equipping a submarine or surface vessel with nuclear-tipped cruise missiles would enable the Pakistan Navy to engage in intra-war coercion through the threat of horizontal escalation, thus potentially compelling Indian ground forces to withdraw. Indeed, some analysts have suggested that Pakistani security managers might be considering a mix of different potential targets in the event of nuclear use, separated into low-, medium-, and high-end options. The low end might involve demonstration nuclear strikes against Indian conventional assets—primarily as a means of demonstrating Islamabad's willingness to escalate even further. This would bear certain similarities to Russia's thinking with regard to the use of tactical nuclear weapons as a means of brutally "de-escalating" (in Russian parlance) high-end conventional conflict.

If such a decision were to be made, a demonstration nuclear strike at sea would no doubt be considered a much more attractive—and potentially less escalatory—option than an attack on land.

Strategic Depth

The quest for strategic depth has long constituted one of the core components of the Pakistani military's geopolitical mind-set.

Strategic depth would allow Pakistan to more effectively respond to a putative Indian incursion by focusing the entirety of its forces on the Indo-Pakistani front. This would enable it to achieve greater parity with an Indian military that is obliged to deploy a substantial portion of its forces along the Sino-Indian border. In order to achieve strategic depth, Islamabad needs to make sure that it does not face a threat on both of its frontiers, and therefore it must rely on a friendly or compliant regime in Afghanistan.

The notion of strategic depth became particularly popular at the end of the 1980s, when both India and Pakistan were covertly developing nuclear weapons programs. General Mirza Aslam Beg, Pakistan Army chief of staff from 1988 to 1991, advocated the scattering of nuclear assets and air force bases across Afghan territory, from where Pakistan could continue to launch strikes against India in the event that its territory was overrun or destroyed. Pakistan has thus consistently viewed Afghanistan both as its strategic backyard and as a launchpad for its war of a thousand cuts against India in Kashmir, whether by actively supporting the Taliban during the long period of factional struggle that followed the Soviet Union's departure from Afghanistan or by continuing, more recently, to aid insurgent groups such as the Haqqani network based in North Waziristan.

Pursuing a sea-based nuclear strike capability allows Pakistan to acquire the strategic depth that it has traditionally sought to acquire across the Hindu Kush. For even though, at the time of writing, Western nations are projected to have withdrawn the vast majority of their troops from Afghanistan within a year, Pakistan's hopes of transforming the country into its Central Asian proxy are likely to remain unfulfilled. The prospect of pursuing a sustained rearguard action or placing hidden second-strike assets deep in Afghan's interior appears particularly untenable. Shifting part of its nuclear arsenal to sea thus allows Pakistan to acquire the greater degree of survivability it was hoping to one day achieve through dispersion in a subservient Afghanistan.

Countering Indian Plans for Ballistic Missile Defense

Since approximately the mid-2000s, India has expressed an interest in developing a ballistic missile defense system to help protect its major cities and infrastructure. While precise information on the progress of India's ballistic missile defense is hard to come by, it would appear that New Delhi has been working toward both an indigenous system and dual ventures incorporating Russian, Israeli, or French technology. Scholars of nuclear issues in South Asia have long warned of the potentially destabilizing effects of introducing missile defense to the subcontinent, equating the danger with that injected by the introduction of counterforce nuclear capabilities during the Cold War.

Pakistan's reactions to India's projected antiballistic missile defenses largely reflect these concerns. One method Islamabad may use to circumvent an operational Indian system, proposed by both Mansoor Ahmed, a strategic studies professor, and Usman Shabbir of the Pakistan Military Consortium think tank, would be to employ submarine-launched, nuclear-tipped cruise missiles.

Insights From the Cold War

Contemporary South Asian nuclear dynamics may be unique in their specificity, yet many interesting, and potentially instructive, parallels—as well as certain revealing differences—can still be gleaned from the past.

At the dawn of the atomic age, Soviet and Western naval strategists found themselves grappling with a set of daunting and unprecedented challenges. Accustomed to the laws of conventional naval warfare, fleet commanders were suddenly compelled to operate under a nuclear shadow. As a result, many of their core assumptions concerning the conduct of naval operations, whether in times of peace or of war, underwent a fundamental revision. Looming in the backdrop of every naval deployment was the possibility, however remote, of tensions escalating into conflict and of conventional maritime combat spiraling into a potentially catastrophic naval nuclear exchange. As Paul Nitze observed in a seminal chapter in 1956, the situation confronting the two superpowers had become analogous to a hair-raising game of chess, whereby

the atomic queens may never be brought into play; they may never actually take one of the opponent's pieces. But the position of the atomic queens may still have a decisive bearing on which side can safely advance a limited-war bishop or even a cold-war pawn. The advance of a cold-war pawn may even disclose a check of the opponent's king by a well-positioned atomic queen.

Using a different metaphor but describing essentially the same phenomenon, French strategists, such as Andre Beaufre, wrote that "the nuclear force may be unseen, but it is always there, and it is this which sets the boundaries of the battlefield."

The problem with the maritime domain, however, was its very lack of boundaries. In contrast to the clear terrestrial delineations among North Atlantic Treaty Organization (NATO) and Warsaw Pact forces in Eastern and Central Europe, the world's oceans provided a vast arena where both superpowers' navies were in almost incessant interaction. The frequency of these contacts inevitably led to moments of friction and occasionally to incidents that severely imperiled strategic stability. As both superpowers aggrandized and diversified their nuclear arsenals, they devoted a great deal of attention to the maritime domain—not only in terms of SSBN operations and CASD—but also as a theater of operations potentially more susceptible to the conduct of tactical nuclear warfare.

As academics such as Francis Gavin have aptly noted, the study of history can prove most useful when it is conducted "horizontally," exposing connections over time and space. Many of the challenges Indian and Pakistani security managers will inevitably come to face in the not-too-distant future were, in fact, discussed at length during the Cold War's multidecadal naval nuclear competition.

CONVENTIONAL NAVAL OPERATIONS UNDER A NUCLEAR SHADOW

For much of the Cold War, the balance of conventional military power on the Eurasian continent was in the Soviet Union's favor. As a result, NATO planners relied heavily on the threat of nuclear use as a means of projecting deterrence.

In the naval domain, the situation was reversed, with Western navies enjoying a distinct superiority—both technological and numerical—over their Soviet rival. From the very beginning of the Cold War, Western planners fretted over the possibility that the Soviets might attempt to offset their conventional naval inferiority by threatening to employ nuclear weapons at sea.

The vulnerability of large surface ships to nuclear attack, in particular, became a source of much concern to nuclear strategists. For instance, Edward Teller, the father of the hydrogen bomb, advised against the deployment of aircraft carriers, writing that in his mind, an aircraft carrier

> *looked to me like quite a good target. In fact, if I project my mind into a time, when not only we, but also a potential enemy, have plenty of atomic bombs, I would not put so many dollars and so many people into so good a target. Come to think of it, I would not put anything on the surface of the ocean—it's too good a target.*

U.S. naval commanders warned that, in the event of conflict, the Soviet Union's Strategic Missile Forces might seek to supplement the actions of a conventionally outmatched Soviet Navy by targeting Western naval task forces or convoys. Writing in the *Naval War College Review* in the late 1960s, one U.S. lieutenant commander made a dire observation:

If one side presented the preponderance of targets the use of nuclear forces could be advantageous to the other side. The preponderance of surface forces in the West makes it extremely strong in a conventional war. However, as soon as the [Soviet] Bloc use of nuclear weapons is conceded, the loss of many of these vessels can be expected with a relatively small amount of effort on the part of the Bloc Forces.

Strategists such as Desmond Ball also noted that

the destruction of large naval assets would disproportionately disadvantage the United States, both because of the enormous U.S. investment in its carrier forces, and because of the greater U.S. dependence on sea lines of communication.

This vulnerability of large, densely concentrated naval formations to nuclear weapons led to something of a conundrum. The natural response to such a threat, argued both Soviet and Western strategists, was to engage in fleet or battle group spacing to reduce the likelihood of multiple kills resulting from a single nuclear blast. The need for dispersal, however, flew in the face of centuries of naval practice. Preeminent Soviet military theorists began to question the very relevance of naval strategy, commenting that in the nuclear missile era, the most deeply ingrained principles of Soviet naval tactics, such as "massed action" (*massirovanie*) and "combined action" (*vzaimodeystvie raznorodnykh sil*), could no longer be considered valid. This presented military planners with a fundamental dilemma, as, notes one former U.S. Army attaché to Pakistan, "Survival in a nuclear environment required dispersal, while success in a conventional fight required mass and concentration."

Within such a heavily nuclearized environment, the prospective operational benefits to be derived from launching a first salvo became even more apparent. Additionally, the escalation dynamics of warfare in the maritime theater appeared, in the eyes of many naval analysts, to be considerably less constrained than those attending military operations on land. In the late 1950s and early 1960s, figures such as Henry Kissinger noted that limited nuclear war between Soviet and Western forces was far more likely to flare up in secondary or peripheral theaters than along the heavily militarized Central European front.

To some theorists, the likelihood of one side initiating limited nuclear war hinged upon two main factors: whether the use of nuclear weapons could be confined to a specific geographical area, and whether they could be used "surgically," without incurring mass civilian casualties or the destruction of strategic centers. Out on the wide-open waters, the use of low-yield nuclear weapons against enemy vessels would result in little to no collateral civilian casualties. As one U.S. naval officer wrote in 1967, "What targets of a tactical or strategic nature can be attacked and destroyed with less direct involvement of civilian populations than naval forces at sea?"

How then, wondered Western nuclear strategists, could the Soviets be deterred from employing—or from threatening to employ—nuclear weapons against NATO's naval forces? Some posited that there was scant likelihood that the Soviet Navy would seek to erode firebreaks between conventional and nuclear forces by genuinely subscribing to a nuclear warfighting strategy. The use of even a few tactical nuclear weapons—however isolated the maritime theater in question—ran the risk of escalating to strategic exchange through the phenomenon of linkage. There was little reason, therefore, for the United States and its allies to emphasize naval nuclear warfare.

Others argued that the only true way to prevent the Soviets from engaging in coercive nuclear escalation at sea was to nuclearize close to the entirety of the combat fleet architecture. The U.S. Navy agreed and adopted a strategy of escalation dominance by engaging in the wholesale nuclearization of its combat fleet while striving to disabuse the Soviet leadership of any notion that a nuclear war at sea could be limited.

This evolution in naval nuclear force posture was greatly facilitated by the wider doctrinal shift, in the mid-1950s and onward, from a deterrent policy predicated on massive retaliation toward one of a more graduated or flexible response. In 1982, Richard Perle, then assistant secretary of defense for international security policy, declared that official U.S. policy was to "discourage the Soviets from believing that they could limit a nuclear war to forces at sea." He also stressed that

the Soviets retain a significant capability to attack ships at sea, and they may, as a consequence, be misled into believing that so long as civilian casualties are not involved in such attacks, as they presumably would not be, they could in fact limit a war to attacks on forces at sea.... The desire on our part is not to permit the Soviets to determine the scope of the battle to give whatever advantages would be inherent in their having the freedom to choose where the battle would be fought.

By the 1980s, however, conventional and nuclear weapons were commingled on U.S. surface and subsurface vessels. The fleet was equipped with a large and impressively broad inventory of tactical nuclear weapons, ranging from nuclear anti-submarine rockets to nuclear-tipped cruise missiles and surface-to-air missiles. For proponents of a strategy of flexible response, such a shift made eminent sense. Supporters argued that this wide dispersal of nuclear assets across the fleet had vastly augmented the allied nuclear reserve, thus effectively dampening any lingering Soviet temptation to conduct a "coordinated, preemptive strike at sea." Moreover, the ubiquitous presence of theater nuclear weapons aboard U.S. vessels served a vital signaling function. It was both a means of communicating resolve, thus dissuading the Soviets from engaging in escalatory naval actions, and a way of demonstrating the strength of U.S. commitment to certain fretful, and geographically distant, allies. The deployment of naval platforms with nuclear-delivery capability, wrote military analyst Richard Fieldhouse, could "critically affect the dynamics of the crisis situation in a number of ways." For example,

perceptions of the stakes involved could be raised by the presence of U.S. tactical nuclear forces; and these forces could significantly alter the actual military capabilities of the forces involved, thus improving escalation control by complicating the adversaries' calculations of success and failure.

Naval Friction and the Risk of Inadvertent Escalation

For many analysts, the generalized commingling of conventional and nuclear assets at sea was dangerously escalatory. In times of conflict, Soviet and Western naval commanders would have no way of determining whether enemy vessels were armed with nuclear weapons or not, and a radioactive fog of war would float over combat operations.

The most controversial dual-capable system was the sea-launched variant of the Tomahawk cruise missile. Fitted aboard both surface and subsurface vessels, the Tomahawk's long range (approximately 2,500 kilometers, or about 1,550 miles) and precision made it an ideal candidate for counterforce missions. This meant, noted one observer, that

with respect to the conventional/nuclear firebreak, the Soviet Union must consider any vessel equipped with Tomahawks to be a nuclear threat even if in fact these missiles are only carrying conventional payloads. The obfuscation of these distinctions is likely to increase Soviet paranoia about U.S. naval deployments in the vicinity of the Soviet homeland; it inevitably reduces the degree of certainty with which Soviet responses can be predicted; it increases the likelihood of escalation from actions that the U.S. might regard as tactical; and it increases the chances of miscalculation and misperception and hence of inadvertent escalation.

The dangers of sudden escalation arising from ill-perceived signaling or deployments were heightened in the maritime domain, where naval interactions frequently led to friction and where conflicts at times continued even after crises had abated on land. A classic example is the tense situation that unfolded underwater during the Cuban Missile Crisis, which almost led to disaster. Historians now know that each of the Soviet submarines deployed off Cuba was armed with nuclear-tipped torpedoes, a fact that was not known by the U.S. Navy at the time. In an attempt to force the Soviet submarines to surface, the U.S. fleet dropped practice depth charges. They were not intended to hit the submarines, but rather to coerce them into revealing themselves. The Soviet submarine officers, however, viewed these actions in a different light, and one harried commander ordered his men to assemble the nuclear torpedo to battle-readiness.

Even after both superpowers signed the 1972 Incidents at Sea Agreement, their naval interactions remained prone to sporadic bursts of tension, such as during the 1973 Arab-Israeli conflict. Episodes of brinkmanship involving games of chicken, aggressive forward intelligence gathering, and accidental collisions were particularly prevalent in the subsurface domain, which had been deliberately excluded from the agreement.

The risks of inadvertent escalation were exacerbated, argued Professor Barry Posen, when conventional naval operations produced "patterns of damage or threat" to structural components of a nation's nuclear reserves, such as its SSBNs. During the administration of U.S. President Ronald Reagan, the U.S. Navy's maritime strategy explicitly called for an aggressive ASW campaign by U.S. and allied naval forces against the entirety of the Soviet submarine fleet, SSBNs included. Conventional attrition of a substantial portion of the Soviet Union's second-strike capability, argued Posen, could be viewed by Moscow as a precursor to a nuclear attack, and this, in turn, might heighten Soviet temptations to engage in a preemptive nuclear strike against NATO forces. John Mearsheimer, a political science professor, also perceived anti-SSBN operations as highly destabilizing, noting that

some strategies also can cause forces to intermingle in a crisis in a manner that produces a tactical or strategic first strike advantage.... Some strategies can raise the risk that forces will collide with one another in a manner that activates one side's rules of engagement, leading it to commence firing. In each instance crisis stability is undermined, and crises are more likely to erupt into war.

Hardline defenders of the 1980s maritime strategy rejected these critiques, and they argued that, to the contrary, threatening Soviet SSBNs provided the allies with significant leverage in times of conflict, which might then be used in favor of war termination. Linton Brooks, who served on the Reagan administration's National Security Council, agreed with this assessment, noting that the maritime strategy also provided a means of eroding the offensive capability of the Soviet SSN fleet, which would find itself compelled to focus its energy on protecting SSBNs, rather than on attacking allied sea lines of communication.

For this school of thinkers, the systemization of dual-use platforms at sea did not weaken but buttressed deterrence—precisely due to the fact that it injected a certain degree of ambiguity. Professor Thomas Schelling famously referred to this as the "threat that leaves something to chance." Thus, for Linton Brooks,

deterrence is enhanced through the deliberate importation of both risk and uncertainty.... Sea-based systems, able to attack a wide spectrum of targets from a large number of platforms, over a broad spectrum of attack azimuths, complicate Soviet defense planning immeasurably, thus strengthening deterrence.

Other observers expressed skepticism over the notion that the Soviet Navy might respond to conventional attacks on its SSBNs by employing sea-based tactical nuclear weapons, arguing that Moscow's political control over nuclear delivery systems was too tight and that the Soviet leadership would never authorize such a response.

Applying Cold War Lessons to Contemporary South Asia

What lessons can be drawn from the Cold War's wealth of deliberations over issues such as sea-based nuclear weapons, naval nuclear warfare, and escalation control? As New Delhi and Islamabad lay out the rudiments of their respective naval nuclear architectures, they will no doubt find themselves wrestling with a remarkably similar array of operational predicaments and deterrence-related challenges.

Both nations are still in the process of shaping their sea-based nuclear force structures, and naval nuclear interactions are likely to remain somewhat sporadic for the next few years. This constitutes a singularly opportune moment, therefore, for security communities in both capitals to engage in a much more granular analysis of past naval nuclear operations and strategies.

The issue of dual-use platforms, whereby conventional and nuclear assets commingle and overlap, is of particular relevance to contemporary South Asia, as are many of the Cold War era's discussions over the tactical quandaries inherent in naval operations under a nuclear shadow.

South Asia's maritime environment remains, for its part, alarmingly unstructured, and the challenges posed by naval friction and misperception will no doubt loom large in future times of crisis. Perhaps most importantly, Cold War theorists' concerns over the considerable risks linked to the conventional targeting of strategic or nuclear-armed platforms will urgently need to be addressed.

The Commingling Issue

Both India and Pakistan appear to be opting for naval nuclear force structures that incorporate dual-capable systems. In India's case, this may only be a temporary phenomenon. It remains unclear whether the Dhanush program is truly envisaged as forming a component of India's nascent sea-based deterrent, or whether the decision to fit surface ships with modified versions of the Prithvi SRBM is simply a stopgap measure while the country's SSBN fleet gradually takes shape. Writing in 2001, a seasoned observer of security developments in South Asia depicted the Dhanush program as the result of mainly bureaucratic calculations, stating that it *is unlikely to result in a sea-based nuclear deterrent—at least on present plans—since it is driven primarily by the Indian Navy's interest in acquiring a land-attack capability vis-à-vis Pakistan in order to assert its own strategic relevance to the larger war-fighting outcomes within the Indian subcontinent.*

There are also some practical considerations that would appear to militate against equipping Indian surface vessels with such a system. First of all, the Dhanush is a liquid-fueled SRBM, and it can prove both difficult and hazardous to handle liquid propellants at sea. Moreover, liquid-fueled missiles take longer to launch than their solid-fueled counterparts, which raises questions over the viability of the Dhanush as a robust second-strike system. Finally, in the event of conflict, India's surface ships could prove highly vulnerable to enemy anti-surface-warfare operations.

Unfortunately, due to the Indian political leadership's traditional reticence to discuss details pertaining to the nation's nuclear force structure, public discourse on the Dhanush has been captured by the scientists of India's DRDO. In 2011, officials from this organization were recorded as saying that the successful launches of the Prithvi from land and sea had established that "different forms of [India's] nuclear deterrence are in place" and that the launches allowed India's Strategic Forces Command to launch (nuclear) attacks "both from land and sea." The Defense Research & Development Organization, however, has developed an unfortunate habit of issuing assertive statements that do not necessarily reflect the views of India's political leadership.

Beyond the practical limitations associated with deploying SRBMs from surface vessels, the debate, as it did during the Cold War, appears to revolve around two very different schools of thought. On the one side are those who believe that deterrence can be strengthened through the injection of ambiguity, and on the other are those who argue that the deliberate blurring of conventional and nuclear platforms is far more likely to heighten the risks of vertical escalation.

One school of thinkers argues that opting to conflate conventional and nuclear assets at sea could have serious ramifications in times of crisis. This problem has been singled out by a trio of U.S. Naval War College professors, who have warned that *if one navy stations nuclear weapons aboard conventionally armed warships, its antagonist could end up inadvertently destroying nuclear forces in the process of targeting conventionally armed forces.*

Echoing the arguments of Linton Brooks during the Cold War, Ashley Tellis, formerly at the RAND Corporation, has taken a different position, arguing that the very ambiguity of the SRBM's payload could provide India with the opportunity to "secure strategic benefits," adding that *the fact that Islamabad can never be certain as to whether these standoff capabilities—especially the ship-based ballistic missile systems—are purely conventional or nuclear-armed make such unorthodox deployment postures particularly attractive from a strategic point of view: These sea-based systems serve to levy a potential threat on Pakistan from what is otherwise a non-traditional axis, and, by that very fact, compel Islamabad to allocate military resources to sanitize them even though the strike systems in question may finally turn out to be no more than conventionally armed vehicles of little strategic significance.*

Whereas it remains unclear whether India has expressly chosen a path that emphasizes commingling, Pakistan's security managers fall squarely into the "blurring is best" school. As discussed in the first section of this report, Pakistan's naval officers and strategists openly advocate nuclearizing a large portion of the Pakistani fleet architecture—not only submarines, but also surface vessels and maritime patrol aircraft.

By wantonly engaging in a horizontal dispersal of its nuclear assets at sea, Islamabad runs the risk of adding a considerable amount of instability to its naval interactions with its larger South Asian neighbor. Pakistan's calculation may be that such a move would effectively neuter the Indian Navy by preventing it from prosecuting Pakistani vessels in the event of hostilities. This assumption, however, may be deeply flawed.

Conventional Operations and Strategic Instability

Several observers have noted that Indian military personnel have openly alluded to the fact that Pakistan's nuclear assets would be targeted by Indian conventional forces in the event of war.

Although India's nuclear doctrine may revolve around countervalue targeting, its conventional operational constructs appear to incorporate some potentially destabilizing counterforce elements. In many ways, this is reminiscent of Barry Posen's discussion of the risks posed by conventional operations that cause patterns of damage or threat to nuclear-armed platforms. India's maritime strategy, for instance, places a heavy emphasis on offensive sea control, as well as on "marking and counter marking" as a means to "clear the cobwebs" in the preliminary phases of conflict.

Going forward, subsurface interactions are liable to become particularly problematic. Andrew Winner, a professor at the U.S. Naval War College, has noted:

Submarine-versus-submarine interactions occur already without any public acknowledgment of increased tensions, but the importance of nuclear weapons may cause both sides to take greater risks both to gather intelligence and to defend a nuclear-armed platform. Similarly, both sides may become more aggressive in patrolling and defending territorial waters, contiguous zones, and even exclusive economic zones if they want to deny the other side from gaining familiarity with a particular stretch of water.

The history of the Cold War is littered with examples of submarine intelligence-gathering operations gone awry, resulting in collisions, accidental groundings, or near confrontations.

A number of key questions about India-Pakistan interactions remain very open and are seldom discussed in either New Delhi or Islamabad. This is cause for concern. As India and Pakistan begin to deploy nuclear-armed submarines, will both navies manage to avoid succumbing to the escalatory pressures tied to such operations? In the event of conflict, would India and Pakistan eschew targeting nuclear-armed or dual-use platforms? If Pakistan engaged an Indian SSBN, or if India destroyed a Pakistani surface ship armed with nuclear-tipped cruise missiles, could strategic stability be preserved?

Greater attention will also need to be paid to naval force disposition and signaling. India is still far from acquiring the capabilities to conduct CASD and to seamlessly maintain SSBNs on deterrent patrol. As a result, it is likely that in times of high tension, New Delhi would surge its undersea nuclear assets from their deepwater ports in the Bay of Bengal. If detected, such a move might be deemed highly provocative by Islamabad and could invite preemptive conventional action. Indian ASW forces, for their part, may feel a similar pressure to engage in early attrition of Pakistan's conventional attack submarines if they were detected moving close to Indian carrier groups or in the vicinity of major Indian port cities such as Mumbai.

Thomas Schelling famously defined brinkmanship as the manipulation of the shared risk of war. By deliberately cultivating uncertainty and importing tactics of intimidation, weak actors may hope to convincingly deter a more risk-averse opponent from effectively leveraging its conventional superiority. In terms of everyday maritime operations, this can dissuade the stronger naval actor from pressing its claims or maintaining a regular presence in certain areas, out of fear of an isolated incident spiraling out of control. Pakistan has displayed a strong attachment to naval brinkmanship over the years, frequently buzzing Indian naval task forces with maritime aircraft, and in some cases threatening to enter into direct collision with Indian naval ships. Both nations have failed to resolve long-standing maritime boundary issues, and they continue to engage in the systematic detention of fishermen they consider to have violated their territorial waters. The most dramatic incident occurred in 1999, when a Pakistani Dassault-Breguet Atlantic aircraft violated Indian airspace, refused to respond to hails, and was shot down by an Indian Air Force MiG-21.

Such episodes are already fraught with risk under normal conditions, and they become even more hazardous in an environment where dual-use systems have become the norm. Until now, both Indian and Pakistani naval officers have been accustomed to operating within a conventional maritime setting. In the future, the Indian Air Force may have no way of ascertaining whether a straying Pakistani maritime patrol aircraft is carrying nuclear ordnance or not. Accurately fathoming an adversary's intentions is a singularly challenging enterprise. It becomes even more arduous when one player relies on a policy of tactical brinkmanship and naval nuclear coercion to compensate for its conventional inferiority.

Bibliography

Ajey Lele: *Strategic Technologies for the Military : Breaking New Frontiers*, Sage, Delhi, 2009.

Akbar S.: *Jinnah, Pakistan, and Islamic Identity: The Search for Saladin*, 1997.

Alam, Aftab : *US Policy Towards South Asia: Special Reference to Indo-Pak Relations*, Raj, Delhi, 1998.

Allana, G.: *Pakistan Movement: Historic Documents*, Karachi, Department of International Relations, University of Karachi, 1967.

Allison, Graham: *Nuclear Terrorism: The Ultimate Preventable Catastrophe*, New York: Times Books, 2004.

Asha Gupta: *Military Rule and Democratization : Changing Perspectives*, Deep & Deep, Delhi, 2003.

Barber B.R.: *Strong Democracy. Participatory Politics for a New Age*. Berkeley, University of California Press, 1984.

Ben Wisner : *At Risk, Natural Hazards, People's Vulnerability, and Disasters*, London, Routledge, 1994.

Budge I: *The New Challenge of Direct Democracy*, Oxford, Polity Press, 1996.

Digumarti Bhaskara Rao: *Military Conversion : Impact on Science and Technology*, Discovery, Delhi, 2003.

Duncan, Francis. *Rickover and the Nuclear Navy: The Discipline of Technology*. Annapolis: Naval Institute Press, 1990.

Eric Herring: *The Arms Dynamic in World Politics*, London: Lynne Rienner Publishers, 1998.

Friedman, G.: *The Future of War of Cyber Crimes*, N.Y., Random House, 1996.

Gerstell, Richard. *How to Survive an Atomic Bomb*. Washington, D.C.: Combat Forces Press, 1950.

Gupta, Asha: *Military Rule and Democratization : Changing Perspectives*, Deep & Deep, Delhi, 2003.

Hoffman, Bruce, *Inside Terrorism*, New York: Columbia University Press, 1998.

Huntington, S.P.: *The China Modernisation Military and the State*, N.Y., Vintage Books, 1964.

Janowitz, M.: *The Professional Soldier: A Social and Political Portrait*, N.Y., The Free Press, 1960.

Jha, Prem Shankar : *India and China : The Battle Between Soft and Hard Power*, Penguin Books India, Delhi, 2010.

Kunju, N. : *Indo-Pak : Nuclear Cold War*, Reliance, Delhi, 2002.

Laquer, Walter, *The New Terrorism: Fanaticism and the Arms of Mass Destruction*, Oxford: Oxford University Press, 1999.

Nevile, P.: *Lahore: A Sentimental Journey*. New Delhi: Penguin, 1993.

Phuskele, Preeti : *Pak and China : Emerging Superpowers*, ICFAI University, Delhi, 2009.

Posen, B.R.: *The Sources of Indian Military Doctrine*, Ithaca, 1984, Cornell Univ. Press.

Prasad, Lal Bahadur : *Indian Political System and Law*, New Delhi, Shree, 2005.

Raj Kumar: *Weapons and Military Technology*, Sumit Enterprises, Delhi, 2009.

Rhodes, Richard, *The Making of the Atomic Bomb*, New York: Simon and Schuster, 1988.

Rosen, P.: *Societies and Military Power: India and its Armies*, Ithaca, Cornell University Press, 1996.

Selden, S.: *The Promise of Representative Bureaucracy: Diversity and Responsiveness in a Government Agency*, New York, M. E. Sharpe, 1997.

Sherwin, Martin J. A World Destroyed: *The Atomic Bomb and the Grand Alliance*. New York: Vintage Books, 1977.

Spector, Leonard S., *Going Nuclear*, Cambridge, MA: Ballinger Publishing Company, 1987.

Spindlove, J. R.: *Terrorism today: The past, the players, the future*, Upper Saddle Creek, NJ: Prentice Hall, 2000.

Stephen Reyna : *The Political Economy of African Famine*, Philadelphia, Gordon and Breach Science Publishers, 1991

Teller, Edward. *The Legacy of Hiroshima*. New York: Doubleday, 1962.

Whitaker, D. J.: *The Terrorism Reader*, New York: Routledge, 2001.

Index

T

❑❑❑